THE CLASSICS OF WESTERN SPIRITUALITY
A Library of the Great Spiritual Masters

President and Publisher
Kevin A. Lynch, C.S.P.

EDITORIAL BOARD

Editor-in-Chief
Richard J. Payne

Editorial Consultant
Ewert H. Cousins—Professor and Director of Spirituality Graduate Program, Fordham University, Bronx, N.Y.

John E. Booty—Professor of Church History, Episcopal Divinity School, Cambridge, Mass.

Joseph Dan—Professor of Kaballah in the Department of Jewish Thought, Hebrew University, Jerusalem, Israel.

Albert Deblaere—Professor of the History of Spirituality, Gregorian University, Rome, Italy.

Louis Dupré—T.L. Riggs Professor in Philosophy of Religion, Yale University, New Haven, Conn.

Rozanne Elder—Executive Vice President, Cistercian Publications, Kalamazoo, Mich.

Mircea Eliade—Professor in the Department of the History of Religions, University of Chicago, Chicago, Ill.

Anne Fremantle—Teacher, Editor and Writer, New York, N.Y.

Karlfried Froelich—Professor of the History of the Early and Medieval Church, Princeton Theological Seminary, Princeton, N.J.

Arthur Green—Assistant Professor in the Department of Religious Thought, University of Pennsylvania, Philadelphia, Pa.

Stanley S. Harakas—Dean of Holy Cross Greek Orthodox Seminary, Brookline, Mass.

Jean Leclercq—Professor, Institute of Spirituality and Institute of Religious Psychology, Gregorian University, Rome, Italy.

Miguel León-Portilla–Professor Mesoamerican Cultures and Languages, National University of Mexico, University City, Mexico.

George A. Maloney, S.J.—Director, John XXIII Ecumenical Center, Fordham University, Bronx, N.Y.

Bernard McGinn—Associate Professor of Historical Theology and History of Christianity, University of Chicago Divinity School, Chicago, Ill.

John Meyendorff—Professor of Church History, Fordham University, Bronx, N.Y., and Professor of Patristics and Church History, St. Vladimir's Seminary, Tuckahoe, N.Y.

Seyyed Hossein Nasr—Professor of Islamics, Department of Religion, Temple University, Philadelphia, Pa., and Visiting Professor, Harvard University, Cambridge, Ma.

Heiko A. Oberman—Director, Insititue fuer Spaetmittelalter and Reformation, Universitaet Tuebingen, West Germany.

Alfonso Ortiz—Professor of Anthropology, University of New Mexico, Albuquerque, N. Mex.; Fellow, The Center for Advanced Study, Stanford, Calif.

Raimundo Panikkar—Professor, Department of Religious Studies, University of California at Santa Barbara, Calif.

Jaroslav Pelikan—Sterling Professor of History and Religious Studies, Yale University, New Haven, Conn.

Fazlar Rahman—Professor Islamic Thought, Department of Near Eastern Languages and Civilization, University of Chicago, Chicago, Ill.

Annemarie B. Schimmel—Professor of Hindu Muslim Culture, Harvard University, Cambridge, Mass.

Sandra M. Schneiders—Assistant Professor of New Testament Studies and Spirituality, Jesuit School of Theology, Berkeley, Calif.

Huston Smith—Thomas J. Watson Professor of Religion, Adjunct Professor of Philosophy, Syracuse University, Syracuse, N.Y.

John R. Sommerfeldt—President, University of Dallas, Irving, Texas.

David Steindl-Rast—Monk of Mount Savior Monastery, Pine City, N.Y.

William C. Sturtevant—General Editor, Handbook of North American Indians, Smithsonian Institution, Washington, D.C.

David Tracy—Professor of Theology, University of Chicago Divinity School, Chicago, Ill.

Victor Turner—William B. Kenan Professor in Anthropology, The Center for Advanced Study, University of Virginia, Charlottesville, Va.

Kallistos Ware—Fellow of Pembroke College, Oxford; Spalding Lecturer in Eastern Orthodox Studies, Oxford University, England.

Other volumes in this series

Julian of Norwich • SHOWINGS

Jacob Boehme • THE WAY TO CHRIST

Nahman of Bratslav • THE TALES

Gregory of Nyssa • THE LIFE OF MOSES

Bonaventure • THE SOUL'S JOURNEY INTO GOD, THE TREE OF LIFE, and THE LIFE OF ST. FRANCIS

William Law • A SERIOUS CALL TO A DEVOUT AND HOLY LIFE, and THE SPIRIT OF LOVE

Abraham Isaac Kook • THE LIGHTS OF PENITENCE, LIGHTS OF HOLINESS, THE MORAL PRINCIPLES, ESSAYS, and POEMS

Ibn 'Ata' Illah • THE BOOK OF WISDOM *and* Kwaja Abdullah Ansari • INTIMATE CONVERSATIONS

Johann Arndt • TRUE CHRISTIANITY

Richard of St. Victor • THE TWELVE PATRIARCHS, THE MYSTICAL ARK, BOOK THREE OF THE TRINITY

Origen • AN EXHORTATION TO MARTYRDOM, PRAYER AND SELECTED WORKS

Catherine of Genoa • PURGATION AND PURGATORY, THE SPIRITUAL DIALOGUE

Native North American Spirituality of the Eastern Woodlands • SACRED MYTHS, DREAMS, VISIONS, SPEECHES, HEALING FORMULAS, RITUALS AND CEREMONIALS

Teresa of Avila • THE INTERIOR CASTLE

Apocalyptic Spirituality • TREATISES AND LETTERS OF LACTANTIUS, ADSO OF MONTIER-EN-DER, JOACHIM OF FIORE, THE FRANCISCAN SPIRITUALS, SAVONAROLA

Athanasius • THE LIFE OF ANTONY, A LETTER TO MARCELLINUS

Catherine of Siena • THE DIALOGUE

Sharafuddin Maneri • THE HUNDRED LETTERS

Martin Luther • THEOLOGIA GERMANICA

Native Mesoamerican Spirituality • ANCIENT MYTHS, DISCOURSES, STORIES, DOCTRINES, HYMNS, POEMS FROM THE AZTEC, YUCATEC, QUICHE-MAYA AND OTHER SACRED TRADITIONS

Symeon the New Theologian • THE DISCOURSES

IBN AL'ARABI
THE BEZELS OF WISDOM

TRANSLATION AND INTRODUCTION
BY
R.W.J. AUSTIN

PREFACE
BY
TITUS BURCKHARDT

PAULIST PRESS
NEW YORK • RAMSEY • TORONTO

Cover Art
The artist, Gloria Ortíz, is a native of Cali, Colombia. Currently a free lance designer and artist in Manhattan, Ms. Ortíz studied art at Marymount College in Tarrytown, New York and has shown her paintings in Bogotá and New York.

Design: Barbini, Pesce & Noble, Inc.

Copyright © 1980 by
The Missionary Society of St. Paul
the Apostle in the State of New York

All rights reserved. No part of this book may be reproduced or transmitted in any form or by any means, electronic or mechanical, including photocopying, recording or by any information storage and retrieval system without permission in writing from the publisher.

Library of Congress
Catalog Card Number: 80-83892

ISBN: 0-8091-2331-2(Paper)
0-8091-0313-3 (Cloth)

Published by Paulist Press
545 Island Road, Ramsey, N.J. 07446

Printed and bound in the
United States of America

Contents

PREFACE	xi
FOREWORD	xvii
INTRODUCTION	1
THE LIFE AND WORK OF MUḤYĪ AL-DĪN IBN AL-ʿARABĪ	1
HIS HISTORICAL AND SPIRITUAL CONTEXT	14
THE BEZELS OF WISDOM	16
HIS THOUGHT	21
THE BEZELS OF WISDOM	
PREFACE	45
I THE WISDOM OF DIVINITY IN THE WORD OF ADAM	47
II THE WISDOM OF EXPIRATION IN THE WORD OF SETH	60
III THE WISDOM OF EXALTATION IN THE WORD OF NOAH	71
IV THE WISDOM OF HOLINESS IN THE WORD OF ENOCH	82
V THE WISDOM OF RAPTUROUS LOVE IN THE WORD OF ABRAHAM	90
VI THE WISDOM OF REALITY IN THE WORD OF ISAAC	96
VII THE WISDOM OF SUBLIMITY IN THE WORD OF ISHMAEL	104
VIII THE WISDOM OF SPIRIT IN THE WORD OF JACOB	111
IX THE WISDOM OF LIGHT IN THE WORD OF JOSEPH	119
X THE WISDOM OF UNITY IN THE WORD OF HŪD	128
XI THE WISDOM OF OPENING IN THE WORD OF ṢĀLIḤ	139

XII	THE WISDOM OF THE HEART IN THE WORD OF SHU'AIB	145
XIII	THE WISDOM OF MASTERY IN THE WORD OF LOT	156
XIV	THE WISDOM OF DESTINY IN THE WORD OF EZRA	163
XV	THE WISDOM OF PROPHECY IN THE WORD OF JESUS	172
XVI	THE WISDOM OF COMPASSION IN THE WORD OF SOLOMON	187
XVII	THE WISDOM OF BEING IN THE WORD OF DAVID	198
XVIII	THE WISDOM OF BREATH IN THE WORD OF JONAH	206
XIX	THE WISDOM OF THE UNSEEN IN THE WORD OF JOB	212
XX	THE WISDOM OF MAJESTY IN THE WORD OF JOHN	218
XXI	THE WISDOM OF DOMINION IN THE WORD OF ZAKARIAH	222
XXII	THE WISDOM OF INTIMACY IN THE WORD OF ELIAS	228
XXIII	THE WISDOM OF VIRTUE IN THE WORD OF LUQMĀN	236
XXIV	THE WISDOM OF LEADERSHIP IN THE WORD OF AARON	241
XXV	THE WISDOM OF EMINENCE IN THE WORD OF MOSES	249
XXVI	THE WISDOM OF RESOURCE IN THE WORD OF KHĀLID	267
XXVII	THE WISDOM OF SINGULARITY IN THE WORD OF MUḤAMMAD	269

BIBLIOGRAPHY	285
INDEXES	288

Editor of this Volume

RALPH AUSTIN was born in 1938 in Willerby, England. He holds an Honours degree in Classical Arabic and a Ph.D. in Islamic Mysticism, both from the University of London. During the year 1962–63 he worked as a Research Assistant at the University of California, Los Angeles. Since 1963 he has taught Arabic and Islamic Studies in the School of Oriental Studies at the University of Durham, firstly as lecturer and currently as senior lecturer. During this period he has done research in Islamic mysticism in general and in the work of Muhyī al-Dīn Ibn al-'Arabī in particular. In this connection he has spent periods of time in Morocco and Turkey studying relevant manuscripts. In 1971 he produced a translation of two of Ibn al-'Arabī's autobiographical works, together with introduction and notes, entitled *Sufis of Andalusia*, published by George Allen & Unwin, and later published in French by Editions Orientales of Paris. In addition he contributed the first part of a Swiss book on the Arab world, as also several articles on Islamic questions published in various journals. He has presented papers at various conferences in England and Europe on the subject of Islamic spirituality. During the past ten years he has been invited to take part in many inter-religious consultations, notably at St. Georges House, Windsor in 1975 and 1976. Currently, he is particularly interested in the symbolic and archetypal significance of the Feminine in Islamic mysticism.

Author of the Preface

TITUS BURCKHARDT, the son of the famous Swiss sculptor Carl Burckhardt, was born in 1908 in Florence. Although at first he followed in his father's footsteps as a sculptor and illustrator, since childhood he had been strongly attracted to oriental art. This interest led him to a theoretical study of eastern doctrines and to repeated sojourns in Islamic countries. He was a guest of the ancient university al-Qarawiyin in Fez. After studying the history of art and oriental languages at the University of Basle for several years, he became the director of a newly founded publishing house, the Urs Graf-Verlag, which specialized in facsimile editions of ancient illuminated manuscripts [*The Book of Kells, The Lindisfarne Gospels, The Ambrosian Iliad*]. He translated several mystical works from Arabic into French [Ibn al-'Arabī's *Wisdom of the Prophets,* Abdul-Karīm al-Jīlī's *The Perfect Man, The Leters of a Sufi Master.*] He also wrote several books on traditional art [*Sacred Art in East and West* and *Art of Islam, Language and Meaning*] as well as three volumes in the series *Abodes of the Spirit* on Chartres, Siena, and Fez. In 1972 Dr. Burckhardt was appointed to UNESCO to work on the preservation of the ancient city of Fez. He collaborated on the World of Islam Festival in London in 1975 and more recently has acted as an advisor for the planning of a new university near Mekkah.

PREFACE

It may well be asked why anyone should enter a magic web to follow the train of thought which, since it is both mystical in nature and Arabic in style, will always remain very foreign to our own. Why not let the experts take the trouble to analyze this work which was considered abstruse even by some of the author's contemporaries? To all of that, the reply may be given: because "truth is one" and it is spiritually comforting to discover it hidden under the most diverse appearances. Obviously we are speaking here of spiritual and eternal truth and not of that wholly external truth which can be measured by science. We recognize eternal, universal truth because we find it in the very depths of our own being, in our heart.

"The only books worth our attention are those which spring from the heart and in turn speak to the heart," the Sufis tell us, and by the word 'heart' they do not mean the source of psychological feelings but something much more profound. 'Heart' can be understood as the very center of our psycho-physical being, as the meeting-place of soul and mind or, more precisely, as the focal point where the mind, which in itself is all knowledge or light, is reflected in the mirror of the soul. We have anticipated, then, one of the principal themes of the book of Ibn 'Arabī, a work concerned essentially with the role of various prophets in revelation. Ibn 'Arabī names some 27 prophets, all of whom are mentioned in the *Koran*; each one is as a vessel of divine Wisdom which, owing to this fact, takes on human nature with

PREFACE

its limitations, all the while remaining one and indivisible in itself. "Water derives its color from the vessel that holds it," Sufi al-Junaid maintains. This law which places in opposition the light of revelation and a plan which reflects and confines it, is repeated on every level of the macrocosm and microcosm, of the world and of man. Now we begin to surmise the importance of this theory for prophetic revelation.

We should point out here that the words 'prophet' and 'Prophecy' do not convey precisely the same ideas in the three monotheistic religions. In Christianity especially, a prophet is one who foretells the future and, more exactly, announces the coming of Christ. Now, according to the *Koran*, each prophet, including Christ, is a messenger sent by God to a particular people. This view depends on a certain elitism and presumes that the prophet has reached the spiritual heights of human nature and that he is, like Adam, "God's representative on earth."

The *Koran* places the prophets outside history, within the framework of the unitarian message of Islam; it speaks in both general and universal terms, as it were. Its prophets run the gamut from Adam to Mohammed and include not only the prophets and patriarchs of the Old Testament, but also an indefinite number of messengers sent by God to ancient Arabic and non-Arabic nations. The Bible stories linked to various prophets reappear in part in the *Koran*, but reduced to their essential features and, as it were, crystallized into symbolic accounts.

Ibn 'Arabī relies on these facts from the Koran to compose what could be called a study of the prophets. This is a central theme in the *Koran* which gives first place to the stories of the prophets. It is of equal importance to Sufic spirituality in which different prophets correspond to various spiritual types and, consequently, to different avenues of approach to God. The theme's centrality together with the spiritual scope of the author justifies Ibn 'Arabī's contention that the Prophet had ordered him in a dream to produce the book *Bezels of Wisdom*.

It is not altogether outside the scope of our discussion to draw a comparison between Ibn 'Arabī's study of the prophets and the representations done by Christian sculptors on the portals of the Gothic cathedrals, notably the northern doorway of Chartres which dates from the same period as *Bezels of Wisdom*. The sacred dimension of the characters is comparable in both traditions. They differ, however,

PREFACE

since on the Christian side, the statues look to the central figure of Christ. Moreover, they are all located on the North side of the sanctuary so as to recall that their place is in the shadow of the Old Testament, before the rising of the spiritual Sun who is Christ.

Ibn 'Arabī's study of the prophets goes beyond the official theology of Islam and does not hesitate to shatter it with such ideas as absolute divinity, which is unattainable, on the one hand, and relative divinity on the other, which does not exist—since it is not of God—outside the polarity between Creator and creature. His study also contains his theory of prototypes or unchanging essences, which have no existence in pure Being but nevertheless refract it in the form of innumerable possibilities.

Ibn 'Arabī's thinking is fundamentally Platonic; thus it is not surprising that in his day he was given the surname "Son of Plato" [*Ibn Aflatun*], apart from his title "supreme master" [*ash-Sheikh al-akbar*]. His thought has a special stamp and lacks a certain cohesion because it is a blending of intellectual speculation, in the true sense of the word *speculare*: to reflect on intellectual reality beyond the reach of the senses; this reflection is accompanied by ecstatic visions. Now speculation is answerable to objective knowledge, while ecstatic vision derives from subjective and mystical inspiration. Such inspiration is not, however, in any sense unreal.

Sometimes the two sources of knowledge coincide and bring to the text an extraordinary spiritual depth. This is true of the first chapter, dealing with Adam, in which the first sentence—very long with many interjections—summarizes the entire Sufic theory on God's manifestation in the world. The text begins with a paraphrase of a divine utterance, well known in Moslem esoterism, that can be translated as: "I was a hidden treasure who longed to be known; therefore I created the world." Ibn 'Arabī continues with a paraphrase of his own: "When God wished to consider the essences of His titles of perfection whose number is inexhaustible—and if you prefer, you can also say: when He wished to consider His own essence—in a global object which, being brought into existence, sums up the whole divine order, in order thereby to manifest His mystery to Himself..." Ibn 'Arabī comments: "for Being's vision of itself within itself is different from that obtained from another reality which Being uses like a mirror. Being is made known to itself in the form resulting from the 'place' of the vision; this form exists with the plan of reflec-

PREFACE

tion and the light which is reflected in it." Using this principle as a starting point, the author, still writing in the same sentence, speaks of the creation of Adam and his receiving the breath of the divine Spirit. Then he says: "And this is simply the realization of the capacity that such a form possesses; having been previously disposed, it receives the inexhaustible pouring out of the essential revelation..." He ends the cycle with these words: Outside the divine Reality, there is only one pure receiver; but this receiver himself springs from the outpouring of the Most High, for the whole of reality, from beginning to end, comes from God alone, and it is to Him that it returns as well..."

Applied to prophetic revelation, this consideration indicates that divine Wisdom is made known according to the recipient who takes on the human form of this or that prophet. The receiving prophet himself is of divine origin inasmuch as he is identified essentially and in an unfathomable way with the prototype of the prophet.

This law of reciprocity between divine revelation and its human recipient also explains the diversity as well as the transcendent unity of religions. In this case, the receptive form which invites and compels the divine light to reveal itself in one way and not another, is the predisposition inherent in a certain sector of humanity.

In order to avoid all misunderstanding we should point out that the works written by Muhyī al-Dīn Ibn al-'Arabī do not have the unqualified approval of all Sufis or Moslem contemplatives; we are not speaking here of "outsiders" who totally reject Sufism in its metaphysical dimension. In the books of Ibn 'Arabī and particularly in his *Revelations Received at Mecca* [*al-futuhat al-mekkiyah*], which is an account of miraculous experiences, there is a quality much like heady wine and certain Sufic masters are afraid of its effect on novices.

I should like to mention a personal recollection along these lines. When I was 24 and living in Fez, in the old quarter where traditional style and clothing were still in evidence, I counted among my friends several members of the Sufic classes. They were recruited mainly from among skilled workers but also included among their adherents men who were learned in the sciences which were taught at the ancient Moslem university Al-Qarawiyin. Both groups frequently spoke with great veneration of the writings of Ibn 'Arabī whom they called *ash-Sheikh al-akbar* [the supreme master]. At that time the old city was full of souvenirs of the great Sufi who had visited it on several occa-

PREFACE

sions and met there some of the greatest and most mysterious spiritual men of his time. I came to know the place to which Ibn 'Arabī would often withdraw to pray and meditate; it was a small mosque situated not far from the central bazaar and had within it a fountain called *'ain al-kheil*, "the fountain of the horses," water from which filled a large pond. The mosque is on two levels, for Summer and Winter, and its eight-sided minaret is built over the adjacent narrow lane. In Fez, there are also enclosed gardens, surrounded by high walls, like the one where Ibn 'Arabī used to meet his friends.

One day while browsing among the bookshops opposite the great mosque and university, I discovered a copy of the seven-volume work, *Futuhat al-Mekkiyah* [*Revelations Received at Mecca*], the greatest and most elaborate of the writings of *Sheikh al-akbar*. While paging through, my eyes fell on a list of titles promising a description of all the spiritual stages leading to the highest union. I bought the work and, carrying my heavy load, found my way back through the narrow streets of the ancient city. On the way I chanced to meet my friend Mohammed ben Makhluf, a dervish with the profile of a hawk and a searching glance. He immediately guessed what I was carrying.

"What are you going to do with that?" he asked me. "It is much too advanced for you. What you need is a primer [of the spiritual life]."

"In that case, the book shall remain on my shelf until I am wise enough to study it."

"When you are wise, you will no longer need the book."

"Whom was it written for then?"

"For men who can see through walls but do not do so, nor even wish to."

Titus Burckhardt

FOREWORD

The *Fuṣūṣ al-ḥikam* or *Bezels of Wisdom*, written in the later years of Ibn al-'Arabī's life, was clearly intended to serve as a summing up of the Andalusian master's mystical teachings and, as such, it is undoubtedly one of his most important works, dealing, as it does, with all the major themes of his highly original and enormously influential thought. The work was probably composed largely in Damascus where Ibn al-'Arabī spent most of the last ten years of his life. Fortunately, a manuscript copy of the work exists which bears his signature of approval. Being a synoptic work, the style is very concentrated and condensed, making it a peculiarly difficult work to translate into another language in a way which makes some sort of sense to the non-Arabic speaking and non-Muslim reader. While it is by no means as comprehensive as his monumental *Meccan Revelations*, which still exists in an autograph manuscript in 37 volumes, it provides more immediate access to an understanding of the overall scheme and pattern of his doctrine and thus, more than others of his works, provides the student with a unique opportunity to come to grips with his teachings as a whole. In doing so, the student is aware that, in grappling with the complexities of Ibn al-'Arabī's thought, he is dealing with an intellectual and spiritual phenomenon which, more than any other in the world of Islam, brings together in a wonderful synthesis a multitude of spiritual traditions and esoteric lore, both Is-

FOREWORD

lamic and non-Islamic, and the influences of which have permeated deeply, not only into all subsequent Sufi thinking, but also into the fabric of Christian mysticism. Indeed, as an expression of profound insights into the very fundamentals of our human spiritual experience, the *Bezels of Wisdom* can have few equals in the spiritual literature of the world.

INTRODUCTION

THE LIFE AND WORK OF
MUḤYĪ AL-DĪN IBN AL-ʿARABĪ

The author of the *Fuṣūṣ al-ḥikam* or *The Bezels of Wisdom* was born on the twenty-seventh of Ramadan in A.H. 560, or the seventh of August, A.D. 1165, in the township of Murcia in Spain, which was ruled at the time by Muḥammad b. Mardanīsh. His full name was Muḥammad b. ʿAlī b. Muḥammad Ibn al-ʿArabī al-Ṭāʾī al-Ḥātimī, which indicates that he came of an ancient Arab lineage. His father, who may have been chief minister to Ibn Mardanīsh, was clearly a well-known and influential figure in the fields of politics and learning. The family seems also to have been a strongly religious one, since three of his uncles became followers of the Sufi Way.

With the defeat of Ibn Mardanīsh at the hands of the Almohads, Ibn al-ʿArabī's family took the precaution of moving to Seville where, thanks to the magnanimity of the ruler, his father very soon established a prominent position in the society of that city. When all this happened, Ibn al-ʿArabī was only eight years old. It was in Seville that he began his formal education, being sent to sit at the feet of the contemporary masters of traditional learning. Among the subjects he studied at this time were the Qurʾan and its exegesis, the Traditions of the Prophet, Arabic grammar and composition, and Islamic Law. Ibn al-ʿArabī has left us quite a detailed account of his masters and the subjects he studied.[1] His education must have been successful, since

---

1. *Al-Andalus*, edited by A. Badawi, XX, 1955, pp. 122–28.

INTRODUCTION

he later obtained employment as a secretary to the governor of Seville. At about this time he married a girl of a good family, called Maryam. Fortunately, this new wife was also well acquainted with men of great piety and clearly shared with her husband his aspiration to follow the Sufi path.[2]

Although Ibn al-'Arabī did not become formally initiated into the Sufi Way until he was twenty years of age, it seems clear, especially from the account he himself gives us of his spiritual masters, that he had kept frequent company with the Sufis and studied their teachings from an early age.[3] One might also deduce from his writings that the youthful Ibn al-'Arabī had attained to considerable spiritual insight while still in his teens. This is shown most strikingly in Ibn al-'Arabī's own account of a meeting, arranged by his father, between him and the celebrated philosopher Averroes.[4]

> I spent a good day in Cordova at the house of Abū al-Walīd Ibn Rushd [Averroes]. He had expressed a desire to meet with me in person, since he had heard of certain revelations I had received while in retreat, and had shown considerable astonishment concerning them. In consequence, my father, who was one of his close friends, took me with him on the pretext of business, in order to give Ibn Rushd the opportunity of making my acquaintance. I was at the time a beardless youth. As I entered the house the philosopher rose to greet me with all the signs of friendliness and affection, and embraced me. Then he said to me, "Yes!" and showed pleasure on seeing that I had understood him. I, on the other hand, being aware of the motive for his pleasure, replied, "No!" Upon this, Ibn Rushd drew back from me, his color changed and he seemed to doubt what he had thought of me. He then put to me the following question, "What solution have you found as a result of mystical illumination and divine inspiration? Does it agree with what is arrived at by speculative thought?" I replied, "Yes and No. Between the Yea and the Nay the spirits take their flight beyond matter, and the necks detach themselves from their bodies." At this

---

2. Cf. *Al-Futūhāt al-makkiyyah*, II, p. 278.
3. Cf. *Sufis of Andalusia*, trans. R. W. J. Austin, London, 1971.
4. *Futūhāt*, I, p. 153.

INTRODUCTION

Ibn Rushd became pale, and I saw him tremble as he muttered the formula, "There is no power save from God." This was because he had understood my allusion.

This passage also reveals a characteristic of Ibn al-'Arabī that is evident in many of his writings, namely a supreme self-confidence that often made him intolerant of the achievements of others.

During the process of his spiritual apprenticeship he must have studied many subjects of a mystical nature, among them the metaphysical doctrines of the Sufis, cosmology, esoteric exegesis, and perhaps the more occult sciences such as astrology and alchemy. There is certainly much evidence of his acquaintance with such matters throughout his works. Although much of this learning may have been received from spiritual masters in a formal way, he must also have culled much from example and constant association with experts in these subjects. In addition to the more theoretical side of the Mystic Way, Ibn al-'Arabī and his fellow disciples were undoubtedly urged by their teachers to cultivate and practice the rites and methods of the orders. These would have included frequent invocation, prayer, fasting, night vigil, retreat, and periods of meditation. Such learning and the accompanying practices often led to experiences of a supersensory nature, many of which Ibn al-'Arabī claims to have had during his life. In order to encourage such experiences, Ibn al-'Arabī, even while he was still a young man in Seville, would spend long hours in the cemeteries communing with the spirits of the dead.

The young man was no ordinary disciple, however, and the self-confidence already referred to, together with a growing sense of his own spiritual authority, often created a rather difficult relationship between him and his masters. On one occasion he disagreed with his Shaikh al-'Uryanī regarding the spiritual state of a certain person. Later, in a vision, he was corrected. He himself readily admits that he was a novice at the time.[5]

Two of Ibn al-'Arabī's spiritual teachers at this time deserve special mention since, unusually perhaps, they were women, both of them considerably advanced in age when he became their disciple. One of them was Shams who lived in Marchena,[6] the other Fatima of Cordova. Of the latter he says, "I served as a disciple one of the lovers of God, a gnostic, a lady of Seville called Fatima bint al-Muthannā

---

5. *Futūḥāt*, I, p. 186. Cf. also *Sufis of Andalusia*, p. 63.

INTRODUCTION

who lived in Cordova. I served her for several years, she being over ninety-five years of age.... with my own hands I built a hut for her of reeds, as high as she was, in which she lived until she died. She used to say to me, 'I am your spiritual mother and the light of your earthly mother.' "[7] A more detailed account of Ibn al-'Arabī's experiences at this time may be had in my translation of his own account of this period of his life, *Sufis of Andalusia*.

Toward the end of this period Ibn al-'Arabī's own reputation as an authority on spiritual matters was growing and he felt himself more and more able to dispute on matters of doctrine with well established shaikhs. He says, "I had heard that a certain shaikh of the order in Andalusia had denied the possibility of assuming the attribute of self-sufficiency. On this point I disputed with him frequently in front of his students, until he finally came round to my point of view on the matter."[8]

Sometime in the 1190s Ibn al-'Arabī left his native shore and traveled in North Africa, spending his time mostly in Tunis, where he took the opportunity of studying *The Doffing of the Sandals* by Ibn Qisyi, the Sufi leader of the rebellion against the Almoravids in the Algarve.[9] He later wrote a large commentary on this work.[10] During his stay in Tunis he visited and consulted with many Sufi shaikhs. It is possible that he met the famous Shaikh Abū Madyan at this time.

Ibn al-'Arabī returned to Seville from Tunis after a relatively short time, perhaps because of political troubles in the region. On his return to Seville he had one of those apparently chance mystical encounters that characterize so many of his spiritual relationships. While he had been in Tunis he had composed a poem about which he told no one.

> On my return to Seville ... a complete stranger came to me and recited, word for word, the poem I had composed, although I had not written it out for anyone. I asked him who had composed the lines, and he replied that they were by Muhammad Ibn al-'Arabī. Then I asked him when he had learned them, and he mentioned the very day on which I had

---

6. *Sufis of Andalusia*, p. 142.
7. Ibid., p. 143.
8. *Futūhāt*, III, p. 45.
9. CF p. 88.
10. Ms. in Konya, Yusuf Aga, 5624 [Eski], 109–338.

INTRODUCTION

composed them, despite the great distance. I then asked him who had recited them to him to learn. He said, "One night I was sitting at a session of the brethren in the eastern part of Seville, when a stranger who looked like a mendicant came and sat with us. After conversing with us he recited the lines to us. We liked them so much that we wrote them down and asked him who had composed them, to which he replied that they were being composed by Ibn al-'Arabī in the oratory of Ibn al-Muthannā. We told him that we had never heard of such a place, to which he replied that it was in Tunis where they had just been composed."[11]

About this time he made a pilgrimage to a shrine at Rota, on the coast, after which he traveled once again to North Africa, this time to Fez, where he heard news of the Almohad victory over the Christian armies at Alarcos in 1194. A conversation he had in Fez at this time helps to illustrate some of the more abstruse aspects of mystical learning with which Ibn al-'Arabī was conversant, that of the science of numbers and letters. "I asked a certain man of God what he thought [of the victory]. He said, 'God promised His Apostle a victory this year . . . in His Book . . . in the words, "Surely we have given to you a clear victory"; the glad tidings being in the two words "clear victory" [*fathan mubīnan*]. . . . consider the sum total of the numerical value of the letters.' This I did and found that the total came to 591 [A.H., the year of the victory]."[12]

The following year he was back in Seville studying the Traditions of the Prophet with his uncle. By this time he was much sought after by aspirants to spiritual learning and many of the would-be disciples who visited him treated him with what, Ibn al-'Arabī thought, was excessive formality. It is an interesting glimpse into his character to read his account of the way in which he tried to modify their approach to him. Speaking of one particular meeting, he says, "Their respect for me prevented them from being relaxed, and they were all very correct and silent; so I sought a means of making them more relaxed, saying to my host, 'May I bring your attention to a composition of mine entitled *Guidance in Flouting the Usual Courtesies*, and expound a chapter from it to you.' He said that he would very much

---
11. *Futūhāt*, III, p. 338.
12. *Futūhāt*, IV, p. 220.

INTRODUCTION

like to hear it. I then pushed my foot into his lap and told him to massage it, whereupon they understood my meaning and behaved in a more relaxed manner."[13] A year later he returned to Fez, primarily to spend time in the mosques and shrines in meditation, but also to gather with other men of the spirit to talk about their experience on the Way. During his stay he had a strange experience of spacelessness.[14] On another occasion, while meeting with some others in a garden, he claims to have met the spiritual Pole of the age.[15] Once more he experienced a growing sense of his own spiritual authority and also of his special status in the spiritual hierarchy. He says of this, "I learned of the Seal of Muhammadan Sainthood in Fez, in the year 594, when God acquainted me with his identity and revealed to me his mark."[16] He later had a vision in which it was revealed to him that he himself was the Seal.[17]

This stay in North Africa, however, was also cut short by the threat of persecution by the Almohad rulers, who were beginning to suspect the Sufi orders of fomenting resistance to their regime. Indeed, at this time, relations between the Sufis and the political rulers were tense and uneasy, since the former often regarded the latter as usurpers of legitimate Islamic authority and offenders against the Sacred Law. The advice generally given by the shaikhs to their disciples was to have as little to do with rulers as possible. In his biographical sketches of his masters, Ibn al-'Arabī tells of the occasion when he refused to eat food the Sultan of Ceuta had provided for a Sufi gathering, which refusal almost resulted in his arrest.[18] He also describes the behavior of one of his shaikhs who was particularly opposed to the rulers of the day.[19]

Ibn al-'Arabī probably spent the next two years or so in his native Andalusia visiting friends and a growing number of his own disciples.[20] Sometime during this period he attended the funeral rites of the philosopher Averroes, whom he had met as a young boy. Averroes had died in Marrakesh and his body was brought to Cordova for

---

13. Ibid., IV, p. 539.
14. Ibid., II, p. 486.
15. Ibid., IV, p. 76.
16. Ibid., III, p. 514; cf p. 67 [this volume].
17. Ibid.
18. *Sufis of Andalusia*, p. 129.
19. Ibid., p. 112.
20. *Futūḥāt*, I, p. 708.

INTRODUCTION

burial. Like most Sufis, Ibn al-'Arabī was rather skeptical of the value of philosophical speculation and this is reflected in lines he composed at the time of the funeral: "This is the Imām and these his works; would that I knew whether his hopes were realized."[21]

The year 1200 found Ibn al-'Arabī in Marrakesh, where he spent some time with a certain Abū al-'Abbās of Ceuta.[22] It was during this visit to what is now Morocco that Ibn al-'Arabī received the call to travel to the East. While in Marrakesh he had a vision in which he was told to go to Fez, where he would meet a certain Muhammad al-Haṣār whom he was to accompany to the eastern Islamic lands.[23] On reaching Fez, Ibn al-'Arabī met al-Haṣār and they traveled together in faith and hope on the road to Egypt. On the way they visited Bijāyah and Tunis visiting fellow Sufis and old friends.[24] They did not linger, however, pressing on with their journey until they reached Egypt, where they stayed in Alexandria and Cairo. Ibn al-'Arabī's companion, al-Haṣār, died there[25], and after a brief stay, Ibn al-'Arabī continued his journey alone to the holy city of Mecca.

He had not been long in the Holy City before the reputation of his spiritual learning and authority spread among the more pious families of Mecca, and he was soon being received with honor and respect by the most learned of its citizens. Foremost among them was Abū Shajā Zāhir b. Rustam, whose beautiful and gifted daughter was to inspire Ibn al-'Arabī to write a fine collection of mystical poetry, *The Interpreter of Desires*, which was later to lead to accusations that he had written sensual love poetry.[26] One suspects that the relationship between Ibn al-'Arabī and this young woman had something of the quality of that between Dante and Beatrice, and it serves to illustrate a strong appreciation of the feminine in him, at least in its spiritual aspect. This insight into the spiritual significance of the feminine is most evident in the last chapter of the present work, where he interprets the saying of the Prophet, "Three things in this world have been made beloved to me, women, perfume, and prayer."[27] He says of the lady in question, "This shaikh had a virgin daughter, a slender

---

21. Ibid., I, p. 153.
22. Ibid., III, p. 292.
23. Ibid., II, p. 436.
24. *Futūḥāt*, IV, p. 559; I, p. 173.
25. Ibid., II, p. 436.
26. *Tarjumān al-ashwāq*, Beirut, 1961.
27. See p. 269.

INTRODUCTION

child who captivated all who looked on her, whose presence gave luster to gatherings, who amazed all she was with and ravished the senses of all who beheld her ... she was a sage among the sages of the Holy Places."[28]

No doubt, while Ibn al-'Arabī was staying in Mecca, he would have visited the Ka'abah regularly to perform the rites and for meditation. On two of these occasions he had important experiences that heightened his spiritual awareness and confirmed him in his feeling that he enjoyed a special spiritual status in the cosmic scheme of things. The first experience was a vision of the "Eternal Youth" who represents, so to speak, the fusion of opposites, the *coincidentia oppositorum* in whose wholeness all tensions are resolved.[29] This archetype has, more recently, been the object of study by C. G. Jung and his school. The second vision confirmed that it was he who was the Seal of Muhammadan Sainthood.[30] It is certainly true to say that, for the Sufi world, Ibn al-'Arabī holds a very special place, being always referred to as the Greatest Shaikh [*al-Shaikh al-akbar*], nor can there be any doubt that his influence on all later generations of Sufis has been enormous and crucial, especially through the work translated here and also *The Meccan Revelations* [*al-Futūḥāt al-Makkiyyah*].[31] However, the relationships that were to cause such influence lay still in the future.

During this time Ibn al-'Arabī would also have been deeply engaged in study and writing. Indeed, he began the composition of his monumental *The Meccan Revelations* at this time. He also completed four lesser works, including the biographical sketches of his Andalusian masters.[32]

In 1204 Ibn al-'Arabī left the Holy City and traveled to Baghdad, staying there only briefly before going on to Mosul, where he spent a year or so in study and writing, the result of which was his *Mosul Revelations* on the esoteric significance of ablution and prayer.[33] Also while he was at Mosul he was initiated for the third time.[34]

---

28. *Tarjumān al-ashwāq*, pp. 7–8.
29. *Futūḥāt*, I, pp. 47–48. Cf. F. Meier, "The Mystery of the Ka'abah," in *The Mysteries*, Papers from the Eranos Year Books, 1955, pp. 149–168.
30. *Futūḥāt*, I, pp. 318–319. Cf p. 67.
31. Published Cairo, A.H. 1329.
32. *Sufis of Andalusia*.
33. Istanbul ms. Murad Molla, 1236.
34. *Sufis of Andalusia*, p. 157.

INTRODUCTION

By the year 1206 Ibn al-'Arabī arrived in Cairo to spend some time with friends. His reputation, however, had gone before him and it was not one that recommended him to the religious authorities of Cairo. The learned divines of that city denounced his teachings and ideas to such an extent that popular reaction promised to threaten his very life.[35] One must understand that much of what Ibn al-'Arabī taught for the benefit of his fellow Sufis was unpalatable to exoteric attitudes, seeming as it did to undermine Islamic verities. Even a cursory study of *The Bezels of Wisdom* will suffice to show clearly how great was the gulf between the insights of the Andalusian master and the received interpretations of Islamic doctrine.[36] This sort of antagonism to Ibn al-'Arabī's teachings has continued down to the present day in certain circles of the Muslim World, since all mystical experience tends to express itself, when it does so, in terms often abhorrent to minds firmly fixed within rigid doctrinal limits.[37] Ibn al-'Arabī's life was saved, however, by the timely intercession of a friend in Tunis who wrote a letter of recommendation to the Egyptian ruler, the Ayyubid, al-Malik al-'Ādil.[38]

Understandably depressed and upset by these developments, Ibn al-'Arabī left Egypt and returned to the more appreciative society of Mecca, there to take up his studies once more and to renew old friendships.[39] After some twelve months or so he traveled by way of Aleppo to Asia Minor, arriving in the city of Konya in 1210. Once more the master's by now formidable reputation went before him, so that he was received with great honor and generosity by the ruler of Konya, Kay Kaus. It is told of Ibn al-'Arabī that he gave away the expensive house allotted to him by Kay Kaus as alms to a beggar.[40]

In a very short time the people and Sufis of Konya took the newly arrived master to their hearts, and it was as a result of the spiritual contacts he made there that his influence became so dominant in all later Sufism down to the present day. The key figure in this process was the local disciple of Ibn al-'Arabī, Ṣadr al-Dīn al-Qunawī,[41] who

---

35. *Futūḥāt*, IV, p. 560.
36. See Chap. 3.
37. Ibn al-'Arabī's works were only recently banned in Cairo as the result of pressure by extremist Islamic groups.
38. *Futūḥāt*, IV, p. 560.
39. Ibid., II, p. 376.
40. Ibid., IV, p. 560.
41. His commentary on *The Bezels of Wisdom* is in the Yusuf Aga Library, 4858.

INTRODUCTION

wrote extensively as a commentator on Ibn al-'Arabī's teachings and who, by his later contacts with such towering exponents of oriental Sufism as Jalāl al-Dīn Rūmī,[42] helped to bring about that remarkable synthesis of oriental and Andalusian Sufism which was later to flower in writers like 'Abd al-Karīm al-Jīlī.[43]

After quite a short stay Ibn al-'Arabī proceeded northward through Kayseri and Siwas toward Armenia, returning southward, through Harran, to arrive in Baghdad once more in 1211. On his travels in northern regions Ibn al-'Arabī relates that he saw the Euphrates frozen over so that whole caravans could move across it.[44]

In Baghdad he had a short, silent meeting with the celebrated author of the *Knowledge of the Mystical Sciences* [*'Awārif al-ma'ārif*], 'Umar al-Suhrawardī, at the end of which the latter described Ibn al-'Arabī as "an ocean of divine truths."[45]

In 1212, Kay Kaus of Konya wrote to him seeking his advice regarding the proper treatment of his Christian subjects, and Ibn al-'Arabī's reply is very revealing of the nonmystical side of his character, since he advised Kay Kaus to impose on them the full rigor of Islamic Law regarding the restriction of their public worship. This letter serves to illustrate an important aspect of Sufism that is not widely understood, namely that, while reaching beyond Law and doctrine in their inward search for experience of the divine Reality, they nevertheless recognize the necessity of law and doctrine for the Community.[46]

After a visit to Aleppo in 1213, Ibn al-'Arabī returned to Mecca in 1214 to deal with the criticisms, which were continuing, of his collection of mystical love poems, *The Interpreter of Desires*. Religious scholars objected to them as being inappropriate to religious feelings, being, they said, too erotic for pious sensibilities. Ibn al-'Arabī therefore composed a full commentary explaining the inner meaning of his verses. In their defense he wrote, "All our poems are related to divine truths in various forms, such as love themes, eulogy, the names and attributes of women, the names of rivers, places, and stars."[47]

During the next few months it is possible that Ibn al-'Arabī visit-

---

42. Author of the celebrated *Mathnawi*, A.D. 1207–1273.
43. Cf. R. A. Nicholson, *Studies in Islamic Mysticism*, Cambridge, 1921, pp. 77–148.
44. *Futūḥāt*, III, p. 459.
45. R. A. Nicholson, "Lives," *J.R.A.S.*, 1906, p. 812.
46. *Futūḥāt*, IV, pp. 547–548.
47. *Futūḥāt*, III, p. 562. See also this volume, p. 7.

INTRODUCTION

ed Medina and Jerusalem. However, in 1215 he was once again in Asia Minor, meeting with Kay Kaus at Malatya, where he seems to have spent much of the next four to five years, instructing and supervising his many disciples.[48] During the year 1220–1221 he was in Aleppo, where a previous ruler had earlier treated him with great honor. Indeed, the increasing respect and confidence shown to Ibn al-'Arabī by more than one ruler seems to have worsened his relationships with jealous jurists and theologians, by reason of the growing influence this respect entailed. His own irritation with such men emerges on several occasions from the pages of his books.[49]

From the year 1223 until his death in November 1240, Ibn al-'Arabī, by now probably exhausted from his many travels, his prodigious literary output, and the sacrifices of his calling, took advantage of an offer by al-Malik al-'Ādil [d. 1227] to settle in Damascus. This ruler's son, al-Ashraf, continued to support Ibn al-'Arabī after his father's death. During this period of semiretirement the master used his time to finish the massive *Meccan Revelations* and his major collection of poetry, the *Dīwān*. More relevantly, it was during this time that he wrote *The Bezels of Wisdom* as the synopsis of his teachings.

As far as we can tell, Ibn al-'Arabī married three times in the course of his life, first Maryam, while he was still a young man in Seville;[50] second Fatima, the daughter of a Meccan nobleman;[51] and third an unnamed lady, the daughter of a judge in Damascus.[52] He had three children, Sa'd al-Dīn, born in Malatya in 1221 and died in 1258; 'Imād al-Dīn, who died in 1268; and a daughter, Zainab. Of these, we know only that Fatima was the mother of 'Imād al-Dīn. In the *Futūḥāt* Ibn al-'Arabī relates a very touching meeting with his young daughter. "When I arrived at the meeting place, I went with a group of people who were with me to look for them in the Syrian caravan. My daughter caught sight of me and cried, 'O Mother, there's my father!' Then her mother looked and saw me in the distance. Zainab went on calling out, 'There's my father! There's my father!' . . . When I reached her she laughed and threw her arms about me, shouting, 'Father! Father!' "[53]

---

48. *Muḥāḍarāt al-abrār*, II, p. 180.
49. Cf. *Sufis of Andalusia*, p. 105.
50. See above, p. 2.
51. *Futūḥāt*, IV, p. 554.
52. Ibid., IV, p. 559.
53. Ibid., IV, p. 117.

INTRODUCTION

Although Ibn al-'Arabī's physical offspring may have been modest, his spiritual and literary legacy is not. Among the many Sufis who have sought to express their insights and experiences in writing, Ibn al-'Arabī was, perhaps, the most prolific of all, having contributed significantly to every aspect of Sufi thought, both qualitatively and quantitatively. He himself lists no fewer than 251 titles.[54] While it is true that many if not most of these titles are relatively small and minor works, the list, nevertheless, includes that massive compendium of Sufi exposition, *The Meccan Revelations*, which by itself would have been considered a major contribution.[55] Unfortunately, most of these works exist today only in manuscript form, some of them in Ibn al-'Arabī's own hand, very few having been printed, even fewer edited, and still fewer translated into non-Arabic languages.

Therefore, the proportion of Ibn al-'Arabī's works available to the non-Arabic reader is very small. Of the two most important and definitive works, *The Meccan Revelations* and *The Bezels of Wisdom*, only a partial translation of the latter by T. Burckhardt, *La Sagesse des Prophetes*,[56] had been published until the present translation. Translations of small sections of *The Meccan Revelations* exist as quotations in other works on Ibn al-'Arabī. Considering that the A.H. 1329 printing of this work contains over 2,500 pages, a translation of the whole work would indeed be a daunting task. Partial or whole translations of smaller and less general works are to be found in Asin Palacios, *El Islam Cristianizado* [Madrid, 1931], in various numbers of *Etudes Traditionelles*, and in A. Jeffrey's *Reader on Islam* [The Hague, 1962]. My own contribution [before the present translation], *Sufis of Andalusia*, is biographical and not really concerned with his teachings.[57]

Of the printings and editions of Ibn al-'Arabī's works, the most readily available are *Al-Futūḥāt al-Makkiyyah* [*The Meccan Revelations*] [printed A.H. 1274, 1282, 1293, and 1329]; A. A. Afifi's edition of the *Fuṣūs al-ḥikam* [the present work] [Cairo, 1946]; H. S. Nyberg, *Kleinere Schriften des Ibn al-'Arabī* [Leiden, 1919], *Rasā'il Ibnul 'Arabī* [Hyderabad-Deccan 1948], and the *Tarjumān al-Ashwāq* [Beirut, 1961].

---

54. A. A. Afifi, "Memorandum by Ibn 'Arabi of His Own Works," in the *Bulletin of the Faculty of Arts*, Alexandria University, VIII, 1954, pp. 109–117.

55. Printed in Cairo A.H. 1329. The Evkaf Museum in Istanbul contains the second copy in Ibn 'Arabī's own hand.

56. Paris, 1955. English version of the French, *Wisdom of the Prophets*, by A. Culme-Seymour, Beshara, 1975.

57. London, 1971.

INTRODUCTION

Books on Ibn al-'Arabī's system of thought and spiritual teachings are also rather few. By far the best of these, especially for the present work, is Izutsu's *Comparative Study of Key Philosophical Concepts in Sufism and Taoism*,[58] which is a very thorough and penetrating study of *The Bezels of Wisdom*. A profound study of certain important themes in Ibn al-'Arabī's thought is H. Corbin's *Creative Imagination in the Sufism of Ibn 'Arabī* [London, 1970]. S. H. Nasr has provided a very useful study of Ibn al-'Arabī in *Three Muslim Sages* [Harvard, 1964]. Two more philosophically oriented studies are A. A. Afifi's *The Mystical Philosophy of Muḥid Din Ibnul Arabī* [Cambridge, 1939] and S. A. Q. Husaini's *The Pantheistic Monism of Ibn al-'Arabī* [Lahore, 1970].

It is clear from the author of these works himself that his writings are not simply the result of long mental and intellectual deliberations, but rather that of inspiration and mystical experiences, which makes the task of translating his writings and of interpreting what he writes a formidable one. He says, "In what I have written, I have never had a set purpose, as other writers. Flashes of divine inspiration used to come upon me and almost overwhelm me, so that I could only put them from my mind by committing to paper what they revealed to me. If my works evince any form of composition, it was unintentional. Some works I wrote at the command of God, sent to me in sleep or through mystical revelation."[59] Sometimes the pressure of mystical revelation was so strong that he felt compelled to finish a work before taking any rest. For example, he claimed that his *Ḥilyat al-abdāl* was written in the space of an hour,[60] that *The Bezels of Wisdom* was all revealed to him in a single dream, and that, while engaged in writing *The Meccan Revelations*, he had filled three notebooks a day. What Ibn al-'Arabī is claiming here is that his written works are as much the result of spiritual revelation as of his own thought processes, the implication being that any attempt to treat what he wrote as a philosophy or ideology is doomed to failure. He would, of course, have admitted that the language in which he expressed his inspirations owed much to the intellectual terminology of the day, educated as it was by the various traditional and cultural influences to which he was exposed throughout his life. This, however, only makes the at-

---

58. Part I, The Keio Institute of Cultural and Linguistic Studies, 1966.
59. Introduction to Afifi's *Memorandum*.
60. Ibid.

INTRODUCTION

tempt at interpretation and classification the more difficult in that, by fixing on the many trees of familiar words, expressions, symbols, and ideas, one may so easily lose sight of the forest of his experience.

HIS HISTORICAL AND SPIRITUAL CONTEXT

In his works, as in his life, Ibn al-'Arabī bestrides the world of Islamic mysticism or Sufism like a colossus and, in doing so, brings unity and cohesion to the phenomenon of esoteric spirituality in Islam, drawing as he does on that great legacy of Islamic spirituality which he inherited, and casting his own peculiar spell on all later generations of Sufis. More than this, he brings together in his writings a whole wealth of spiritual and intellectual disciplines that, in his own special way, he seeks to weld together into a system of thought notable not only for its universality and breadth, but also for its profundity and penetration into the central issues of human experience. He brought to his task not only a great store of traditional and mystical learning and experience but also, in striving for solutions to the great difficulties inherent in the divine-human enigma, a quite brilliant genius and originality of mind. It is indeed the combination of these two things that makes any attempt to fully comprehend the Sufi master so extraordinarily difficult.

Historically speaking, Ibn al-'Arabī's life occurred toward the end of a major phase of Islamic development, in that only eighteen years after his death the Mongol invasions of the Fertile Crescent dealt a terrible blow to Islamic civilization in the East, so that, in a sense, the great gathering together of Islamic spiritual learning in the written works of Ibn al-'Arabī, before the storm of political, social, and cultural upheaval, becomes for later, less secure, generations an invaluable source of spiritual inspiration. Ibn al-'Arabī represents a culmination not only of Sufi exposition but also, in a very significant way, of Islamic intellectual expression.

He was, however, not only a link between one phase of Islamic civilization and another, but also—more importantly for the Sufi tradition itself—an essential link between the Islamic spirituality of the West and that of the Oriental world, between one world influenced more by the Classical and Neo-Classical heritage and the other influenced more by the ancient Iranian spirit and the impact of the Hindu world.

INTRODUCTION

This link was forged, as we have already indicated, when Ibn al-'Arabī went to spend the second half of his life in the Eastern Islamic world and, more particularly, when his travels took him northward into Anatolia, to Konya, which would become later the home of the great Jalāl al-Dīn Rūmī.[61] More specifically, the link was created through the meeting of the Andalusian master with his devoted disciple in Konya, Ṣadr al-Dīn al-Qunawī.[62] It was the latter's contacts in later years with many of the most celebrated Persian Sufis that ensured the continuing presence of Ibn al-'Arabī's spirit in the body of Sufism. Al-Qunawī was later to become the spiritual master of Quṭb al-Dīn al-Shīrāzī and Fakhr al-Dīn al-'Irāqī, both major contributors to Oriental Sufism. He was also a close friend of Jalāl al-Dīn Rūmī, whose monumental *Mathnawī*[63] did so much to encourage the flowering of Sufi spirituality in Iran and beyond. Apart from the vital meeting of master and disciple in Konya, Ibn al-'Arabī also had contact both with 'Umar Shihāb al-Dīn al-Suhrawardī, himself a major influence in Sufi circles, and with Ibn al-Fāriḍ, perhaps the greatest mystical poet of Arab Islam.[64]

Although Ibn al-'Arabī spent so many years in the East, he was not forgotten in the western Islamic world, since, through the medium of Abū al-Ḥasan al-Shādhilī and his order,[65] his influence has been felt throughout western Islam down to the present day.

The influence of the Andalusian master, however, also spread beyond the confines of the Islamic world to touch, among others, no less a figure than Dante. Asín Palacios, in his controversial book *Islam and the Divine Comedy*,[66] seeks to show that certain elements in the work of Dante indicate the influence of Ibn al-'Arabī, albeit secondhand. Indeed, it is hardly surprising that the ideas and images of so influential a man as Ibn al-'Arabī should have percolated into the mystical and poetical imagery of Europe at a time when the influence of Muslim Spain, in general, was very considerable. Whether affected by

---

61. D. A.D. 1273. Founder of the famous Mevlevi order or "Whirling Dervishes."
62. See above, p. 9
63. Trans. R. A. Nicholson, 8 vols. London, 1925–1940.
64. A.D. 1182–1235. When Ibn al-'Arabī asked his permission to write a commentary on his poem *al-Tā'iyyah*, Ibn al-Fāriḍ replied that *The Meccan Revelations* was commentary enough.
65. A.D. 1196–1258. His order gave rise to many other important orders in North Africa and the Middle East.
66. London, 1926.

INTRODUCTION

such influences or not, the celebrated German mystic Meister Eckhart taught a form of Christian mystical theology that in certain respects bears a striking resemblance to the monistic teachings of Ibn al-'Arabī. The German master, like the Andalusian master, also fell foul of the religious authorities of his day.

All in all, the contribution of Ibn al-'Arabī to Islamic mystical thought and devotion was great and extensive, both in time and area, so that there is hardly a Sufi order or teacher since his time not influenced by his perspective.

THE BEZELS OF WISDOM

The work of Ibn al-'Arabī here presented in translation is called in the original Arabic *Fuṣūṣ al-ḥikam*, which literally translated is *The Bezels of the Wisdoms*. The latter translation is too literal and is cumbersome in English. In calling the translation *The Bezels of Wisdom* I am following R. A. Nicholson, since it is the only English title that at once accurately translates the Arabic title and conveys adequately the intention of the work. T. Burckhardt has called his partial translation of the work into French *La Sagesse des Prophetes*,[67] the English version of which is entitled *The Wisdom of the Prophets*.[68] While these titles do indeed convey, in a general way, the original Arabic and the intention of the author, they do not convey to the non-Arabic reader the precise meaning Ibn al-'Arabī wished to convey by calling his work *Fuṣūṣ al-ḥikam*. The Arabic word *faṣṣ*, which is the singular form of *fuṣūṣ*, means the bezel or setting in which the gem, engraved with a name, will be set to make a seal ring. It is true that the word can also be used to denote the gem itself, but that is not what is intended here by the author. By calling his work *Fuṣūṣ al-ḥikam*, Ibn al-'Arabī means that each prophet, after whom each chapter is entitled, is the human setting in which the gemstone of each kind of wisdom is set, thus making of each prophet the signet or sign, by selection, of a particular aspect of God's wisdom. This is expressed in another way in the chapter headings. For example, the title of the first chapter is "The Wisdom of Divinity in the Word of Adam."[69] In

---

67. Lyons, 1955.
68. Beshara Publications, 1975.
69. See p. 47.

INTRODUCTION

this chapter the divine truth or wisdom is expressed or set in the form or word of Adam, Adam being in this context, so to speak, a divine utterance of a particular wisdom. In this case the Word is equivalent to the bezel in the main title.

The text I have used in translating this work is the excellent manuscript from the Evkaf Museum in Istanbul, No. 1933, which, according to a certificate of authenticity incorporated in the manuscript, was written down by no less a person that Sadr al-Dīn al-Qunawī and signed by the author, Ibn al-'Arabī, in the year A.H. 630.[70]

In preparing the translation I have also used several of the many commentaries on this work by Ibn al-'Arabī's disciples and followers. They are, first, al-Qāshānī, *Sharḥ 'alā fuṣūṣ alḥikam* [Cairo, A.H. 1321]; second, *Al-Fukūk* by Sadr al-Dīn al-Qunawī [Yusuf Agha Library in Konya, 4858]; third, Al-Nābulusī's *Sharḥ jawāhir al-nuṣūṣ* [Cairo, A.H. 1304–1323] and fourth, the *Sharḥ* of al-Jāmī [Cairo, A.H. 1304–1323]. These commentaries have not, however, been used as quotations in the footnotes to the translation, since the intention is to let the author speak for himself as much as possible.

As Ibn al-'Arabī says in the preface to the work, he composed *The Bezels of Wisdom* during the year A.D. 627 [A.H. 1230] after he had settled in Damascus. He says,

> I saw the Apostle of God in a visitation granted to me during the latter part of the month of Muḥarram in the year 627, in the city of Damascus. He had in his hand a book and he said to me, "This is the book of the bezels of Wisdom; take it and bring it to men that they might benefit from it." I replied, "All obedience is due to God and His Apostle; it shall be as we are commanded." I therefore carried out the wish, made pure my intention, and devoted my purpose to the publishing of this book, just as the Apostle had laid down, without any addition or subtraction."[71]

Whether this means that Ibn al-'Arabī is claiming that he took down what had been dictated to him in the vision, or whether he expressed

---

70. Cf. Osman Yahia, *Histoire et classification de l'oeuvre d'Ibn 'Arabi*, Damascus, 1964, I, pp. 240–257.
71. See p. 45.

INTRODUCTION

the principal themes in his own way, is not clear. Suffice it to say that the work, apart from its arrangement into twenty-seven chapters, lacks any real system or organization of its subject matter.

As the title suggests, the intention of the work is to present particular aspects of the divine wisdom within the context of the lives and persons of twenty-seven prophets.[72] Although the first of the twenty-seven chapters is concerned with Adam, the first of the prophets according to Islam, and the last with Muḥammad, the prophets in between are not arranged in any chronological order. Indeed, they do not seem to be arranged according to any particular pattern. In some cases, for example the chapters concerned with Noah, Moses, and Jesus, the teaching is related specifically to the lives and utterances of those prophets, as recorded in the Qur'an, while in others there would seem to be very little relationship between the prophet whose name appears in the chapter heading and the topics discussed in the chapter itself.

Whatever may have been the circumstances of its composition, *The Bezels of Wisdom* is clearly a most important resumé or synopsis of Ibn al-'Arabī's principal themes and, as such, deserves serious attention and careful study, and must be counted as perhaps his greatest work, apart from the much larger and more diffuse *Meccan Revelations*.[73] Distributed throughout the work are the main topics of his teaching, the nature of God and man and their relationship, the divine Mercy, the Creative Imagination, and so forth. However, it is precisely because the author tried to include so many cardinal points in such a relatively short work in such an haphazard way that *The Bezels of Wisdom* is very difficult to understand, let alone translate into the language of another culture. The synoptical character of the work also leads Ibn al-'Arabī to great concentration of expression on the one hand, and to extremes of exegesis on the other.

Indeed, it is mystical exegesis, sometimes of a startling and unusual kind, that is the dominant feature of this work, since throughout it Ibn al-'Arabī draws heavily on qur'anic material to illustrate his points. In common with many other Sufi writers, he approaches the qur'anic text in a way different from that of the more familiar exoteric commentators. That is to say, he deals with the texts on the premise that every verse of the Qur'an has many more meanings than the

---

72. See above, p. 16.
73. See above, p. 12.

INTRODUCTION

one that might be obvious to the ordinary believer, who sees merely the surface of things. Beneath the surface, according to the Sufis, there lies an ocean of meaning, both subtle and spiritual, that is accessible only to those whose inner eye is open, whether by divine grace or by proper training.[74] In this way, the Sufi considers that the qur'anic text acts, so to speak, as a mirror to the reader, in that the latter will perceive in it only what his own spiritual state permits him to see.

Thus the mystic exegete claims to see in the sacred texts meanings that are not apparent to ordinary mortals. In *The Bezels of Wisdom*, especially in the chapter on Noah, Ibn al-'Arabī goes one step further and actually interprets verses from the last part of *Sūrah Nūh* as meaning the very opposite of what the words appear to mean.[75] For example, interpreting the words of the Qur'an [LXXI, 24], "It only increases the oppressors in confusion," he sees them as meaning, "It only increases those who oppress their own souls by self-denial in spiritual perplexity." Now it is quite clear from the context of this verse that such an interpretation could have been arrived at only by completely ignoring the context, and also the meaning the words "oppressors" and "confusion" have throughout the Qur'an.[76] Here we see Ibn al-'Arabī at his most "perverse" in forcing the issue of the Oneness of Being according to which all contrast and opposition is resolved in the *coincidentia oppositorum*.

In much the same spirit, Ibn al-'Arabī is not afraid, in *The Bezels of Wisdom*, to express his ideas in ways equally unacceptable to the religious establishment. One has only to mention his treatment of such ideas as the apparent conflict between the divine Will and the divine Wish or Command,[77] the very interesting and challenging notion of "the god created in belief"[78] and the suggestion, in the last chapter, that it is in woman that man may most perfectly contemplate God,[79] to see that a work like this would be open to all manner of misinterpretation and misunderstanding. This is because, in the last analysis, the implications of Ibn al-'Arabī's teachings on such subjects are in danger of leading the reader far beyond the familiar borders of tradi-

---

74. Cf. H. Corbin, *Creative Imagination*, Chaps. 2 and 3.
75. See pp. 80ff.
76. See pp. 80–81.
77. See p. 117.
78. See p. 137.
79. See p. 275.

INTRODUCTION

tional Islam into realms of spiritual universality and direct experience in which dogmatic certainties suffer the torments of the mystical perplexity, mentioned above. In the author's defense, it must be said that such works as *The Bezels of Wisdom* were certainly not intended for public consumption, but rather for his fellow Sufis, who knew how to deal with the apparent theological dangers implicit in it. Ibn al-'Arabī knew better than most the essentially incommunicable nature of mystical experience,[80] and it is clear from his letter of advice to the ruler Kay Kaus that he recognized fully the validity and necessity of Islamic doctrine and law.[81] This contrast, and apparent conflict, between daring mystical expression and a more sober caution is illustrated in two poems in *The Bezels of Wisdom*. In the first he utters what appears to be pure heresy in the line, "I worship Him and He worships me,"[82] while in the second he warns against spiritual inflation with the words, "Be the servant of the Lord, not the lord of the servant."[83] Despite this, however, Ibn al-'Arabī, like other Sufis before him and like Meister Eckhart in Christendom, was often the object of extreme suspicion and passionate denunciation, as during his visit to Cairo in A.D. 1206.[84]

However, despite the undoubted profundity and originality of this important work, there is no denying that the overall impression on the reader is one of a lack of proper organization and continuity. As has already been observed, the subject matter of most of the chapters bears little or no relation to the name of the prophet in the title. Indeed, there is often but scant connection between the subjects discussed in a chapter and the particular Wisdom of the title. Within the chapters also there is often a considerable measure of discontinuity in the topics dealt with. The main themes of his thought occur again and again from chapter to chapter in a rather haphazard way. It is for these reasons that I have tried, in my introductory notes, to isolate from each chapter the most important themes and to introduce them within the context of his own thought.

In addition to the general lack of organization, the reader is also likely to be sorely tried by the devious and tortuous methods Ibn al-

---

80. Cf. *Futūḥāt*, I, p. 31.
81. See above p. 10.
82. See p. 95.
83. See p. 103.
84. See above, p. 9.

INTRODUCTION

'Arabī employs in commenting on and interpreting not only material from the *Qur'an* and elsewhere but also the associated meanings of the Arabic words themselves.

All in all, *The Bezels of Wisdom* is a difficult and perplexing work, requiring considerable patience, sublety, and imagination from the reader, who must be prepared to follow the Sufi master along all the tortuous alleyways of his thought and exposition. Nevertheless, the work also affords many profound and often amazing insights into the deeper and more recondite aspects of mystical experience and expression.

It is recommended that the reader refer frequently to the qur'anic passages quoted in such a piecemeal fashion in this work, in order to form a clearer picture of the context.

HIS THOUGHT

Any attempt, at the present time, to define the nature of Ibn al-'Arabī's thought or to assess its significance must, of necessity, be a tentative one, since no really satisfactory appreciation of his system of mystical thought will be possible until the immense task of editing and interpreting his many still unpublished works is nearer to completion, or, at least, until an exhaustive study has been made of *The Meccan Revelations*.[85] Athough he was, without doubt, a thinker of great stature and although there has come down to us a considerable corpus of his works, comparatively little study has been devoted to him. The student of Ibn al-'Arabī has to approach what has been said of him previously with caution and to be constantly aware of the provisional nature of his own conclusions. A. J. Arberry summed up the situation very well when he said,

> When all is said and done, however, it remains indisputably true that thorough research on this the greatest mystical genius of Islam is still in its infancy, and there are few subjects in the whole field of human studies more attractive to the student or more likely to yield important results. Ibn 'Arabī may be compared to an unexplored mountain peak. Much of

---

85. See above, p. 12.

INTRODUCTION

the territory on all sides is known, but it has yet to be determined by what precise paths the way to the summit lies, or in what remote heights those fountains spring that well into the mighty river of all subsequent mystical thought, Muslim and Christian alike.[86]

In more recent years this situation has been improved somewhat by the excellent work of H. Corbin and T. Izutzu.[87]

This neglect of one who is undeniably one of the greatest figures in the Muslim mystical tradition and probably one of the world's greatest mystics is a curious one in view of the fact that so much more attention has been given to other great exponents of Sufism, such as Ghazālī and Rūmī.

The reason for this neglect can probably be traced to the daunting nature of the task facing the would-be exponent. First of all, there is the enormous corpus of written material, not only by the master himself, but also by the many commentators and disciples who came after him. Second there is the bewildering diversity and richness of his sources and, last, the variety of levels at which he expresses his teachings, reflecting his brilliant originality of thought together with his profound spiritual experience. The first requires of the student both a good knowledge of the Arabic language and a thorough acquaintance with Sufism—not to speak of time. The second requires a reasonable knowledge of comparative mysticism, Neoplatonism, astrology, alchemy and some of the other more obscure sciences of the Middle Ages. The last requires, if not an actual experience of the mystic path, then at least some real sympathy and insight into its premises and aims.

Ibn al-'Arabī's two main sources were, by his own admission, the Qur'an and the Traditions of the Prophet Muhammad. In this he followed established Sufi practice and, by so doing, confirms the Muslim origins of his inspiration. These sources, however, he freely interpreted, both linguistically and theologically, to corroborate his spiritual experience. In common with other Islamic thinkers of the time, whether philosophers or theologians, he draws heavily for many of his terms and concepts on the Neoplatonic writers, includ-

---

86. *An Introduction to the History of Sufism*, Oxford, 1942, p. 58.
87. See above, p. 13.

INTRODUCTION

ing the celebrated and wrongly attributed *Theology of Aristotle*.[88] The relationship, however, between the original connotations of the terms and those he gave them is still by no means established. As an initiated Sufi, he also drew much inspiration from both Andalusian and Eastern exponents of the Sufi tradition. Of the former the most prominent were Ibn Barrajān[89] and Ibn al-'Arīf,[90] while of the latter al-Tirmidhī,[91] al-Ḥallāj,[92] and al-Bistāmī[93] are frequently quoted by him. Within the pale of orthodox Islam, the Mashā'is and the 'Ash'aris exerted some influence on his thinking, while among the less orthodox, the various schools of the Isma'ilis and the Brethren of Purity seem to have left some mark.[94]

Although not definitely established, it is quite possible that Ibn al-'Arabī used material from the Jewish writers of the Kabbalistic tradition, especially in his studies on the mystical significance of the letters of the alphabet. Similarly, some of his cosmological ideas would seem to suggest some acquaintance with the Gnostic tradition in Christianity. Another possible source of inspiration, but one that has been little studied, is that of the various schools of Hinduism and, perhaps, Buddhism. Both Hindu and Buddhist ideas must be assumed to have infiltrated into the Muslim world,[95] and it is of particular interest to note that an Arabic version of a Persian translation of a Sanskrit work on Tantric Yoga has been attributed to Ibn al-'Arabī.[96] In this connection also, his important theory of the Creative Imagination bears a striking resemblance to the Hindu concept of *māyā*.[97] It is certainly true that a comparative study of Hindu and Sufi metaphysics often produces some surprising parallels.[98]

All of these sources and influences appear in various guises with-

---

88. In fact a Neoplatonic abridgement of the last five Enneads of Plotinus.
89. Died A.H. 536.
90. Cf. *Maḥāsin al-majālis*, ed. Asin Palacios, Paris, 1933.
91. *Kitāb khatm al-awliyā'*, ed. O. Yahya, Beirut, 1965.
92. Cf. L. Massignon, *La Passion d'al-Ḥosayn Ibn Mansour al-Ḥallaj*, 2 vols., Paris, 1922.
93. Cf. R. C. Zaehner, *Hindu and Muslim Mysticism*, London, 1960.
94. Cf. A. A. Afifi, *Mystical Philosophy*, p. 183.
95. Cf. M. Horten, *Festgabe Jakobi*, Bonn, 1926, pp. 397–405.
96. *Mir'āt al-ma'ānī*, unedited ms. Cf. C. Brockelmann, *Geschichte der arabischen Literatur*, GI, p. 579.
97. Cf. H. Corbin, *Creative Imagination in the Sufism of Ibn 'Arabi*, London, 1970.
98. Cf. R. C. Zaehner, *Hindu and Muslim Mysticism*, London, 1960.

INTRODUCTION

in his works where they become grist to the mill of his own unique enunciation of a vision of the Oneness of Being [*waḥdat ak-wujūd*]. It requires only a general survey of his works to realize that he managed to combine in himself the genius and resources of the philosopher, the poet, the traumaturge, the occultist, the theologian, and the practical ascetic. He combines the scholastic expertise of Ghazālī with the poetic imagery of Ibn al-Fāriḍ, the metaphysical daring of al-Ḥallāj with the stringent orthodoxy of al-Muḥāsibī, the abstract categories of the Neoplatonists with the dramatic imagination of Rūmī, and the abstruse science of the Kabbalist with the practical wisdom of the spiritual guide.

A further difficulty presents itself in dealing with the writings of Ibn al-'Arabī and that is the degree to which he inevitably restrained himself in expressing certain of his experiences or disguised them in elliptical language to avoid serious charges of heresy from the religious authorities. He refers to this when he says, "This kind of spiritual insight and knowledge must be hidden from the majority of men by reason of its sublimity. For its depths are far reaching and the dangers involved great."[99]

Too often various studies on Ibn al-'Arabī's thought have been limited to one or another aspect of his teaching, to the exclusion or insufficient appreciation of other dimensions. Thus, A. A. Afifi and T. Izutzu, in their different ways, see in him a predominantly philosophical thinker, while H. Corbin, in his very timely appreciation of Ibn al-'Arabī's intuitive and imaginative genius, does not fully recognize his undoubtedly precise and systematic mind.[100] As has been the case with mystics of other traditions, so also with Ibn al-'Arabī, Western scholars have too often tried, rather unsuccessfully, to judge him by the criteria of rational philosophy and to understand his concepts within that framework, ignoring in the process his own frequent criticism of rational approaches to reality and forgetting that most non-Western religious traditions have very different perspectives from our own. The very systematic way in which he expressed his ideas, his use of familiar philosophic terms, and his often apparently philosophic train of thought have led certain scholars to suppose that he was primarily a philosopher, whereas, on his own testimony, he was first and foremost a mystic. Therefore, in attempting to form a

---

99. *Al-Fanā' fī'l-mushāhadah*, in *Rasā'il Ibnul-'Arabī*, Hyderabad, 1948, I, 1, p. 3.
100. See above, p. 13.

INTRODUCTION

comprehensive picture of Ibn al-'Arabī's contribution to Islamic thought, one must take into consideration all aspects of it, and not simply concentrate on that which is immediately familiar.

Above all, it is the mystical and therefore experiential dimension underlying the whole of Ibn al-'Arabī's work that must necessarily prove the greatest obstacle to any thorough comprehension of his teachings, since the most essential experience of spiritual mysteries is, by the very nature of the case, incommunicable except, in the last analysis, to those who have shared in the same or a similar experience. This is, of course, the dilemma faced by all nonparticipant students of mysticism in whatever tradition. Ibn al-'Arabī himself draws attention to this in *The Meccan Revelations*: "Knowledge of mystical states can only be had by actual experience, nor can the reason of man define it, nor arrive at any cognizance of it by deduction, as is also the case with knowledge of the taste of honey, the bitterness of patience, the bliss of sexual union, love, passion or desire, all of which cannot possibly be known unless one be properly qualified or experience them directly."[101] This means, in effect, that however good one's knowledge of Arabic, Islam, history, or comparative religion may be, one must realize, in trying to understand Ibn al-'Arabī's thought, that all the external and relatively familiar forms of his exposition, drawing as he did on the intellectual *koine* of the period, are no more than vehicles of expression, imperfect ones at that, for the realities he claimed to have experienced.

It remains, having explained the many factors to be taken into account in studying Ibn al-'Arabī, to consider the main themes of his teaching, indeed those themes that dominate *The Bezels of Wisdom*, which he composed as a synopsis of his principal ideas.

Of his main themes, the one that predominates over the rest and to which they are subordinate is that of the Oneness of Being [*wahdat al-wujūd*]. The concept of the Oneness of Being is an all-embracing one, in that all Ibn al-'Arabī's other concepts are but facets of it, just as he would say that all distinction, difference, and conflict are but apparent facets of a single and unique reality, the "seamless garment" of Being, whose reality underlies all derivative being and its experience.

Certain Sufi writers seem to think that there is an important difference between this concept of the Oneness of Being and that of

---

101. *Futūḥāt*, I, p. 31.

INTRODUCTION

waḥdat al-shuhūd or the Oneness of Perception, having regard to a very important tension in human experience between perception and being, subject and object, the knower and the object of knowledge.[102] Ibn al-'Arabī, however, in coining the term *waḥdat al-wujūd* [Oneness of Being], did not intend to make any distinction but, by choosing the word *wujūd*, to convey the meaning of the Oneness of both Being and Perception in the perfect and complete union of the one and only Reality [*al-ḥaqq*]. This is because the Arabic root word *wajada* carries both ideas, that of being and therefore objectivity, and that of perception and therefore subjectivity, both of which he sees as being one in *the* Reality.[103] Of this sole and, essentially, undifferentiated Reality, Ibn al-'Arabī does not use the word *Allāh* or God, since to speak of divinity, as is evident in this work, is also to imply that which is not divine and thus to introduce differentiation, polarity, tension, and ultimately conflict. Naturally, since the experience of differentiation and polarity is inevitably an aspect of the whole and complete Reality, and since we are, as human beings, patently a part of that aspect, Ibn al-'Arabī necessarily spends much of the time writing about the macrocosmic and microcosmic implications of that aspect of the Reality, the divine and the nondivine, the substantial and the accidental, the existent and the nonexistent, and so forth. He is, however, constantly returning from such considerations of a differential nature to his great underlying concept of the sole perfect and complete Reality, which is its own sole Being and its own sole Perception of its own Being, a concept succinctly expressed in the Hindu term *sachidananda* [Being-Consciousness-Bliss]. As has already been mentioned, in returning to this concept, Ibn al-'Arabī often makes statements that scandalize those of the religious whose outlook is irrevocably fixed in an attitude of distinction and differentiation.[104]

This characteristic and fundamental concept of Ibn al-'Arabī has led Western scholars, at various times, to categorize or to attempt to categorize his teachings in different ways. Many have called him a pantheist, while others have, perhaps more accurately, assigned the term "monism" to his thought. Although helpful in certain ways, this sort of categorization according to Western criteria impedes rather

---

102. Cf. A. Valiuddin, "A Reconciliation between Ibn 'Arabi's wahdat al-wujud and the Mujaddid's wahdat al-shuhud," *Islamic Quarterly*, 25, 1951, pp. 43–51.
103. See Lane's *Arabic-English Lexicon*, art. *wajada*.
104. See above, p. 9.

INTRODUCTION

than assists in understanding his vision of Reality. To say that he was a pantheist is to ignore his often strongly transcendental view of divinity. What he says of the relationship between the Cosmos and God is that the Cosmos is not and cannot be other than God, not that it is God or that God is the Cosmos. His doctrine of the Oneness of Being/Perception means that the sole, whole Reality is far more than the sum of its parts or aspects and that, however things may seem from the standpoint of differentiated being or perception, all being is nothing other than Its Being, and all perception, however limited, is nothing other than *the* Perception in a particular mode.

Within the context of the Real, however, there is eternally being played the great drama of polarity with all its implicit experience of relationship, affinity, tension, and conflict. The original emergence of the principle of differentiation within the Reality is accounted for by the Sufis according to the Holy Tradition: "I was a hidden treasure, and longed to be known, so I created the Cosmos." This tradition indicates that the primordial and fundamental polarization to take place within the Reality is that of Self-consciousness, that is to say the original Self-polarization of the Reality into subject and object, knower and known. This is by no means as simple as it sounds, since it is not a question of the one being active and dominant while the latter is passive and dominated, as often tends to be assumed in our consciousness-oriented society, but there is rather a relationship of mutual conditioning going on by which each, at once, experiences and determines the other.

Furthermore, because each of the poles is nothing other than the Reality, each must imply, potentially and latently, the other within itself. The process of Self-polarization is then one by which each projects onto the other what is latent of the other within itself. There is of course, at this stage, no real otherness, since it is a case of divine Self-consciousness for which the principle of otherness is simply for Self-realization, as is the case with human self-awareness. In dealing with this matter, as also its cosmic and human reverberations, Ibn al-'Arabī often uses the image of the mirror in attempting to explain this process.[105] More importantly, however, he uses two other powerful images, the one more masculine and the other distinctly feminine in its connotations.

The first of these images is that of the Creative Imagination or

---

105. Cf. p. 69.

INTRODUCTION

khayāl by which the essentially latent images of reality are projected onto the screen of the illusion of otherness, so that the divine might perceive Itself as object.[106] Thus this Imagination is no less than the link between the Real as perceiver and knower and the Real as object and what is to be known, between the creator and the created, worshiped and worshiper.[107] It is, indeed, that which effects the apparent alienation of the Real as consciousness from the Real as becoming and, as such, may be said to be the very principle of creation itself, creation, that is, in the sense of polarization *in divinis*, since, for Ibn al-'Arabī, nothing is ultimately other than the Reality.[108] Indeed, for Ibn al-'Arabī, there is no such thing as *creatio ex nihilo* in the usual sense, since all that is thus caused, apparently, to exist derives from their essences implicit within the divine knowing, which although they may be nonexistent are, nevertheless, of the Reality.[109] In being released into existence by the Creative Imagination they become confirmed by being recognized by the divine Subject, just as the consciousness implicit, essentially, without being finds its own corroboration in the affirmation by "created" being of the Supreme Consciousness. Distant echoes of this original and fundamental Creative Imagination in the human sphere are the dreaming of the sleeper, the vision of the craftsman, and the fantasies of the Walter Mitty.

The second striking image Ibn al-'Arabī uses to illustrate the original process of Self-realization is similarly inspired by the Holy Tradition quoted above, although in this case the image is more earthy and immediate. Having stated that the origin of the divine longing to be known is love, he goes on to describe the precreative state of the Reality as one of anxiety or distress [*karb*], of a primordial labor pressing for birth and manifestation, of an original urge to overflow, to pour out into patent existence the realities latent within.[110] This birth image is reinforced when Ibn al-'Arabī describes the relieving of the distress as a breathing or sighing [*tanaffus*], which at once expresses and relieves the distress.[111] He goes on, however, to call this creative and existential exhalation the Breath of the Merciful

---

106. Cf. p. 121. This aspect of Ibn al-'Arabī's thought has been thoroughly studied by H. Corbin in his *Creative Imagination in the Sufism of Ibn 'Arabi*, London, 1970.
107. *Futūḥāt*, II, p. 311.
108. Ibid.
109. See p. 64.
110. See p. 181.
111. Ibid.

INTRODUCTION

[*nafas al-raḥmān*], and Ibn al-'Arabī, with his keen insight into the meanings of Arabic roots, cannot have been unaware of the basic meaning of the root *raḥima*, which is the womb, the meaning of mercy being derivative. Indeed, for him, the term "mercy" [*raḥmah*] did not simply denote an attitude or feeling of compassion, as usually understood, but rather the very principle of creation by which all created things exist and by which all the latent potentialities within the "divine mind" are released into actuality, as objects of the divine perception and witness. For Ibn al-'Arabī, then, love and mercy, both of which require polarity and relationship, that is to say they require "another," an object, lie at the center of the creative process.[112] However, as if to complete the circle of Self-realization, the love and compassion for "the other" leads inevitably to the longing for reunion, for the obliteration of otherness in oneness. Thus, the bipolarization of the Reality into divine subject and "created" object leads once more to reidentification in the One Real, but this time enriched and enhanced by the experience of Self-consciousness.[113] Thus, also, the Mercy operates in two directions, outwardly in creating the necessary object of the divine love, which Mercy is called *raḥmān*, and inwardly in reestablishing the original synthesis of the Reality, which is called *raḥīm*.[114] Although the latter is also a movement of love, a longing for reunion, it nevertheless threatens the otherness of the object, thus appearing to the object in its otherness as wrath and destruction.[115] Thus we have here that eternal enigma and paradox, the reverberations of which are manifest in all human relationships, of the double and inevitable necessity of otherness and nonotherness for love, whether divine or human, which creates the tension necessary for the experience and awareness of Self-consciousness, whether divine or human. As we shall see, however, divine Self-consciousness or identity is Self-subsistent, whereas human identity is truly other-related.[116]

Yet another image used by Ibn al-'Arabī, and one he shares with many other Muslim and Sufi writers, is that of the divine Pen, equat-

---

112. *Futūḥāt* II, p. 310, where he speaks of the "breathing out" as being accompanied by joy [*ladhdhah*].
113. It is this reunion in full awareness that the mystic seeks, and not merely the unconscious, ontological identity of contingency.
114. Cf. p. 190.
115. Cf. p. 130.
116. Thus God is called in the *Qur'an* [II:255], the Self-subsistent [*al-Qayyūm*].

INTRODUCTION

ed with the Universal Intellect of Hellenistic philosophy, and the Tablet, which was equated with Universal Nature.[117] In all these images, Ibn al-'Arabī, as a Muslim mystic, naturally regards the consciousness pole as active and dominant and therefore primarily divine, and the becoming pole as passive and dependent, so that the relationship between the Cosmos as created object and God as creating subject is envisaged within the context of the patriarchal perspective in which woman, as the human image of Universal Nature, is always seen as being derivative from and dependent on man, as the human agent of the Spirit. In certain passages, however, it is clear that Ibn al-'Arabī was well aware that, within the context of the primordial polarity, the dependence, as between the two poles, is mutual, and not as one-sided as traditional attitudes compelled him to suggest. This awareness is more obvious when he writes on the subject of the Oneness of Being.

This leads to a consideration of the various terms Ibn al-'Arabī uses in discussing the matters outlined above. When speaking of the Reality within the context of the Oneness of Being, or of the Reality as contrasted with that which imagines falsely that it is real or that it is other or separate from the Reality, he calls it *al-Ḥaqq* [the Real, the Reality, the True].[118] When he is writing about the Reality as polarized into the spiritual or intellectual pole and the cosmic or existential pole, he calls the former God [*Allāh*] or the Creator [*al-Khāliq*] and the latter creation [*khalq*] or the Cosmos [*al-'ālam*].[119] The term *Allāh* is also the Supreme Name, the Name of names, which as the title of divinity establishes the whole quality of the relationship between the two poles, the one being divine and necessary while the other is nondivine and contingent. The other Names represent the infinite aspects or modes of the relationship in its infinite variety of qualities.[120] The term *Allāh*, however, when used precisely by Ibn al-'Arabī, is not the same as the Reality, since, as he would say, divinity as such is in a state of mutual dependence with that which affirms or worships it as divine.[121] The same is true of the term "Lord" [*rabb*], which denotes

---

117. These two terms are based on the *Qur'an* [LXVIII:1 and LXXXV:22].
118. Ibn al-'Arabī does not always use this or the other terms in such a precise way, often using *al-Ḥaqq* and *Allāh* as synonyms. In the translation I have given the former as the Reality and the latter as God.
119. See p. 153.
120. See p. 52.
121. See p. 93.

INTRODUCTION

not the universal position of the Creator God vis-à-vis creation, Cosmos, but rather the particular position of a particular aspect of God vis-à-vis a particular, individual creation, so that, while *Allāh* is the God of creation as a whole, the Lord denotes a private and special relationship between a particular creature and its corresponding archetype *in divinis*. The status of Lord, however, like that of divinity, is dependent on the existence of the slave or servant [*'abd*], since dominion requires what is dominated and thus has no function outside the context of the polarity discussed above. Indeed, all such distinctions are unreal as far as the Oneness of Being is concerned, something of which Ibn al-'Arabī never tires of reminding his reader.

Another of his important themes that relate to the primordial polarity of Divinity-Cosmos is his, in certain quarters, highly controversial teachings on the subject of the Divine Will. This he divides into two aspects or modes, one of which he calls the Will [*al-mashī'ah*], and the other the Wish [*al-irādah*].[122] Alternatively, he calls the first the Creative Command [*al-amr al-takwīnī*], and the second the Obligating Command [*al-amr al-taklīfī*].[123] The Will of God, as opposed to the Wish of God, is the infinitely creative power that effects the endless becoming of the primordial other in all the complexity of its aspects and derivations. It is indeed the volitive aspect of the creating Mercy, and everything it wills comes into existence, there being no question, in the case of the Will, of obedience or disobedience, being purely existential in its effects. The Wish of God, however, or the Obligating Command, is concerned not so much with creation as with reintegration and concentration. This Obligating Command has everything to do with obedience and disobedience, since conformity with the Divine Wish is the sine qua non of salvation, which is to say the salvation of man, whose place in Ibn al-'Arabī's scheme will be considered below. It is clear from this that this notion of the two modes of the Divine Will implies considerable tension between the two modes and presents theology with a major paradox. In other words, while the Will is dedicated to cosmic actuality, irrespective of its implications for faith, morality, or ethics, the Wish demands the recognition of certain truths and behavior appropriate to such recognition, the one serving the existential pole of the Reality, the other the sapiential or spiritual pole.

---

122. See p. 190.
123. See p. 183.

INTRODUCTION

Linked very closely with these two ideas is another pair of concepts, namely that of Destiny [*al-qadar*] and Decree [*al-qadā'*], the latter being that power which determines what shall be and not be in existence, while the former determines more exactly when, where, and how such coming into existence will be. In certain respects, therefore, the concepts of Destiny and Decree may be regarded as modes of the divine Will and Wish, especially the former. Thus, Destiny and Decree may be said to concern more the realization of the creative process in actuality, while the Will and the Wish are concerned with the subjective intention to create.[124]

At first glance this theory of creation might seem to be unduly deterministic and to leave no room for freedom of action or determination by the creature, especially man. It is therefore very necessary for any proper understanding of Ibn al-'Arabī's thought in this regard to bear two things always in mind. The first of these is his concept of the latent essences or archetypes, and the second is the fundamental and all-pervading concept, already discussed, of the Oneness of Being.[125] It is in the concept of the latent essences that there lies the mystery of free will and divine omniscience. Indeed, this concept is one of the most important of Ibn al-'Arabī's contributions to Sufi metaphysics. The latent essences are the potential, latent, nonexistent ideas or archetypes, within the divine consciousness, of all actual, apparent, created things in the projected Cosmos. Thus each created, existent thing is not something in itself, independent and isolated, but rather the existential becoming or actualization of an essential, potential, and latent reality that, hidden within the divine consciousness, constitutes, so to speak, the inner object of Self-knowledge, the essential core of divine identity. Once again, the existent thing and its latent archetype form yet another polarity of mutual dependence, since the former depends utterly on the latter for its reality and essence, while the latter depends on the former for its becoming and existence. Thus, the one is the outer and the other the inner mode of the one real object.[126]

Since, therefore, each one of us, as created beings, also has eternal and essential being *in divinis* and since, in our essential latency, we cannot be anything other than what God is and, furthermore, as con-

---

124. Cf. p. 165.
125. See above, p. 25.
126. Cf. p. 64.

INTRODUCTION

stituents of the inner object of His knowledge we contribute to what He knows Himself to be—which knowledge, in turn, informs the divine Will and Decree—we therefore share in the most essential way, by our inevitable essentiality, in the divine free will.[127] As Ibn al-'Arabī says, quoting the Qur'an, ultimately and originally, *in divinis*, the responsibility for what we are and how we are falls on us, since, in our latent essences, it is we ourselves who contribute to the divine knowing the very data that is the basis on which God ordains the nature and term of our becoming and existence.[128] Of course, as has been mentioned above, this view of our own eternal answerability assumes the the undifferentiated and inalienable reality of the Oneness of Being, in which the whole dialectic of self-other is fused into the unimaginable and inexpressible experience of the Reality. Connected with this question of existence-latency is the further concept of eternal predisposition [*isti'dād*], which means that each created thing, in its state of existence, is and can be no more or less than it is eternally predisposed to be or become *in aeternis*.[129] In relation to the Obligating Command, as opposed to the Creative Command, this means, for example, as the Qur'an itself indicates, that only those will heed the call to God who are, from eternity, predisposed to do so, which idea would seem to make nonsense of any notion of divine punishment and reward.[130] The concept of predisposition, however, is closely linked with the notion of our implicit and essential participation in the forming of our own destiny within the cosmic context. Thus, we mortals in our apparent state of otherness and separation, while seemingly pawns of the divine Will, are, in reality and essentially, none other than He Who wills.

In all these pairs of concepts, in their polar interrelationships, we can perceive another aspect of the original polarization within the Divine Self or the Reality, and that is the paradoxical and problematic tension between the divine Self-manifestation or Theophany [*tajallī*] and the divine Self-reservation or occultation, between the longing to experience Itself as object and other and the insistence on maintaining uniqueness and singularity of identity, or between the urge to pour out Its infinite possibility into actuality and the necessity to re-

---

127. Ibid.
128. *Qur'an*, XIV:27; see also this volume, p. 64.
129. See P. 167.
130. *Qur'an*, XXXVI: 10–11.

INTRODUCTION

tain the absolute inalienability of Its Truth. This tension is indeed the tension between polarization and nonpolarization, between an absolute consciousness that would contain all object latently and essentially within Itself and an infinite becoming that would absorb all subject into the infinite process of Self-actualization. Thus the absolute subject is eternally seeking to define and order the infinite becoming of the object with a view to annihilating its otherness, while the infinite object is eternally striving to relativize and involve the absolute knowing of the subject with the intention of ending its detachment. Needless to say, all these tensions, together with all the complex mutual experience they entail, are at once resolved in and a harmonious part of the Reality Itself.

These observations lead naturally to a consideration of the subject of man in Ibn al-'Arabī's thought, since, within the context of the divine-cosmic polarity, man, and especially the Perfect Man, constitutes the all-important link or medium between the two poles of Reality; the Isthmus [*barzakh*] as Ibn al-'Arabī calls him.[131] Having called man the link, however, it is necessary to point out that any link is important only so long as it serves to effect communication and relationship between things that are real in themselves, the link itself having no meaning per se, except by reference to the things it links. Thus man, considered in himself and by himself, is an absurdity, while assuming enormous significance when considered within the context of the polarity God-Cosmos.

The human condition, then, considered not as something in itself but only within the proper frame of reference, is at once representative of both poles and of the interrelationship between them, all of which confers on it, potentially, the most important status of all, in that as link it constitutes, so to speak, the microcosmic experience of the Reality Itself. On the other hand, when falsely regarded as an entity in itself, it is none of these things and an absurdity. Thus man may be said to combine in himself, simultaneously, the possibility of supreme significance and utter insignificance, just as he combines in himself a strong sense of the Absolute and the Infinite, without being either. Half animal and half angel, he serves to transmit to the Cosmos the truth of the divine subject, while also acting as the reflecting image of the cosmic object to the divine observer. As the first, he is God's agent and vicegerent, while as the second he is His obedient

---

131. Cf. Afifi, *Mystical Philosophy*, p. 82.

INTRODUCTION

slave. As representative of Heaven, as mouthpiece of the divine Word, man is male, while as representative of Earth, man is female, so that just as Earth or the Cosmos came forth from God the Creator, so did Eve, the woman, come forth from Adam.[132] At the heart of his humanity, however, man is both vicegerent and slave, male and female, spiritual and sensual, in one human selfhood, being never either one exclusively or completely.[133] Whatever his degree of spiritual attainment, man remains, in his human nature, forever a slave, and whatever the degree of his involvement in the Cosmos, he remains, in his human spirit, an agent, and it is his charge never to forget either aspect on pain of absurdity and nothingness. It is precisely the Perfect Man who perfectly combines within himself, in harmony, Heaven and Earth within the context of the realization of the Oneness of Being, who is at once the eye by which the divine subject sees Himself and the perfectly polished mirror that perfectly reflects the divine light.[134]

The Perfect Man is, thus, that individual human being who realizes in himself the reality of the saying that man is created in God's image, who combines in his microcosmic selfhood both the macrocosmic object and divine consciousness, being that heart which, microcosmically, contains all things essentially, and in which the Reality eternally rediscovers Its wholeness.[135] He is also, at once, the original and ultimate man whose archetype and potential for realization is innate in every human being.[136] Most human beings, however, are caught up in the currents of tension and interrelationship between the two poles, which meet and struggle in the human state, forever forgetting, in their vice-regal sense of identity, that they are also created slaves, and always shirking, in their cosmic animality, their responsibility as spiritual beings.

As a spiritual being, man shares with God, in Whose image he is created, in the divine power to create, as also in the power to articulate and give expression to knowledge and consciousness. As regards creative power, man's share in it is twofold. First, at the animal level, his natural instincts urge him, for the most part unconsciously and

---

132. Cf. p. 277.
133. Cf. Corbin, *Creative Imagination*, pp. 221–236.
134. See p. 88.
135. Cf. p. 148.
136. See p. 55.

INTRODUCTION

involuntarily, into the cosmic process of life and death. Second, at the spiritual and intellectual level, man's intelligence prompts him to impress on the Cosmos the forms and images of his own imagination and awareness. In the case of high spiritual attainment this human capacity may become a microcosmic channel of the divine creative act. This spiritual power is called by Ibn al-'Arabī *himmah*, a word that is rather difficult to translate accurately into English.[137] Its reflection at the purely mental level is the ability to concentrate mental energy on an object or situation with the intention of controlling it or determining its development. This concept is also linked with that of the imagination in that it also involves the ability to create, by concentration, an inner image of what one intends or would wish to realize objectively.[138]

In the case of most men, this ability goes no further than the skill involved in impressing a form or image on cosmic matter, and does not extend to the ability to bring about the existence, objectively, of one's inner image. In other words, for most people, no matter how they concentrate on the wish-image, it remains a dream and a fantasy and no more. In the Tibetan mystical tradition, however, certain adepts claim to be able to materialize inner images when they exert intense concentration on them for a prolonged period.[139] It is this degree of creative, imaginative power that is most like the concept of *himmah*, which Ibn al-'Arabī attributes to the saint or man of advanced spiritual attainment.[140] In other words, when the individual consciousness has been reintegrated into its divine subject by faith and submission, and when the mind and spirit have been strengthened and refined by asceticism and self-denial, the concentrative power of the saint is brought into alignment with the divine creative power to effect new conditions and states in the Cosmos, states that often appear miraculous or paranormal. Such phenomena as bilocation, telekinesis, abnormal auditory and sensory powers, and communication with the dead are among the claimed effects of such powers. However, being human and not divine, the saint can maintain such effects only for limited periods. The divine *himmah*, on the other hand, is maintained eternally, at every level and in every instance,

---

137. Corbin, *Creative Imagination*, pp. 222–224; see also this volume, p. 158.
138. Ibid., pp. 179–183; see also this volume, p. 121.
139. Cf. W. Y. Evans-Wentz, *The Tibetan Book of the Great Liberation*, Oxford, 1965, p. 29, n. 1.
140. See p. 158; also *Sufis of Andalusia*, pp. 63, 92.

INTRODUCTION

since anything that ceases to receive the divine attention ceases therefore to exist at all.[141]

Ibn al-'Arabī was well aware of the great dangers inherent in the possession of such power and, while encouraging its development as a spiritual attainment, was very careful to warn his fellow Sufis against any egotistical preoccupation with its often miraculous effects, urging them rather to abjure any residual individual interest they might have in such power, as true slaves of God.[142] This facility of *himmah* together with other side effects of the spiritual path resulted in much abuse and deception among the would-be gurus of his day.[143]

The concept of the Perfect Man may further be elaborated in the context of its particular human manifestations. As has been mentioned, the Perfect Man is that human individual who has perfectly realized the full spiritual potential of the human state, who has realized in himself and his experience the Oneness of Being that underlies all the apparent multiplicity of existence. The concept of the Perfect Man is, however, in itself more of a spiritual archetype than an actual human condition. Its principal manifestation in the human individual is that of Sainthood or *wilāyah*, within the context of which all other spiritual functions are performed.[144] Ibn al-'Arabī lays particular emphasis on the fact that the Arabic word for a saint [*walī*] is also one of the Names of God, the Friend [*al-Walī*], as if to stress the very intimate connection between Sainthood and divinity.[145] In other words the title of "saint," strictly speaking, may be conferred only on one whose individual identity has become spiritually annihilated in the Supreme Identity, who has become the "friend" of One whose "friendship" allows of no sense of otherness. This is the one who sees beyond "the God created in belief," beyond the conflicts and tensions implicit in cosmic and human complexity and variety, to the undifferentiated truth of the ever-present Reality. For Ibn al-'Arabī, indeed, Islam proper is nothing other than the truth and experience of the saint, all actual religions being particular manifestations of it. He does, however, maintain that the Islam brought by the Prophet Muḥammad, as the final and synoptic version of *the* Islam of universal Sainthood, now enshrines that truth most

---

141. See p. 102.
142. See p. 158.
143. Cf. R. A. Nicholson, *The Mystics of Islam*, London, 1914, chap. 5.
144. See p. 169.
145. See p. 168.

INTRODUCTION

perfectly.[146] The most important particular functions of the saint are, when he is so appointed, those of prophet [*nabī*] and apostle [*rasūl*], the office of prophet being higher than that of apostle.[147] Thus, all prophets and apostles are saints and all prophets are apostles, while not all apostles are prophets. The prophet is one who has special knowledge of the Unseen, while the apostle is one who is aware of a special responsibility toward the community to which he has been sent. The prophet may either be the bringer of a new dispensation or may function within an existing one.[148] Whatever the case may be, it is the sainthood of the prophet or the apostle that alone confers validity on the more particular functions. Thus, as the Qur'an says, every prophet and apostle brings not only a scripture, but also, deriving from his sanctity, wisdom that is the wisdom of realization.[149]

Just as the Prophet Muhammad is regarded by Islam as the last or Seal of the prophets, so Ibn al-'Arabī himself claimed to have had visionary evidence that he was the Seal of Muhammadan Sainthood.[150] To understand the meaning of this term, one must first understand that by the word "Muhammadan" Ibn al-'Arabī does not mean simply what pertains to the particular earthly mission of the Prophet Muhammad, but rather with the Spirit of Muhammad or Light of Muhammad, which he equates with the whole principle of prophecy, regarded as having been perfectly manifested in the Prophet Muhammad. Thus the Seal of Muhammadan Sainthood carries a double significance, in that he embodies not only the wisdom inherent in the final mission of the Prophet Muhammad, but also, and more importantly, the special, universal wisdom inherent in the epitome of the Muhammadan Spirit. Thus, although there may be many saints after the Seal, whether of the Muhammadan tradition or otherwise, it is he who is the culmination of that special and essential Sainthood associated with Muhammad as the name peculiar to the notion of the Perfect Man, and as that Spirit of which all prophetic and apostolic missions are manifestations.[151] This, then, is the Seal, which Ibn al-'Arabī claimed to be, although there were and are many who

---

146. *Futūḥāt*, I, p. 174.
147. See p. 169.
148. See p. 168.
149. Cf. *Qur'an*, III:47.
150. *Futūḥāt*, I, pp. 318–319.
151. Ibid., II, p. 64.

INTRODUCTION

would dispute that claim. There is no disputing, however, the fact that *al-Shaikh al-Akbar* possessed unusual spiritual gifts and insights, which have penetrated deeply into the fabric of Islamic spirituality.

As has been stressed many times above, the underlying theme to which Ibn al-'Arabī is always returning and which is implicit in all his teachings is that of the Oneness of Being-Perception. One may be forgiven, however, in reading through his many works, for feeling that one is being drawn deeper and deeper into a spiritual maze of frightening complexity, a complexity that, in the light of the fundamental theme, seems somehow strangely unnecessary and perhaps even irrelevant. On the one hand one is ever being reminded of the all-pervading presence of the Reality, and on the other hand of the polemic of interreligious conflict. In other words, one becomes more and more conscious that the whole edifice of Ibn al-'Arabī's thought is itself polarized, just as many of his secondary themes are characterized by polarity. Thus, while anchored in the dominant theme of the Oneness of Being as the original and eternal truth to which all other considerations are related, he leads his reader through all the complexity of the implications and ramifications inherent in the aboriginal desire of the Reality to know Itself, striving as he does to capture the most distant reverberations and reflections of the divine Love, on the very edge of nothingness. In doing so he presents us with that most baffling of mysteries, the relationship between reality and illusion, between what is apparent and what is, and between knowing and not knowing. However, as Ibn al-'Arabī himself demonstrates in dealing, for example, with the concept of the "God created in belief," the solution to the mystery is by no means as simple as rejecting illusion and affirming reality, since it is clear from the whole system of his thought that the principle of illusion or appearance, far from being a purely negative concept, is an important aspect of the Reality's consciousness of Itself. This is not to say that this same principle, from certain viewpoints, is not constantly threatening deception and alienation.[152]

This paradox is nowhere more vividly in evidence than in a story Ibn al-'Arabī tells about one of his Andalusian shaikhs. This man had met someone at the Ka'abah in Mecca who had asked him whether he knew what had brought them both to that place. When he asked the

---

152. Cf. pp. 191, 179.

INTRODUCTION

man to explain he replied, "Heedlessness, my brother!" and then he wept.[153] In other words, the idea that one has to travel to Mecca to be nearer to God or, indeed, that one must travel the Sufi path to become one with Him is an illusion, albeit a necessary one. As Ibn al-'Arabī pointed out on numerous occasions, the notion that we can ever be in a state of separation from God, so that it should be necessary for us to make ourselves nearer to Him, is an illusion, since we would have no being or consciousness, however apparently separate, were we anything other than the Reality. He is saying, therefore, that it is not a case of the Sufi striving to reach a goal from which he is, in reality, distant, but only that he is trying to realize and become aware of a oneness and identity that is inexorably and eternally real. The question then arises as to why the illusion of separation, which has then to be painstakingly seen through, arises at all or, more to the point, why it is capable of exerting such power over us, and why the whole phenomenon of religion and mysticism is necessary. The answer to that question lies in the primordial tension inherent in the polarization of the Reality into knower and known, in the inherent necessity for apparent separation in that polarization, and in the inevitably spiritual bias of Ibn al-'Arabī himself, referred to above, although he was always ready to admit that, in the words of the Qur'an, "There can be no refuge from God, but in Him," and "Wherever you turn, there is the face of God."[154] Thus, ultimately, whether we throw ourselves into the infinite ocean of cosmic "illusion," in conformity with the all-creating Will, or whether we annihilate our identity in the absolute truth of His identity, in conformity with the all-commanding Wish, we can never be, in reality, other than the Real, on pain of absurdity.

Perhaps the best clue to Ibn al-'Arabī's vision of the nature of things is to be found in another paradoxical but nonetheless profound saying of his. He said, "It is part of the perfection of Being that there is imperfection in it."[155] That is to say that Reality, to be real, must embrace within its reality both the wholeness that includes all possibilities, including the partial and incomplete, and the perfection that excludes all but the highest and the best. As has been noted above, the implications of this idea, as of the concept of illusion, were not missed

---

153. *Sufis of Andalusia*, p. 131.
154. See above, p. 25. *Qur'an*, IX:118, II:115.
155. *Futūḥāt*, II, p. 307.

INTRODUCTION

by the religious authorities of Ibn al-'Arabī's time, nor should he have expected the representatives of a Wish-oriented religious tradition to accept the, from their point of view, extremely dangerous implications of his teachings on the divine Will.[156]

In writing this survey of the main themes of Ibn al-'Arabī's thought, I am conscious of the fact that I have not explored the many parallels and similarities in other traditions, nor related his ideas specifically to earlier Sufi writers. The ommission is, indeed, deliberate, since I consider that his system of thought is original enough to merit presentation without the further complication of detailed religious, philosophical, and mystical comparisons that, while of great interest for the wider history of Islamic thought, are for the most part of relatively little assistance in understanding the way in which Ibn al-'Arabī himself saw the nature of reality. As has been mentioned above, although his terminology and the intellectual models he uses are often clearly traceable to other sources, nevertheless the particular way in which he uses the terms and the models to express his ideas is, in essence, peculiarly his own.[157]

---

156. See above, p. 31.
157. See above, p. 23.

IBN AL 'ARABI
THE BEZELS OF WISDOM

THE CLASSICS OF WESTERN SPIRITUALITY

PREFACE

In the name of God, the Compassionate, the Merciful.

Praise be to God Who has sent down the [revelations] of Wisdom upon the hearts of the *logoi* in a unique and direct way from the Station of Eternity, even though the sects and communities may vary because of the variety of the nations. May God bless and protect him who provides the aspirations from the treasuries of bounty and munificence, Muḥammad and his family.

I saw the Apostle of God in a visitation granted to me during the latter part of the month of Muharram in the year 627, in the city of Damascus. He had in his hand a book and he said to me, "This is the book of the Bezels of Wisdom; take it and bring it to men that they might benefit from it." I said, "All obedience is due to God and His Apostle; it shall be as we are commanded." I therefore carried out the wish, made pure my intention and devoted my purpose to the publishing of this book, even as the Apostle had laid down, without any addition or subtraction. I asked of God that, both in this matter and in all conditions, He might number me among those of His servants over whom Satan has no authority. Also that, in all my hand may write, in all my tongue may utter, and in all my heart may conceal, He might favor me with His deposition and spiritual inspiration for my mind and His protective support, that I may be a transmitter and not a composer, so that those of the Folk who read it may be sure that it comes from the Station of Sanctification and that it is utterly free from all the purposes of the lower soul, which are ever prone to deceive. I hope that the Reality, having heard my supplication, will heed my call, for I have not set forth here anything except what was set before me, nor have I written in this book aught but what was revealed to me. Nor yet am I a prophet or an apostle, but merely an heir preparing for the Hereafter.

> It is from God, so hear!
>   And to God do you return!
> When you hear what
>   I bring, learn!
> Then with understanding see the details in the whole
>   And also see them as part of the whole.
> Then give it to those
>   Who seek it, and stint not.
> This is the Mercy that
>   Encompasses you; so extend it.

From God I hope to be of those who are aided and accept aid, of those bound by the pure Law of Muḥammad, who accept to be bound and by it bind. May He gather us with Him as He has made us to be of His community.

CHAPTER I

THE WISDOM OF DIVINITY IN THE WORD OF ADAM

INTRODUCTORY NOTE

This chapter, as the title suggests, is largely concerned with the relationship between Adam, who here symbolizes the archetype of humankind, and God. More particularly it is concerned with Adam's function in the creative process, as the principle of agency, transmission, reflection, and, indeed, as the very reason for the creation of the Cosmos. The chapter also discusses the nature of angels and the relationship between pairs of concepts essential to the understanding of the creative process, such as universal-individual, necessary-contingent, first-last, outer-inner, light-darkness and approval-anger.

Ibn al-'Arabī opens the chapter, however, with the subject of the divine Names and their relationship with the divine Essence. By the term "Names," he means the Names of God, the Name *Allāh* being the supreme Name. These Names serve, essentially, to describe the infinite and complex modalities of the polarity God-Cosmos. The supreme Name itself, as being that of God Himself, clearly describes the overall and universal nature of that relationship, namely that it is God Who is the real, the Self-sufficient, while the Cosmos is, essentially, unreal and completely dependent. By the term "Essence" [*dhāt*], he means what the divine being is in Itself, beyond any polarity or relationship with a cosmos. This term should not be confused

IBN AL-'ARABĪ

with "the Reality," which denotes rather that primordial Being and eternal Perception which unites both polarity and nonpolarity. Thus the Names, including the supreme Name, have relevance or meaning only within the context of the polarity Divinity-Cosmos, and Adam represents precisely that principle which at once mediates and resolves the whole experience of that polarity, being that vital link without which the whole occurrence of divine Self-consciousness would not be possible.

Ibn al-'Arabī goes on to illustrate this Adamic function with one of his favorite images, that of the mirror, by which he seeks to explain the mystery of "the reflection of reality in the mirror of illusion." In this subtle image there are two elements, the mirror itself and the observing subject who sees his own image reflected in the mirror as object. Adam, being the linking factor in the process of reflection and recognition of the reflection, is representative of both the mirror and the observing subject, the mirror itself being a symbol of the receptivity and reflectivity of cosmic nature, and the observing subject being God Himself. Thus, Adam is described by Ibn al-'Arabī as "the very principle of reflection" and the "spirit of the [reflected] form." However, Ibn al-'Arabī was not thinking of the specially coated glass mirrors of our day, but rather of the highly polished metal mirror of his own time. Such mirrors served to illustrate better the metaphysical problems with which he was dealing. To begin with, such mirrors had to be kept polished in order to preserve their reflective qualities and, furthermore, it required great skill by the craftsman to make a perfectly flat surface. With such a mirror, therefore, there was always the possibility of surface deterioration and distortion. Thus, so long as the mirror was perfectly polished and flat, the observing subject might see his own form or image perfectly reflected on its surface, in which case the otherness of the mirror itself is reduced to a minimum in the observing consciousness, or even effaced completely. To the extent, however, that the mirror reflects a dulled or distorted image, it manifests its own otherness and detracts from the identity of image and subject. Indeed, the distorted and imperfect image presents something alien to the subject, who then may become involved in efforts to improve and perfect the mirror, so that he might achieve a more perfect self-consciousness. Thus, in the mirror we have a very apt symbol of the divine-cosmic polarity. At one extreme of the relationship cosmic Nature threatens to absorb and assimilate the subject in the infinity and complexity of his creative urge, while, at the other, the divine Subject seems to annihilate Nature in the reassertion of identity, each being, at once, another and non-other.

Adam, as the archetype of humankind, is therefore in his essential nature at once the medium of sight by which the observing Subject beholds His own cosmic image or reflection and the medium of reflection by which the cosmic "other" is restored to Itself. As medium, therefore, it is Adam who is the very principle of the polar relationship, and who, as such, knows the Names of God, which he is ordered in the Qur'an to teach to the angels.

The subjects of the angelic state has always been a problematic one for theology. For Ibn al-'Arabī the angels seem to have been particularizations of divine power, whether creative or recreative, beings who, while close to the divine presence, nevertheless had no share in the physical and formal actuality of cosmic creation. Thus, they are purely spiritual beings, quite unlike the bipolar and synthetic Adamic being who alone, of all creation, shares in the Self-consciousness of the Reality. Similarly, the animal creation, as particularization of purely cosmic life, lies outside the uniquely synthetic experience of the human state.

Another image Ibn al-'Arabī employs in this chapter, and which is particularly appropriate to this work, is that of the seal-ring. In this image, man is seen as the seal that seals and protects the cosmic treasure house of God and on which is stamped the signet of its Owner. Thus Adam, as man, is the receptive wax that bears the image of the all-embracing and supreme Name of God, the breaking of which seal means the end of all cosmic becoming.

However, as has been pointed out above, while in the main insisting on the eternal supremacy of the cognitive and volitive pole, Ibn al-'Arabī always returns, as in this chapter, to the underlying mutuality of the polar experience, in keeping with the fundamental concept of the Oneness of Being. Thus, as he points out here, the term "origin" is meaningless without assuming the existence of what is "originated," and so on with all polar concepts, including the terms "God" and "Lord," which are significant only if the corresponding terms "worshiper" and "slave" are implied.

In keeping with this basic premise of Ibn al-'Arabī's thought, it is not surprising to find that his notion of the Devil or Satan is somewhat different from that of ordinary theology. Indeed, he sees the diabolic principle in two ways. First, it is for him that principle which resists the Self-realizing urge to create the own-other object and in-

IBN AL-'ARABĪ

sists on the sole right of pure spirit and transcendence, this being the reason for Satan's refusal to obey God's command to prostrate himself to Adam, from jealousy for the integrity of pure spirit. Second, it is also that principle which insists on the separate reality of cosmic life and substance and which denies all primacy to the Spirit. In other words, it is that principle which would seek to insist on the separate reality of either pole, at the expense of the other, and thus to impair the original wholeness of the divine experience as the Reality by trying to sever the all-important link between "own" and "other" and consign each to mutually exclusive isolation in absurdity.

THE WISDOM OF DIVINITY IN THE WORD OF ADAM

The Reality wanted to see the essences of His Most Beautiful Names or, to put it another way, to see His own Essence, in an all-inclusive object encompassing the whole [divine] Command, which, qualified by existence, would reveal to Him His own mystery. For the seeing of a thing, itself by itself, is not the same as its seeing itself in another, as it were in a mirror; for it appears to itself in a form that is invested by the location of the vision by that which would only appear to it given the existence of the location and its [the location's] self-disclosure to it.

The Reality gave existence to the whole Cosmos [at first] as an undifferentiated thing without anything of the spirit in it, so that it was like an unpolished mirror. It is in the nature of the divine determination that He does not set out a location except to receive a divine spirit, which is also called [in the Qur'an] *the breathing into him*.[1] The latter is nothing other than the coming into operation of the undifferentiated form's [innate] disposition to receive the inexhaustible overflowing of Self-revelation, which has always been and will ever be. There is only that which is receptive and the receptive has been only from the most Holy Superabundance [of the Reality], for all power to act [all initiative] is from Him, in the beginning and at the end. All command derives from Him,[2] even as it begins with Him.

---

1. *Qur'an*, XXI:91.
2. Cf. ibid, II:210.

THE BEZELS OF WISDOM

Thus the [divine] Command required [by its very nature] the reflective characteristic of the mirror of the Cosmos, and Adam was the very principle of reflection for that mirror and the spirit of that form, while the angels were only certain faculties of that form which was the form of the Cosmos, called in the terminology of the Folk, the Great Man. In relation to it the angels are as the psychic and physical faculties in the human formation. Each of these [cosmic] faculties or powers is veiled [from knowing the whole] by its own self [being limited by its relative individuality], so that it cannot know anything that excels it. It also claims that it has the qualification for every high position and exalted abode with God by virtue of its participation in the divine Synthesis, deriving both from the Sphere of Divinity and the Reality of Realities and, finally, with respect to the formation assuming these characteristics, from the exigencies of the Universal Nature, which contains and comprises all the receptivities of the Cosmos, higher and lower.

This [knowledge] cannot be arrived at by the intellect by means of any rational thought process, for this kind of perception comes only by a divine disclosure from which is ascertained the origin of the forms of the Cosmos receiving the spirits. The [above-mentioned] formation is called Man and Vice-Regent [of God]. As for the first term, it stems from the universality of his formation and the fact that he embraces all the realities. For the Reality, he is as the pupil is for the eye through which the act of seeing takes place. Thus he is called *insān* [meaning both man and pupil], for it is by him that the Reality looks on His creation and bestows the Mercy [of existence] on them. He is Man, the transient [in his form], the eternal [in his essence]; he is the perpetual, the everlasting, the [at once] discriminating and unifying Word. It is by his existence that the Cosmos subsists and he is, in relation to the Cosmos, as the seal is to the ring, the seal being that place whereon is engraved the token with which the King seals his treasure. So he is called the Vice-Regent, for by him God preserves His creation, as the seal preserves the king's treasure. So long as the king's seal is on it no one dares to open it except by his permission, the seal being [as it were] a regent in charge of the kingdom. Even so is the Cosmos preserved so long as the Perfect Man remains in it. Do you not see that when he shall cease to be present in it and when the seal [on the treasury] of the lower world is broken, none of what the Reality preserved will endure and all of it will depart, each part thereof becoming reunited with every other part, [after which] the whole will be transferred to the Final Abode where the Perfect Man will be the seal forever.

All the Names constituting the Divine Image are manifest in the human formation so that this information enjoys a degree by which it encompasses and integrates all existence. It is for this reason that God holds the conclusive argument against the angels [in their protest at His command to prostrate to Adam]. So take care, for God warns you by the example of another, and consider carefully from whence the arraigned one is charged. For the angels did not grasp the meaning of the formation of God's Regent nor did they understand the essential servitude demanded by the Plane of Reality. For none knows anything of the Reality save that which is itself implicit in the Essence [of the Reality].

The angels do not enjoy the comprehensiveness of Adam and comprehend only those Divine Names peculiar to them, by which they glorify and sanctify the Reality, nor are they aware that God has Names of which they know nothing and by which they cannot glorify Him, nor are they able to sanctify Him with the [complete] sanctification of Adam. Their condition and limitation being what it is, they said, concerning his formation, *Will You put in it one who will work mischief in it?*[3] meaning [his] rebellion, which is precisely what they themselves evince, for what they say of Adam applies equally to their own attitude toward the Reality. But for the fact that their own formation imposes this [limitation of knowledge], they would not have said what they said concerning Adam; but they are not aware of this.

If they indeed knew their own [essential] selves they would know [their limitation], and if that were so, they would have been spared [their mistaken utterance]. Furthermore, they would not have persisted in their challenge by calling attention to their own [more restricted] glorification of God, as also their [limited] sanctification.

Adam enshrines divine Names the angels have no part in, nor are they able to glorify their Lord by them or by them to exalt His transcendence, as Adam does.

God expounds the whole affair to us so that we might bear it in mind and learn from it the proper attitude toward Him and lest we [ignorantly] flaunt what [little] individually restricted insight or un-

---

3. Ibid., II:30.

derstanding we might have realized. Indeed, how can we make claims concerning something the reality of which we have not experienced and concerning which we have no knowledge, without exposing ourselves to ridicule? This divine instruction [concerning the angels] is one of the ways by which the Reality instructs His most trusted servants, His representatives.

Let us now return to this Wisdom. Know that the universals, even though they have no tangible individual existence in themselves, yet are conceived of and known in the mind; this is certain. They are always unmanifest as regards individual existence, while imposing their effects on all such existence; indeed individual existence is nothing other than [an outer manifestation] of them, that is to say, the universals. In themselves they are always intelligibles. They are manifest as being individual beings and they are unmanifest as being [purely] intelligible. Every individual existence is dependent on the universals, which can [never] be disassociated from the intellect, nor can they exist individually in such a way that they would cease to be intelligible. Whether the individual being is determined temporarily or not, its relationship, in both cases, is one and the same. However, the universal and the individual being may share a common determining principle according as the essential realities of the individual beings demand, as for example [in] the relationship between knowledge and the knower or life and the living. Life is an intelligible reality, as also knowledge, each being distinguished from the other.

Thus, concerning the Reality, we say that He has life and knowledge and also that He is Living and Knowing. This we also say of Man and the angels. The reality of knowledge is [always] one, as is the reality of life, and the relationship of each respectively to the knower and the living remains [always] the same.

Concerning the knowledge of the Reality we say that it is eternal, whereas of man's knowledge we say that it is contingent. Consider then how attachment to the determinant renders something in the intelligible reality contingent and consider the interdependence of the universals and individual existence. For, even as knowledge determines one who applies it as being a knower, so also does the one thus described determine knowledge as being contingent in the case of the contingent [knower], and eternal in the case of the Eternal One, both determining and determined.

Further, even though the universals are intelligible, they enjoy no real existence, existing only insofar as they determine [existent beings], just as they themselves are determined in any relationship with individual existence. As manifest in individual existence, they may admit of being [in a sense] determined, but they admit of no particularization or division, this being impossible. They are essentially present in each thing they qualify, as humanity is present in every human being, while not being particularized or divided according to the number of individual beings [in which they are manifested], remaining [purely] intelligible.

If, therefore, it is established that there is an interrelationship between that which has individual existence and that which has not, the latter being nonexistent relations, the interconnection between one individual being and another is the more comprehensible because they have, at least, individual existence in common, whereas in the former instance there is no unifying element.

It is established that the originated is [completely] dependent on that which brings it about, for its possibility. Its existence is [entirely] derived from something other than itself, the connection in this case being one of dependence. It is therefore necessary that that which is the support [of originated existence] should be essentially and necessarily by itself, self-sufficient and independent of any other. This it is that bestows existence from its own essential Being on dependent existence, in this way becoming related to it.

Furthermore, since the former, because of its essence, requires the latter [the dependent], the latter has [in a certain sense] necessary being. Also, since its dependence on that from which it was manifested is [implicit in] its own essence, it follows that the originated should conform to all the Names and attributes of the cause [origin], except that of Self-sufficient Being, which does not belong to originated existence, since what necessary being it has derives [entirely] from other than itself.

Know that if what has been said concerning the manifestation [of the originated] in the form [of the originator] be true, it is clear that God draws our attention to what is originated as an aid to knowledge of Him and says [in the Qur'an] that He will show forth His signs in it.[4] Thus He suggests that knowledge of Him is inferred in knowledge of ourselves. Whenever we ascribe any quality to Him, we are ourselves [representative of] that quality, except it be the quality of His Self-sufficient Being. Since we know Him through ourselves and

---

4. Ibid., XLI:53.

from ourselves, we attribute to Him all we attribute to ourselves. It is for this reason that the divine revelations come to us through the mouths of the Interpreters [the prophets], for He describes Himself to us through us. If we witness Him we witness ourselves, and when He sees us He looks on Himself.

There is no doubt that we are, as individuals and types, many, and that, though representatives of a single reality, we know definitely that there is a factor distinguishing one individual from another, but for which, multiplicity would not be [implicit] in the One. In the same way, even if we describe ourselves as He describes Himself, in all possible aspects, there would still remain an inevitable factor of distinction [between Him and us]. This [factor] is our dependence on Him for existence, which, in our case, derives entirely from Him because we are originated while He is free of all dependence whatsoever. Thus is He rightly called the One without beginning, the Ancient of Days, contradicting all priority in the sense of existence starting from nonexistence. For, although He is the First, no temporal priority may be attributed of Him. Thus He is called also the Last. Even if He were the First in the sense of being the first-determined existence, He could not be called the Last in this sense, since contingent being has no end, being infinite. He is called the Last only in the sense that all reality, though reality be attributed to us, is His. His Finality is essentially [implicit] in His Priority as is His Priority essentially [implicit] in His Finality.

Know also that the Reality has described Himself as being the Outer and the Inner [Manifest and Unmanifest]. He brought the Cosmos into being as constituting an unseen realm and a sensory realm, so that we might perceive the Inner through our unseen and the Outer through our sensory aspect.

He has also attributed of Himself pleasure and wrath, having created the Cosmos as [expressing] both fear and hope, fear of His wrath and hope for His pleasure. He has also described Himself as being possessed of beauty and majesty, having created us as combining awe [of His majesty] and intimacy, and so on with all His attributes and Names. He has expressed this polarity of qualities [in the Qur'an] as being His Hands devoted to the creation of the Perfect Man who integrates in himself all Cosmic realities and their individual [manifestations].[5]

---

5. Ibid., XXXVIII:75.

IBN AL-‘ARABĪ

The Cosmos is the sensory realm [both subtle and gross] and the Vicegerent is unseen. For this reason the Ruler [God] is veiled, since the Reality has described Himself as being hidden in veils of darkness, which are the natural forms, and by veils of light, which are the subtle spirits. The Cosmos consists of that which is gross and that which is subtle and is therefore, in both aspects, the veil [covering] its [own] true self [reality]. For the Cosmos does not perceive the Reality as He perceives Himself, nor can it ever not be veiled, knowing itself to be distinct from its Creator and dependent on Him. Indeed, it has no part in the [divine] Self-sufficiency [of being] of the Reality, nor will it ever attain to that. In this sense the Reality can never be known [by cosmic being] in any way, since originated being has no part in that [Self-sufficiency].

God unites the polarity of qualities only in Adam, to confer a distinction on him. Thus, He says to Lucifer, *What prevents you from prostrating to one whom I have created with my two hands?*[6] What prevents Lucifer is the very fact that he [man] unites [in himself] the two modes, the [originated] Cosmos and the [originating and original] Reality, which are His two hands.

As for Lucifer, he is only a part of the Cosmos and has no share in this Synthesis, by virtue of which Adam is the Regent. Were he not manifest [in the Cosmos] in the form of Him Whom he represents, he would not be the Regent, and were he not to comprise all that his dependent charges require or were he unable to meet all their requirements, he would not be the Regent. In short, the Regency is fitting only for the Perfect Man.

His outer form He composed of the cosmic realities and forms, while his inner form He composed to match His Own form. Thus He says in the Sacred Tradition, "I am his hearing and his sight,"[7] and not, "I am his eye and his ear," in order to show the distinction between the two forms [the imperceptible and the perceptible]. Likewise He is [implicit] in every cosmic being according as the essential reality [manifested] in that being requires it, providing it is understood that no other being enjoys the Synthesis [of divine realities] possessed by the Regent. It is only by virtue of this Synthesis that he is superior [to all other beings].

---

6. Ibid.
7. Bukhārī, LXXXI:38.

THE BEZELS OF WISDOM

Were it not that the Reality permeates all beings as form [in His qualitative form], and were it not for the intelligible realities, no [essential] determination would be manifest in individual beings. Thus, the dependence of the Cosmos on the Reality for its existence is an essential factor.

> All is dependent [upon another], naught is independent,
>   This is the pure truth, we speak it out plainly.
> If I mention One, Self-sufficient, Independent,
>   You will know to Whom I refer.
> All is bound up with all, there is no escaping
>   This bond, so consider carefully what I say.

You are now acquainted with the Wisdom involved in the corporeal formation of Adam, his outer form, as you have become acquainted with the spiritual formation of Adam, his inner form, namely, that he is the Reality [as regards the latter] and that he is creature [as regards the former]. You have also learned to know his rank as the all-synthesizing [form] by which he merits the [divine] Regency.

Adam is that single soul, that single spiritual essence from which humankind was created, as He says, *O Men, fear your Lord Who created you from a single soul and created from it its mate, so that from them both there issued forth many men and women.*[8] His saying *Fear your Lord* means "Make your outer [transient] selves a protection for your Lord [your inner essential reality], and make your inner [reality], which is your Lord, a protection for your outer selves."

All creation [*amr*] involves censure [negation] and praise [affirmation], so be His protection as regards censure [as being relative beings] and make Him your protection as regards praise [as being identified with the Adamic reality], so that you are of those who act properly and are possessed of knowledge.

Then He, Most High and Glorious, caused Adam to look on all He had deposited in him and held it in His Hands [Active and passive, Essential and formal], in the first Hand the Cosmos and in the other Adam and his seed, expounding their degrees.

When God revealed to me, in my innermost center, what He had deposited in our great progenitor, I recorded in this book only that

---

8. *Qur'an*, IV:1.

IBN AL-'ARABĪ

which he dictated to me, not all I was given, since no book could contain all of it, nor yet the Cosmos as now existing.

Of what I witnessed [in the spirit] and, of that, what I recorded in this book as laid down by the Prophet, are the following chapters:

I	The Wisdom of Divinity in the Word of Adam
II	The Wisdom of Expiration in the Word of Seth
III	The Wisdom of Exaltation in the Word of Noah
IV	The Wisdom of Holiness in the Word of Enoch
V	The Wisdom of Rapturous Love in the Word of Abraham
VI	The Wisdom of Reality in the Word of Isaac
VII	The Wisdom of Sublimity in the Word of Ishmael
VIII	The Wisdom of Spirit in the Word of Jacob
IX	The Wisdom of Light in the Word of Joseph
X	The Wisdom of Unity in the Word of Hūd
XI	The Wisdom of Opening in the Word of Ṣāliḥ
XII	The Wisdom of the Heart in the Word of Shu'aib
XIII	The Wisdom of Mastery in the Word of Lot
XIV	The Wisdom of Destiny in the Word of Ezra
XV	The Wisdom of Prophecy in the Word of Jesus
XVI	The Wisdom of Compassion in the Word of Solomon
XVII	The Wisdom of Being in the Word of David
XVIII	The Wisdom of Breath in the Word of Jonah
XIX	The Wisdom of the Unseen in the Word of Job
XX	The Wisdom of Majesty in the Word of John
XXI	The Wisdom of Dominion in the Word of Zakariah
XXII	The Wisdom of Intimacy in the Word of Elias
XXIII	The Wisdom of Virtue in the Word of Luqmān
XXIV	The Wisdom of Leadership in the Word of Aaron
XXV	The Wisdom of Eminence in the Word of Moses
XXVI	The Wisdom of Resource in the Word of Khālid.
XXVII	The Wisdom of Singularity in the Word of Muḥammad

The seal of each Wisdom is the Word assigned to it. I have restricted myself in what I have written concerning the [divine manifestations of] Wisdom in this book to what is confirmed in that respect in the Heavenly Book. I have transcribed faithfully according as was vouchsafed to me. Even had I wished to add to it I would not have been able to do so, since the plane [from which it came] would prevent anything of the kind. God it is Who grants success and He is Sole Lord.

CHAPTER II

THE WISDOM OF EXPIRATION IN THE WORD OF SETH

INTRODUCTORY NOTE

The chapter named after Seth deals with two main topics, that of divine giving and the subject of the respective functions of the Seal of Saints and the Seal of Apostles. In connection with the first of these topics, Ibn al-'Arabī touches also on the subject of latency and predisposition and the possibility of knowing one's own predisposition.

In the first part of the chapter he deals with the question of divine giving and favor. He divides the divine giving in various ways and discusses the whole relationship between requesting and giving in response to a request, whether uttered or implicit.

This first topic of the chapter provides, perhaps, a clue to the title of the chapter, *The Wisdom of Expiration in the Word of Seth*. The Arabic word used for "expiration" is from the root *nafakha*, which literally means "to blow." Now, the divine gift par excellence is that of existence itself, the bringing about of which is closely related to Ibn al-'Arabī's concept of the creating Mercy, which creativity is often termed the Breath of the Merciful [*nafas al-raḥmān*]. In other words the blowing referred to in the title is precisely that outgoing projection inspired by the divine desire for Self-consciousness which, from the standpoint of created existence, is the supreme act of divine giving and generosity, all other particular gifts of God being aspects of that original gift of existence, since each particular gift to a particular creature serves only to confirm that existential covenant by which God affirms the ontological significance of the Cosmos. It is the universal gift of becoming that is the gift of the Essence, while the gift of the Names is the particular manifestation of that supreme Self-giving of God. Ibn al-'Arabī returns to this theme in the chapter on the Prophet David.

As already mentioned, this notion of divine giving is closely related by Ibn al-'Arabī to the concept of latent predisposition *in divinis*. This means that the quality and nature of one's existence as creature, in general and in detail, may be no more or less than that which it is eternally predisposed to be in one's latent essence. Furthermore, not only the gift or response but also the making of the request itself is determined by the latent predisposition to do so.

Awareness or knowledge of what one is disposed to be *in aeternis* is, for Ibn al-'Arabī, an essential part of what he calls *ma'rifah* or gnosis, since it involves the knowledge of oneself that is, at the same time, knowledge of the divine Reality of which one is, latently and essentially, inescapably an aspect, which is the meaning of the saying "Whosoever knows himself, knows his Lord." Gnosis, according to our author, is not the acquired knowing of profane learning, but rather, as the Arabic root suggests, an immediate recognition and grasp not of something new or strange but rather of the state and status of things as they really are, have always been, and eternally will be, which knowledge is inborn in man but later covered over and obscured by the spiritual ignorance encouraged by preoccupation with ephemeral and partial data.

It is precisely this gnosis, which is potential in all humankind, that is the realized spiritual heritage of the saints, prophets, and apostles, and particularly of the Seal himself. Indeed, it is the normative cognition of the Perfect Man who perceives all difference and identity in terms of the Reality, other than which nothing is or exists.

Ibn al-'Arabī concludes this chapter with a curious prediction concerning the fate of man as defined in his teachings. He says that the last true human, in the line of Seth, will be born in China and that he will have an elder sister. He goes on to prophesy that thereafter men will become as beasts, bereft of spirit and law, until the coming of the Hour. Thus, he indicates that that particular human synthesis of spirit and nature, of which we are all a part, will come to an end and the link be broken.

THE WISDOM OF EXPIRATION IN THE WORD OF SETH

Know that the [divine] gifts and favors manifest in the realm of determined being, whether through His servants or not, are divided into two kinds, gifts of the Essence and gifts of the Names, just as there are those gifts [bestowed in answer] to a specific request and those [given in answer] to a general request. There are those gifts also that are bestowed without any request, whether they derive from the Essence or the Names.

An example of a request for something specific is one who says, "O Lord, grant to me such and such," specifying something to the exclusion of anything else. An example of a general request is one who says, "Grant to me what You know to be in my interest, whether for my subtle or physical being."

Those who ask are of two kinds: The first kind is urged to make a request by a natural eagerness, for, *Man was created hasty*,[9] while the second kind is moved to make the request because he knows that there are certain things with God that cannot, in accordance with the divine Prescience, be obtained except by asking for them. He says [to himself], "Perhaps what we are about to ask for from God is of this kind." Thus his request is by way of taking full account of the possibilities inherent in the divine Command [the thing asked for]. He cannot know what is in the knowledge of God, nor can he know his own eternally determined predisposition to receive, for to be, at each instant, aware of one's [eternal] predisposition is one of the most difficult kinds of knowledge. Indeed, were it not for that with which the predisposition imbues the request, he would not make the request at all.

For those practicing the Presence of God who do not usually know this, the most they attain to is to know it [their predisposition] at the time [of receiving or asking]. This is because, by reason of their presence with God, they know what the Reality bestows on them at

---

9. *Qur'an*, XXI:37.

that time and they know that they receive it only because of their predisposition to receive it. They are of two kinds: those who know their predisposition by knowing what they receive, the others knowing what they [will] receive by knowing their predisposition. Of these, the latter is the more complete knowledge of the predisposition.

There are also those who ask, not because of any natural impulse, nor yet through knowledge of the possibilities, but simply to conform with God's command, *Call upon Me and I will answer you.*[10] Such a one is eminently a servant, for in such a supplication there is no trace of self-interest, the concern being directed solely to conformity with the behest of his Master. If his state necessitates a request on his part, he asks for more servanthood, whereas if it necessitates silence and resignation, he is silent.

Job and others were sorely tried, but they did not ask that their affliction from God be lifted from them. At a later time their state necessitated their making such a request and God answered them. The speed or tardiness in granting what is requested depends entirely on the measure appointed for it with God. If a request is made at just the right moment for it, the response is swift, but if its time is not yet due, either in this life or until the next life, the response will be postponed until that time. By this is meant the granting of the thing requested, not the principle of divine response, which is always, "I am here," so consider well.[11]

As regards our reference to those gifts bestowed without any request being made, I meant a request that is articulated, for in the case of any [divine] action [gift] there must be a request [a recipient], whether it be expressed in words or is inherent in the state or predisposition.

Similarly the praising of God usually means its articulation, whereas in the inner sense the praise is necessitated by the [spiritual] state, for that which impels you to praise God is that essential element in you that binds you to a Divine Name, whether expressing His activity or transcendence. The servant is not aware of his predisposition, but only of the spiritual state, which he knows as that which impels him, since knowledge of the predisposition is the most hidden. Those who [receive God's gifts and] do not make a request omit to make a request only because they know that God possesses, in respect

---

10. Ibid., XL:60.
11. Ibid., II:186.

of them, predetermining knowledge. They have made themselves ever ready to receive whatever comes from Him and have withdrawn completely from their separative selves and their aims.

Of these persons there are those who know that God's knowledge of them, in all their states, corresponds to what they themselves are in their state of preexistent latency. They know that the Reality will bestow on them only that which their latent essences contribute to Him [as being what He knows Himself to be]. Thus they know the origin of God's [predetermining] knowledge concerning them. Of the Folk there are none higher or more intuitive than this kind [who do not ask], for they have grasped the mystery of the divine Premeasurement. This group is itself divided into two parts: those who possess this knowledge in a general way and those who have a detailed knowledge, the latter [knowledge] being more elevated and complete. In this case he knows what God knows concerning himself, either because God informs him of what his essence has contributed to His knowledge of him, or because God has revealed to him his essence in all its infinite fluctuations of spiritual state. This is higher than the general knowledge.

Such a one, in respect of his knowledge of himself, knows himself as God knows him, since the object [of knowledge] is the same in both cases. However, in respect of his creatureliness, his knowledge is nothing but a favor from God, one of a multitude of predetermined [spiritual] states [inherent] in his essence. The recipient of such a revelation recognizes this fact when God shows to him the states [inherent] in his essence; for it is not possible for a creature, when God shows to him the states of his essence, on which the created form will be cast, to look on it as the Reality looks on the latent essences in their state of nonbeing, since they are formless attributions of the Essence.

If all of this is understood, we can say that this parity [in knowledge, as between God and the servant] is a divine favor predetermined for that servant. In this regard is His saying, [*We will try you*] *until we know* [*which of you strive*],[12] which bears a very exact meaning, quite other than that imagined by those who have no direct experience [of the divine mysteries]. Concerning this verse, the most the transcendentalist could say, using the highest of his mental powers, would be that the [apparent] temporality in God's knowledge is due to its dependence [on creatures], except that he maintains the distinc-

---

12. Ibid., XLVII:31.

tion of the knowledge from the Essence, and so ascribes the dependence to it and not to the Essence. By this he is distinguished from the true knower of God, the recipient of revelation.

Returning to the subject of the divine gifts, we have already maintained that these stem either from the Essence or from the Divine Names. As for favors or gifts of the first kind, they can result only from a divine Self-revelation, which occurs only in a form conforming to the essential predisposition of the recipient of such a revelation. Thus, the recipient sees nothing other than his own form in the mirror of the Reality. He does not see the Reality Itself, which is not possible, although he knows that he may see only his [true] form in It. As in the case of a mirror and the beholder, he sees the form in it, but does not see the mirror itself, despite his knowledge that he sees only his own and other images by means of it. God makes this comparison so that the recipient of a divine Self-revelation should know that it is not Him Whom he sees. The analogy of a mirror is the closest and most faithful one for a vision of a divine Self-revelation.

Try, when you look at yourself in a mirror, to see the mirror itself, and you will find that you cannot do so. So much is this the case that some have concluded that the image perceived is situated between the mirror and the eye of the beholder. This represents the greatest knowledge they are capable of [on the subject]. The matter is [in fact] as we have concluded, and we have dealt with it also in *The Meccan Revelations*.[13] If you have experienced this [in the spirit] you have experienced as much as is possible for a created being, so do not seek nor weary yourself in any attempts to proceed higher than this, for there is nothing higher, nor is there beyond the point you have reached aught except the pure, undetermined, unmanifested [Absolute]. In your seeing your true self, He is your mirror and you are His mirror in which He sees His Names and their determinations, which are nothing other than Himself. The whole matter is prone to intricacy and ambiguity.

Some of us there are who profess ignorance as part of their knowledge, maintaining [with Abū Bakr] that "To realise that one cannot know [God] is to know."[14] There are others from among us, however, who know, but who do not say such things, their knowl-

---

13. *Futūhāt*, I, p. 162ff.
14. Cf. Ábū Nar al-Sarrāj, *Kitāb al-luma'*, ed. R. A. Nicholson, 1914, p. 36 [Arabic text].

edge instilling in them silence rather than [professions] of ignorance. This is the highest knowledge of God, possessed only by the Seal of Apostles and the Seal of Saints.[15] Thus, none of the prophets and apostles can attain to it except from the Niche of the Seal of Apostles, nor are any of the saints able to attain to it except from the Niche of the Seal of Saints, so that, in effect, none of the apostles can attain to it, when they do so, except from the Niche of the Seal of Saints.

This is because the office of apostle and prophet [by prophet I mean the bringer of Sacred Law] comes to an end, while Sainthood never ceases. Thus the apostles, as being also saints, attain only to what we have mentioned from the Niche of the Seal of Saints, this being even more the case with the lesser saints. For, although the Seal of Saints follows the Law brought by the Seal of Apostles, this does not in any way diminish his station or contradict what we have said, since he is, in one sense, below the apostle and, in another sense, higher. What we have maintained here is supported by events under our own dispensation, as when 'Umar's judgment was the better one in respect of the prisoners taken at Badr, as also in the matter of the pollination of palms.[16]

It is not necessary for one who is perfect to be superior in everything and at every level, since men of the Spirit have regard only to precedence in the degrees of the knowledge of God, which is their [sole] aim. As for the passing phenomena of created beings, they do not concern themselves with such things. Therefore, mark well what we have said.

The Prophet likened the office of prophet to a wall of bricks, complete except for one brick. He himself was the missing brick. However, while the Prophet saw the lack of one brick, the Seal of Saints perceived that two bricks were missing. The bricks of the wall were of silver and gold. Since he saw himself as filling the gap, it is the Seal of Saints who is the two bricks and who completes the wall. The reason for his seeing two bricks is that, outwardly, he follows the Law of the Seal of Apostles, represented by the silver brick. This is his outer aspect and the rules that he adheres to in it. Inwardly, however, he receives directly from God what he appears [outwardly] to follow, because he perceives the divine Command as it is [in its essence], represented by the golden brick. He derives his knowledge

---

15. Cf. al-Tirmidhī, *Kitāb khatm al-awliyā'*, ed. O. Yahya, Beirut, 1965.
16. Cf. A. Guillaume, *Life of Muhammad*, O.U.P., 1955, p. 301.

from the same source as the angel who reveals it to the Apostle. If you have understood my allusions you have attained to the most beneficial knowledge.[17]

Every prophet, from Adam until the last of the prophets, derives what he has from the Seal of Prophets, even though he comes last in his temporal, physical manifestation, for in his [essential] reality he has always existed. The Prophet said, "I was a prophet when Adam was between the water and the clay,"[18] while other prophets became such only when they were sent forth [on their missions]. In the same way the Seal of Saints was a saint "when Adam was between the water and the clay," while other saints became saints only when they had acquired all the necessary divine qualities, since God has called Himself *the Friend [al-Walī], the Praised One*.[19]

The Seal of Apostles, as being also a saint, has the same relationship to the Seal of Saints as the other prophets and apostles have to him, for he is saint, apostle, and prophet.

As for the Seal of Saints, he is the Saint, the Heir, the one whose [knowledge] derives from the Source, the one who beholds all levels [of Being]. This sainthood is among the excellencies of the Seal of Apostles, Muḥammad, first of the Community [of apostles] and Lord of Men as being he who opened the gate to intercession. This latter is a state peculiar to him and not common [to all apostles]. It is in this state that he precedes even the Divine Names, since the Merciful does not intercede with the Avenger, in the case of those sorely tried, until intercession has been made [to It]. It is in the matter of intercession that Muḥammad has attained to preeminence. Whoever comprehends the levels and stations will not find it difficult to understand this.

As for favors deriving from the Names of God, they are of two kinds: a pure mercy, such as a good pleasure in the world that leaves no taint on the Day of Resurrection, which is bestowed by [God] the Merciful, or a mixed mercy, such as an evil-tasting medicine that brings relief, which is a gift of God in His Divinity, although in His Divinity He always bestows His gifts through the medium of one of the holders of the Names.

Sometimes God bestows a gift on His servant in His Name the Merciful, in which case the gift will be free of all that is contrary to

---

17. Cf. Bukhārī, LXI:18.
18. Ibid., LXXVIII:119.
19. *Qur'an*, XLII:28.

the servant's nature at the time, or of anything that might fail him. Sometimes God gives in His Name the Encompassing, so that the effect is universal, while at other times He gives in His Name the Wise, to serve the best interests of His servant. He may give in His Name the Bestower, in which He gives as an [unsolicited] favor, so that the recipient is under no obligation to render thanks or to perform works to merit the favor. He may give in His Name the Powerful, in which case His action is in accordance with the requirements of the situation. He may give in His Name the Forgiver, in which He considers the situation or state as it is at the time. If punishment is merited, He will [under this Name] protect the servant from it, and if no punishment is merited, He protects from a state that would incur punishment.

In this way are such servants [the saints] spoken of as being immune and protected [from sin]. The giver is God as Keeper of the treasuries [of His Grace], which only He dispenses according to a prescribed measure through the appropriate Name. *He bestows [appropriately] on all He has created,*[20] in His Name the Just and similar attributes.

The Names of God are infinite because they are known by all that derives from them which is infinite, even though they derive [ultimately] from a [known] number of sources, which are the matrices or abodes of the Names. Certainly, there is but one Reality, which embraces all these attributions and relations called the Divine Names. This Reality grants that every Name, infinitely manifest, should have its own reality by which to be distinguished from every other Name. This distinguishing reality is the essence of the Name [the Name itself], not that which it may have in common [with others]. In the same way every [divine] gift is distinguished from every other by its own individual quality; for, even though all derive from a single source, it is evident that one gift is not the same as another. The cause of that is the mutual distinction of the Names, there being no repetition on the Plane of Divinity with all its extensiveness. This is the indisputable truth.

Such was the knowledge possessed by Seth and it is his spirit that moves every other spirit expressing this kind of truth, except the spirit of the Seal, for his spiritual constituent comes directly from God and not from any other spirit. Further, it is from his spirit [the Seal]

---

20. Ibid., XX:50.

that all other spirits derive their substance, even though the Seal may not be aware of the fact while in the physical body. In respect of his essential reality and his [spiritual] rank he knows it all essentially, whereas in the body he is ignorant of it. He at once knows and does not know, taking on himself the attribution of opposites, as does the Source Itself, as being at once the Majestic and the Beautiful, the Manifest and the Unmanifest, the First and the Last, this [*coincidentia oppositorum*] being his own essence. He knows and does not know, he is aware and he is not aware, he perceives and yet does not perceive.

It is because of this knowledge that Seth is so named, his name meaning "Gift of God." In his hand is the key to the [divine] gifts in all their variety and their relations. God bestowed him on Adam, as his first unconditional gift, bestowing him as coming from Adam himself, since the son is the inner reality of the father, issuing from him and to him returning. Thus it is nothing alien to him that comes [as God's gift]. He whose understanding is inspired by God will know this.

Indeed, every gift in the manifested universe is after this fashion. There is nothing in anyone from God [as other], and there is nothing in anyone but what comes from his own self, however various the forms. Though this be the eternal truth of the matter, none knows it [directly] save certain of the elite of the saints. Should you meet one who possesses such knowledge you may have complete confidence in him, for he is a rare gem among the elite of the Folk.

Whenever a gnostic receives a spiritual intuition in which he looks on a form that brings him new spiritual knowledge and new spiritual graces, [he should know] that the form he contemplates is none other than his own essential self, for it is only from the tree of his own self that he will garner the fruits of his knowledge. In the same way his image in a polished surface is naught but he, although the place or plane in which he sees his image effects certain changes in the image in accordance with the intrinsic reality of that plane. In this way something big appears small in a small mirror, long in a long mirror, and moving in a moving mirror. It may produce the inversion of this image from a particular plane, or it may produce an exactly corresponding image, right reflecting right [and left reflecting left]. However, it is more usual with mirrors for the right to reflect the left. In contradiction to this, however, the right sometimes reflects the right and reversion takes place. All this applies [equally] to the modes and properties of the plane in which the divine Self-revelation occurs, which we have compared to a mirror.

Whoever has knowledge of his [eternal] predisposition knows what [divine gifts] he will receive, although not every one who knows what he will receive knows also his predisposition except after he has received, even though he may know it in a general way.

Certain theorists of weak intellect, having agreed that God does what He wills, go on to state things about God that contradict Wisdom and the truth. They go so far as to deny contingency as also self-sufficient and relative essential being. The one who truly knows confirms contingency and knows its plane; he knows what is the contingent and in what way it is so, even though it be in its essence self-sufficient [necessary] by virtue of something other than it, as also [he knows] in what way its [source] may be considered as "other," when it makes it self-sufficient [necessary]. Only those possessing special knowledge of God understand this in detail.

It will be in the line of Seth that the last true Man will be born, bearing his mysteries [of divine Wisdom], nor will such be born after him. He will be the Seal of Offspring. There will be born with him a sister who will be born before him, so that his head will be at her feet. He will be born in the land of China and will speak the language of that land. Sterility will then overcome the men and women of this land and, although there will be much consorting, there will be no bringing forth of children [as true men]. He will call them to God without success and when God has taken him and those of his time who believed, the others will remain living like beasts with no sense of right and wrong, given over to the law of the [lower] nature, devoid of intellect and Sacred Law. The Last Hour will overtake them.

CHAPTER III

THE WISDOM OF EXALTATION IN THE WORD OF NOAH

INTRODUCTORY NOTE

This is, perhaps, the most difficult and controversial of the chapters of *The Bezels of Wisdom* by reason of the unusual and extraordinary interpretations of the Qur'an that feature in it. Certainly, from the standpoint of exoteric theology, Ibn al-'Arabī's approach to the qur'anic material in this chapter is, at best, reckless, and, at worst, flagrantly heretical. The chapter is also unusual among the chapters of this work in that it not only confines its subject matter to the situation of the Prophet Noah, named in the title, but draws almost all its quotational material from the *Sūrah* of Noah in the Qur'an. Thus, this chapter is in effect a commentary on the issues raised in that *Sūrah*.

The situation described in the *Sūrah* concerns Noah's attempts to persuade his people of their folly and wickedness in worshiping their idols and of the urgent necessity to repent and recognize the transcendent unity of the true God. Throughout the *Sūrah* Noah calls on God to vindicate him and to punish his heedless and stubborn contemporaries. Ibn al-'Arabī uses this situation not so much to confirm the rightness of Noah but rather to explore and expound on a whole series of polar concepts, the relationship of which he discusses from the point of view of the Oneness of Being.

IBN AL-'ARABĪ

He begins by discussing the tension between the notion of transcendence and that of immanence or comparability, and it becomes clear, on reading further into the chapter, that he regards Noah as representative of the former and the people of Noah as committed to the latter view. The explanation early in the chapter that both positions are mutually related and cannot, properly, be considered in isolation from each other also makes it clear that he regards both sides of the dispute in the Qur'an not as right or wrong, but as both necessarily representing the two fundamental modalities of divine Self-experience as being, at one and the same time, involved in and assimilated into Cosmic creation, and utterly removed from and beyond it. Indeed, all the other pairs of concepts he discusses in the chapter are derived from this pair.

He goes on to consider the concepts outer-inner, form-spirit, and elaborates yet again on the saying of the Prophet, "Whoso knows himself, knows his Lord," with the clear implication that the Adamic being, as isthmus, as created in the image of the Reality, is the microcosmic synthesis of form and spirit, being the spirit of the form and the form of the spirit. In the same vein, Ibn al-'Arabī indulges in his tendency to manipulate Arabic roots to illustrate a point. Thus he takes the word *qur'ān*, which derives from the root *qara'a*, and treats it as if it derived from the root *qarana*, meaning to correlate, link. He then contrasts this novel interpretation of the word with *furqān*, so that we have the pair of concepts, correlation-distinction, in other words, that which on the one hand correlates God with cosmic manifestation, and on the other hand asserts His absolute separation from it.

In this context, Ibn al-'Arabī does not regard the people of Noah as necessarily misguided, but rather as exponents, albeit unconscious ones, of the reality of the divine Self-manifestation [*tajallī*] in the ever-changing multiplicity of cosmic forms, implying that, had Noah tempered his extreme transcendentalism with a little concession to divine immanence, his people might have been more responsive to his exhortations.

It is toward the end of the chapter that Ibn al-'Arabī's interpretations of qur'anic verses are, seemingly, most outrageous, since he seems indeed to be suggesting meanings diametrically opposed to those usually accepted. In short, he interprets the "wrongdoers," "infidels," and "sinners" of the last verses of the *Sūrah* of Noah as saints and gnostics drowning and burning not in the torments of Hell but rather in the flames and waters of gnosis, bewildered in the divine perplexity of their awareness of the paradox of God.

Although at first sight incomprehensible and extraordinary, such interpretations would seem to be a deliberate attempt on the part of Ibn al-'Arabī to demonstrate, as vividly as possible, the full implications of the concept of the Oneness of Being, within the context of which all possible oppositions and conflicts are resolved in the unimaginable wholeness and unity of the Reality.

THE WISDOM OF EXALTATION IN THE WORD OF NOAH

For those who [truly] know the divine Realities, the doctrine of transcendence imposes a restriction and a limitation [on the Reality], for he who asserts that God is [purely] transcendent is either a fool or a rogue, even if he be a professed believer. For, if he maintains that God is [purely] transcendent and excludes all other considerations, he acts mischievously and misrepresents the Reality and all the apostles, albeit unwittingly. He imagines that he has hit on the truth, while he has [completely] missed the mark, being like those who believe in part and deny in part.[21]

It is known that when the Scriptures speak of the Reality they speak in a way that yields to the generality of men the immediately apparent meaning. The elite, on the other hand, understand all the meanings inherent in that utterance, in whatever terms it is expressed.

The truth is that the Reality is manifest in every created being and in every concept, while He is [at the same time] hidden from all understanding, except for one who holds that the Cosmos is His form and His identity. This is the Name, the Manifest, while He is also unmanifested Spirit, the Unmanifest. In this sense He is, in relation to the manifested forms of the Cosmos, the Spirit that determines those forms.

In any definition of Man, his inner and outer aspect are both to be considered, as is the case with all objects of definition. As for the Reality, He may be defined by every definition, for the forms of the Cosmos are limitless, nor can the definition of every form be known,

---

21. Cf. *Qur'an*, IV:150.

except insofar as the forms are implicit in the [definition] of the Cosmos.

Thus, a [true] definition of the Reality is impossible, for such a definition would depend on the ability to [fully] define every form in the Cosmos, which is impossible. Therefore, a [complete] definition of the Reality is impossible.

It is similar in the case of one who professes the comparability of God without taking into consideration His incomparability, so that he also restricts and limits Him and therefore does not know Him. He, however, who unites in his knowledge of God both transcendence and immanence in a comprehensive way, it not being possible to know such a thing in detail, owing to the infinitude of Cosmic forms, knows Him in a general way, but not in a detailed way, as he may know himself generally but not in detail.

In this connection the Prophet said, "Who [truly] knows himself knows his Lord,"[22] linking together knowledge of God and knowledge of the self. God says, *We will show them our signs on the horizons*, meaning the world outside you, *and in yourselves*, self, here, meaning your inner essence, *till it becomes clear to them that He is the Reality*,[23] in that you are His form and He is your Spirit. You are in relation to Him as your physical body is to you. He is in relation to you as the spirit governing your physical form.

This definition of you takes account of your outer and inner aspects, for the form that remains when the governing spirit is no longer present may no longer be called a man, but only a form resembling a man, there being no real difference between it and the shape of wood or stone. The name "man" may be given to such a form only figuratively, not properly.

On the other hand, the Reality never withdraws from the forms of the Cosmos in any fundamental sense, since the Cosmos, in its reality, is [necessarily] implicit in the definition of the Divinity, not merely figuratively as with a man when living in the body.

Just as the outer form of Man gives praise with its tongue to its spirit and the soul that rules it, so also did God cause the Cosmic Form to give praise to Him, although we cannot understand its praise by reasons of our inability to comprehend all the forms of the Cosmos. All things are the "tongues" of the Reality, giving expression to

---

22. I have not been able to trace this tradition.
23. *Qur'an*, XL:53.

the praise of the Reality. God says, *Praise belongs to God, Lord of the worlds,*[24] for all praise returns to Him Who is both the Praiser and the Praised.

> If you insist only on His transcendence, you restrict Him,
>   And if you insist only on His immanence you limit Him.
> If you maintain both aspects you are right,
>   An Imām and a master in the spiritual sciences.
> Whoso would say He is two things is a polytheist,
>   While the one who isolates Him tries to regulate Him.
> Beware of comparing Him if you profess duality,
>   And, if unity, beware of making Him transcendent.
> You are not He and you are He and
>   You see Him in the essences of things both boundless
>   and limited.

God says, *There is naught like unto Him,* asserting His transcendence, and He says, *He is the Hearing, the Seeing,*[25] implying comparison. On the other hand, there are implicit in the first quotation comparison [albeit negative] and duality [in the word "like"], and in the second quotation transcendence and isolation are implicit [He alone being named].

Had Noah combined the two aspects in summoning his people, they would have responded to his call. He appealed to their outer and inner understanding saying, *Ask you Lord to shield you [from your sins], for He is Forgiving.*[26] Then he said, *I summoned them by night [inwardly] and by day [outwardly], but my summons only made them more averse [outer].*[27] He states that his people turned a deaf ear to his summons only because they knew [innately] the proper way for them [maintaining God's immanence in many forms] to respond to his summons [made from the standpoint of unity and transcendence]. Those who know God understand the allusion Noah makes in respect of [what he knows to be the real state of] his people in that, by blaming them he praises them, since he knows the reason for their not responding [positively] to his summons; the reason being that his sum-

---

24. Ibid., I:1.
25. Ibid., XLII:11.
26. Ibid., LXXI:10.
27. Ibid., LXXI:5.

mons was made in a spirit of discrimination [seeking to oppose transcendence to immanence]. The whole truth is a conjunction [*al-qur'ān* [*qarana*] as the whole revelation] and not a discrimination [*al-furqān* [*faraqa*] a chapter of the Qur'an, i.e., a part].[28]

One who is firmly established in [his knowledge of] the conjunction does not dwell on the discrimination, for the former [*al-qur'ān*] includes the discrimination [the chapter—both aspects in their apparent opposition] and not vice versa. It is for this reason that the Qur'ān [the union of the two aspects] was vouchsafed to Muḥammad and this Community, which is the best granted to mankind.

The quotation *There is none like unto Him*[29] combines the two aspects. Had Noah uttered this kind of saying [in summoning his people], they would have responded [positively] to him, for he would have combined in the single verse the transcendental and immanental modes; nay, even in half a verse.

Noah summoned his people *by night,* in that he appealed to their intellects and spirits, which are unseen, and *by day,*[30] in that he appealed to the [evidence of] their external senses. But he did not unite the two as in the verse *There is none like unto Him.*[31] For this reason their inner selves [given to the immanental aspect] recoiled [from his summons] because of its discriminatory nature, making them even more averse [outer]. Then he told them that he summoned them in order that God might shield them [from the sin of excessive immanence] and not to reveal [uncover] for them [His transcendence as an absolute]. This they understood from him [according to their outer senses] so that *they put their fingers in their ears and tried to cover themselves with their clothes.*[32] This is an [external] form of shielding to which he had summoned them, although they responded literally by their actions and not in humble surrender [to God's shielding].

In the verse *There is none like unto Him,*[33] similarity is at once implied and denied. Because of this Muḥammad said that he had been granted [knowledge of God] integrating all His aspects. Muḥammad

---

28. Cf. ibid., LXXV:17 and VIII:29. Here Ibn al-'Arabī seeks to derive *qur'ān* from *qarana* rather than *qara'a.*
29. Ibid., XLII:11.
30. Ibid., LXXI:5.
31. Ibid., XLII:11.
32. Ibid., LXXI:2.
33. Ibid., XLII:11.

[unlike Noah] did not summon his people *by night* and *by day*,[34] but by night during the day [an inner summons implicit in the outer one], and by day during the night [the outer truth being implicit in the inner].

Noah, in his wisdom, said to them, *He causes the heaven to rain upon you copiously,*[35] meaning intellectual knowledge and reflection, and *has provided you with reserves [of wealth]*[36] by which He reserves you to Himself. When He does this you will see your form in Him. Whoever imagines that he sees the Reality Himself has no gnosis; he has gnosis who knows that it is his own essential self he sees. Thus are the Folk divided into those who know and those who do not know. And, ... *his offspring,*[37] meaning that which results from their ordinary discursive thinking, while what is required is the devotion of knowledge to contemplation, far removed from the fruits of ordinary thought. [*It will only increase them*] *in loss*[38] and *Their commerce will not profit them,*[39] meaning that that which they had within their grasp and which they imagined to be theirs departed from them. In respect of Muḥammad's heirs, He says, *Make use of that over which you have been appointed regents.*[40] In the case of Noah [and his people] He says, *Have you not taken a trustee other than Me?*[41] By this He confirms that, in their case, the power was theirs, God being trustee for them, while, in the case of the heirs of Muḥammad, they are God's regents in His kingdom, God being both Possessor and Trustee, while they are possessors only in the sense that they are regents.

Thus the Reality is *Ruler of the Kingdom* as indicated by at-Tirmidhī.[42]

And they hatched a great conspiracy,[43] meaning that summoning to God [in one mode] is [in a sense] a deception played on the one summoned, since God is no more nonexistent in the first mode [that of the one summoned] than in the second. *I call to God*, which is the de-

---

34. Ibid., LXXI:5.
35. Ibid., LXXI:11.
36. Ibid., LXXI:12.
37. Ibid., LXXI:21.
38. Ibid.
39. Ibid., II:16.
40. Ibid., LVII:7.
41. Ibid., XVII:2.
42. Cf. ibid., III:26.
43. Ibid., LXXI:22.

ception itself, *with clear vision,*⁴⁴ indicating that the whole [both modes] belong to Him. Thus they [for their part] responded to him with a deception, as he had summoned them with one.

The heir of Muḥammad knows that the summons to God is not a summons to His Ipseity [Essence], but to Him in respect of His Names [modes]. He says, *On the day when we will gather together the guarding ones in a band,*⁴⁵ indicating that they will come before God in the [all-embracing] Name the Merciful [not before God in His Essence]. We know that the Cosmos is under the rule of a divine Name that makes all in it guarding [guarded].

In their deception they say, *Do not abandon your gods, neither Wadd, Suwā', Yaghūth nor Ya'ūq, nor Nasr.*⁴⁶ If they had abandoned them they would have become ignorant of the Reality, to the extent that they deserted them, for in every object of worship there is a reflection of the Reality, whether it be recognized or not.

In the case of Muḥammad's heirs He says, *Your Lord has decreed that you serve only Him,*⁴⁷ meaning He has determined it. The one who knows, knows Who is worshiped and in what form He is manifest to be worshiped. He also knows that the distinction and multiplicity [of forms] are merely like parts of a sensible form or the powers of a spiritual image. Indeed, in every object of worship it is [in truth] God Who is worshiped.

The ignorant man imagines the object to be invested with divinity and, were it not for such a notion, neither the stone nor anything similar would be an object of worship. For this reason He says, *Bid them name them.*⁴⁸ Had they done so they would have called them stones, trees, or stars. Had they been asked whom they worshiped, they would have said "a god" and not "God" or "the God."

The man endowed with knowledge does not imagine thus, but knows that the object of worship is the vehicle of divine manifestation, worthy of reverence, while not restricting himself [to that particular object].

The ignorant man says, *We only worship them that they might bring us nearer to God.*⁴⁹ The man of knowledge says, *Your God is only One, so*

---

44. Ibid., XII:108.
45. Ibid., XIX:85.
46. Ibid., LXXI:23.
47. Ibid., XVII:23.
48. Ibid., XIII:33.
49. Ibid., XXXIX:3.

THE BEZELS OF WISDOM

submit yourselves to Him, howsoever He is manifest, *and bring glad tidings to those who conceal,*[50] that is, who conceal the fire of their [lowly] nature. They would say "a god" and not "a nature" [something passive].

He also says, *They have caused confusion to many,*[51] meaning that they have caused them to become perplexed in the face of the [apparent] multiplicity of the One in respect of His aspects and attributions.

It only increases the oppressors [in confusion],[52] meaning those who oppress themselves [by self-denial], who inherit the Book [of unitary knowledge]. These are the first of the three [categories] [described by God elsewhere], since He places the self-oppressor before the *moderate one* and the *doer of good works.*[53] *In confusion,*[54] that is, in [spiritually self-effacing] perplexity on the part of the heirs of Muḥammad, who said, "My Lord increase my perplexity concerning You."[55] *When it [the Self-revelation of the One] shines for them they proceed, but when it shines not [because of the multiplicity of forms] they stop [in perplexity].*[56] He who experiences this perplexity is ceaselessly centered on the Pole [God], while he who follows the "long" path [to a distant God] is always turning aside from the [Supreme] Goal to search after that which is [eternally] within him, running after imagination as his goal. He has an [imaginary] starting point and [what he supposes to be] a goal and what lies between them, while for the God-centered man there is no restriction of beginning or end, possessing [as he does] the most comprehensive existence and being the recipient of [divine] truths and realities.

Because of their transgressions,[57] going beyond themselves so that they drowned in the seas of the knowledge of God, which is what is meant by perplexity. *And they were cast into the fire,*[58] which means the same as drowning according to the heirs. *When the seas swell,*[59] where the same verbal root is used to denote the heating of an oven. *Nor will*

---

50. Ibid., XXII:34.
51. Ibid., LXXI:24.
52. Ibid.
53. Ibid., XXXV:32.
54. Ibid., LXXI:24.
55. I have not been able to trace this saying.
56. *Qur'an,* II:20.
57. Ibid., LXXI:25.
58. Ibid.
59. Ibid., LXXXI:6.

they find any helpers apart from God,[60] since their helpers are [in essence] nothing other than God and they are annihilated in Him forever.

Were He to deliver them [from the seas of gnosis] onto the shore of Nature He would be lowering them from an eminent stage [of spiritual attainment], [that is, relatively eminent] although [in truth] all is God's, through God, indeed is God.

Noah said, "O my Lord!"[61] He did not say, "O my God," because [God as] the Lord is fixed, whereas the Divinity is manifold according to [the variety] of His Names and *every day He is engaged in some matter.*[62] [God] as the Lord denotes a constancy of mode without which the appeal would not be appropriate. [*O my Lord*], *do not leave* [*any of the deniers dwelling*] *upon Earth,*[63] [that is on the level of devotion to formal manifestation], beseeching that they be brought to the inner aspect [of knowledge of essential Unity].

In respect of Muḥammad's heirs, [it might be said], "If you let down a rope it would fall upon God [He being below and above],"[64] and, *His is what is in the Heavens and the Earth.*[65] When you are buried in it you will be in it and it will be your covering, *to it We will return you and from it We will bring you forth a second time,*[66] because of the variety of aspects.

... *of the deniers,*[67] who *seek to cover themselves in their clothes and put their fingers into their ears,*[68] seeking cover because he summoned them that He might shield [forgive] them, which is a kind of covering. *Dwelling,*[69] that is, any of them at all, so that the benefit might be general as was the summons. *If you spare them,* that is leave them [as they are], *they will confuse your servants,*[70] meaning that they will perplex them and cause them to depart from their servanthood to [assert] the mysteries of Lordship in themselves, so that they will consider themselves as Lords after being servants. They will indeed be servants be-

---

60. Ibid., LXXI:25.
61. Ibid., LXXI:26.
62. Ibid., LV:29.
63. Ibid., LXXI:26.
64. Tirmidhī, V:58.
65. *Qur'an*, II:116.
66. Ibid., XX:55.
67. Ibid., LXXI:26.
68. Ibid., LXXI:7.
69. Ibid., LXXI:26.
70. Ibid., LXXI:27.

come as Lords. *They will only bring forth,* they will only produce and make manifest *one who breaks open [wrong doer],* that is one who makes manifest what is hidden, and *one who denies,*⁷¹ that is one who conceals what is manifest after its manifestation. They will bring forth what is hidden and then conceal it after its manifestation, so that the beholder will be perplexed, not knowing what the discloser intends by his action nor the concealer by his, though they are [in truth] the same.

*My Lord, shield [forgive] me,*⁷² that is, conceal me [from my separate self] and cover for my sake [other than You] and render my [relative] span and station unknowable [in You] since You are without measure; You say, *They do not assess God to the fullness of His measure.*⁷³ *And my parents,* from whom I derived, namely, the Intellect and Nature. *And whoever enters my house,* that is, into my heart, *believing,* that is, confirming the divine communications, having himself received them. *And the believers, both men,* meaning the intellects, *and women,* the souls.

And do not increase the oppressors, those in darkness who belong to the Unseen, concealed behind dark veils, *except in destruction,*⁷⁴ that is, in annihilation [in God]. They have consciousness of themselves because their contemplation of the face of the Reality absorbs them to the exclusion of their [separative] selves. Among the heirs is remembered the verse, *All perishes save His face,*⁷⁵ the *destruction*⁷⁶ in the above verse meaning this "perishing."

Whoever wishes to gain access to the Noah mysteries must ascend to the Sphere of the Sun. These matters are also dealt with in our book, *The Mosul Revelations.*⁷⁷

---

71. Ibid.
72. Ibid., LXXI:28.
73. Ibid., VI:91.
74. All other quotations are from LXXI:28.
75. *Qur'an,* XXVIII:88.
76. Ibid., LXXI:28.
77. This work has not been published. There is an autograph Ms. in Istanbul, Murad Molla, 1236.

CHAPTER IV

THE WISDOM OF HOLINESS IN THE WORD OF ENOCH

INTRODUCTORY NOTE

To understand the significance for this chapter of the word "holiness" in the title, it is necessary to know that the meaning of the Arabic root *qadasa* is "to be far removed," which in this context means the spiritual remoteness of God from the trammels of the world or Cosmos. To demonstrate the relevance of this notion further, it must be pointed out that, in most spiritually oriented religious traditions, the notion of spiritual remoteness, in the sense of transcendence, is closely associated with the notion of height or elevation, which is precisely the main topic of discussion in this chapter.

Ibn al-'Arabī divides the concept of elevation into two kinds, elevation of position, which relates to cosmic activity by the soul, and elevation of degree, which relates to the knowing of the spirit. He discusses also the meaning and significance of the term "elevation" in connection with God. In other words, elevation of position is according to a cosmic scale and elevation of degree is according to a divine scale, although it is only God, as the worshiped element in the polarity Creator-creation, Who may be said to be elevated, since the Reality Itself is beyond and, at the same time, embraces such a concept, whether it be of position or degree. It all depends on whether one views God as the One in the sense of the Unique, or as the One, the First of many.

This leads us on to the next subject dealt with in the chapter, namely that of the mystical theory of number. Here he discusses the implications for his teachings of considering the number one, either as the number par excellence from which all other numbers derive and of which they are merely manifestations, or the number one as a unique reality in itself, unrelated to and beyond any possibility of multiplication. For Ibn al-'Arabī, this question relates, once more, to the polarity God in Himself–God in the Cosmos. In other words, are we to see God as unique, and therefore as unrelating and unrelatable, or as the relating and related origin of all created existence? Ibn al-'Arabī's answer is, of course, that both perspectives are true of the Reality.

Going on to discuss the relationship of cosmic Nature with God, Ibn al-'Arabī compares it to the father-son and Adam-Eve relationship, by which he seeks to show that the Cosmos, deriving as it does from God, is essentially none other than He. He returns to these analogies later in the work. However, as he points out earlier in the chapter, regarded from the standpoint of the Reality Itself, there is no clear bias in favor of the Creator rather than creation, since, from this standpoint, we may speak of a "created Creator" and a "creating creation," as he himself expresses it.

The chapter ends with another look at the subject of the divine Names. Since all the Names that, as we have seen, serve to describe the nature of the relationship Creator-creation are the Names of God, which term is itself the universal Name, each particular name must needs express, if only essentially, all the other Names, while in itself denoting some particular aspect of the divine connection with the Cosmos. Thus each particular creation in its own particular relationship with its Lord, as determined by its own latent predisposition *in divinis,* partakes in reality in all possible creation, since even in its own particularity it is, and cannot be, other than He.

THE WISDOM OF HOLINESS IN THE WORD OF ENOCH

Elevation may be attributed in two ways, either with respect to position [created being] or to degree [of essential reality]. An example of the former is provided in His saying, *We raised him to a high position.*[78] The most elevated [cosmic] position is that point round which the Spheres revolve, which is the Sphere of the Sun where the spiritual form of Enoch resides.

There revolve round it seven higher Spheres and seven lower Spheres, being fifteen in all.

The higher Spheres are those of Mars, Jupiter, Saturn, the Mansions, the Constellations, the Throne, and the Seat.

The lower Spheres are those of Venus, Mercury, the Moon, Ether, Air, Water, and Earth.

As being the pivot of the Spheres he is elevated as regards position. As for degree, it belongs to the heirs of Muhammad. God says, *You are the elevated ones and God is with you*[79] in this elevation, since, although He is far above all position, He is not so in respect of degree.

When the soul in us, concerned with activity, fears [the loss of attainment], He follows with His saying, *He will not nullify your deeds,* for action seeks position while knowledge seeks degree. God unites the two kinds of elevation for us, elevation of position through action and of degree through knowledge.

Then He says, rejecting any suggestion of co-partnership in His words *God is with you, Exalt the name of your Lord, the Sublime,*[80] that is, beyond any idea of partnership.

Man, namely, the Perfect Man, is the most elevated of existing beings, but his elevation depends on an elevation of position or degree, not deriving it from himself [as a created being]. He is elevated either because he occupies a high position [in the cosmic order] or because he has a high degree, the elevation residing in them and not in him.

Elevation of position is as He says, *The Merciful is established on the Seat,*[81] which is the highest position. Alluding to elevation of degree, He says, *All perishes save His face,*[82] and *All reverts to Him,*[83] and *Can there be a god with God?*[84]

---

78. *Qur'an*, XIX:57.
79. Ibid., XLVII:35, the source also of the following two quotations.
80. Ibid., LXXVIII:1.
81. Ibid., XX:5.
82. Ibid., XXVIII:88.
83. Ibid., XI:123.
84. Ibid., XXVII:60.

When God says, *And We raised him to a high position*,[85] He connects the adjective "high" to the noun "position," whereas His saying, *When your Lord said to the angels, "I am going to place on the Earth a regent,"*[86] refers to elevation of degree. He also says, with reference to the angels, *Are you displaying pride or are you of the elevated ones?*[87] connecting elevation to the angels themselves. If this ascription were implicit in their being angels, all angels would share in it. Since, however, it is not a general ascription, even though they are all defined as being angels, we know that it refers to elevation of degree with God.

Similarly in the case of the Caliphs, if their elevation were implicit in their being men, all men would partake of it. Since it is not general however, we know that the elevation belongs to the degree.

The Elevated is one of God's Beautiful Names; but above whom or what, since only He exists? More elevated than whom or what, since only He is and He is Elevated in Himself? In relation to existence He is the very essence of existing beings. Thus, in a certain sense, relative beings are elevated in themselves, since [in truth] they are none other than He and His elevation is absolute and not relative. This is because the [eternal] essences are immutable unmanifest, knowing nothing of manifested existence, and they remain in that state, despite all the multiplicity of manifested forms. The Essence is Unique of the whole in the whole. Multiplicity exists only in respect of the divine Names, which are themselves purely relationships and thus not manifest [in themselves].

Naught is except the Essence, which is Elevated in Itself, its elevation being unrelated to any other. Thus, from this standpoint, there is no relative elevation, although in respect of the aspects of existence there is [a certain] differentiation. Relative elevation exists in the Unique Essence only insofar as It is [manifest in] many aspects.

Thus, in a certain sense, it may be said that He is not He and you are not you. Al-Kharrāz,[88] who is an aspect of the Reality and one of His tongues by which He expresses Himself, said, "God cannot be known except as uniting the opposites," in determining them through them. He is the First and the Last, the Manifest and the Un-

---

85. Ibid., XIX:57.
86. Ibid., II:30.
87. Ibid., XXXVIII:75.
88. Abū Saʿīd al-Kharrāz died in A.D. 899. Cf. Al-Hujwīrī, *Kashf al-maḥjūb*, trans. R. A. Nicholson, London, 1911, pp. 241–246.

manifest, the Essence of all that is manifest and all that is not yet manifest, even as He is manifesting Himself. Thus, only He sees Him and only He is hidden from Him, for He is manifest to Himself and hidden from Himself. It is none other than He who bears the name Abū Sa'īd al-Kharrāz and all the other names given to relative beings. The Unmanifest says "No" when the Manifest says "I [am]" and the Manifest says "No" when the Unmanifest says "[Only] I [am]." This is the nature of opposition, but the speaker and listener [in both cases] are One, the Unique. The Prophet said, "... and what they told themselves,"[89] they being the tellers, the ones told, and the telling, knowing what was to be told.

The Essence is Unique while the determinations are various. This situation is well known, since every man knows this of himself, being the form of the Reality. The realities are mingled [some with others]. The numbers derive from the one according to the well-known groupings [10s, 100s, etc]. Thus the one makes number possible, and number deploys the one. Furthermore, enumeration is possible only because of the existence of that which is enumerated. The latter may exist or not exist, since something may be nonexistent physically but exist intellectually. Therefore there must be number and that which can be numbered, just as there must be the one to initiate the process by which it is itself developed.

Each unit is a reality in itself, like nine or ten down to the lowest [two] or upward *ad infinitum*, although none of them are comprehensive, each of them being a [particular] collection of ones. Two is unique and three and so on, even though all are one [in being made up of ones], nor does a particular number embrace other numbers [essentially]. For the fact that all numbers are collections of ones establishes at once that, as being different collections, they are [relatively] unique and that, as being all multiples of one, they derive entirely from the one. Inherent in all this are the twenty groups [1, 2, 3, 4, 5, 6, 7, 8, 9, 10, 20, 30, 40, 50, 60, 70, 80, 90, 100, 1,000], according to a particular construction. Thus, in saying that all numbers are one reality, one must also say that the one is not the numbers [being the origin].

Whoever has understood what I have said about the numbers,

---

89. Bukhārī, II:15.

namely, that to deny them is to affirm them, will know that the transcendent Reality is [at the same time] the relative creature, even though the creature be distinct from the Creator. The Reality is at once the created Creator and the creating creature. All this is One Essence, at once Unique and Many, so consider what it is you see.

[Isaac said to his father], *O Father, do as you are commanded*,[90] for the son is the essence of the father. Abraham saw only his own self to be sacrificed. *Then We ransomed him with a mighty sacrifice*,[91] so that that which had appeared in human form appeared as a ram, whereas it had appeared in the form of a son or, more precisely, in a form distinguishing father and son, since the son is [in reality] the essence of the father.

He created from it [Adam's soul] its mate,[92] so that Adam's consort was nothing other than his [essential] self. From him came forth both mate and child, for the [Creative] Command is one in multiplicity.

Who [else] is the Universal Nature and who [else] is manifest in her [many forms]? We observe that Nature suffers no loss in displaying [her forms] nor yet any increase in reassimilating them. What is manifest is She Herself, just as She is not what is manifest from the standpoint of formal distinction. One particular manifestation is cold and dry, while another is hot and dry. They are both one as regards dryness, but otherwise distinct. Nature, or rather the Essential Nature, is that which unites all of them. The natural order may thus be regarded [at once] as [many] forms reflected in a single mirror or as a single form reflected in many mirrors. This notion causes nothing but confusion [to the sense-bound mind] because of the divisive nature of its apprehension.

He who truly understands what we are discussing here is not confused. Even if his knowledge is extended, the extension is only the result of the determination of the location, which is nothing other than the immutable essence in respect of which the Reality is [formally] diversified within the theater [of His Self-revelation]. These locational determinants seem to diversify Him, but it is He Who absorbs every determinant, He Himself being determined only by His Own Self-manifestation. There is naught but He.

---

90. *Qur'an*, XXXVII:102.
91. Ibid., XXVII:107.
92. Ibid., IV:1.

IBN AL-'ARABĪ

In one sense the Reality is creature, so consider,
   In another He is not, so reflect.
Who grasps my saying, his perception will not dim,
   Nor may one grasp it save he be endowed with perception.
Whether you assert unity or distinction, the Self is Unique.
   As also the Many that are and yet are not.

He Who is Elevated in Himself enjoys that [complete] perfection in which all realities and relationships, determined or undetermined, are immersed, since none of the attributes can possibly apply to other than He. This means all realities and relationships, whether they be, in the eyes of convention, reason or law, praiseworthy or otherwise. This applies only to the Reality as "God" [the Name uniting all Names]. As for the Reality as other than God, [as manifested] in some place or form, then qualitative disparity [necessarily] occurs, as between one location and another. If the form be a [synthetic] form [the Perfect Man], it embraces [essentially] the essential perfection, since it is identical with the [universal] location in which it is manifest. The [all-embracing] totality inherent in the Name "God" is implicit in that form, which is at once not He and not other than He.

Abū al-Qāsim b. Qissī alludes to this in his book *The Shedding of the Sandals*, where he says, "Every Divine Name is invested with all the Names."[93] This is because every Name implies the Essence as well as the particular aspect it enshrines. Therefore, insofar as it implies the Essence Itself, it partakes of all the Names, whereas, as evincing the particular aspect [of the Essence] it is distinct and unique [relatively]. In this latter sense it is differentiated from every other Name, such as Lord, Creator, Fashioner, and so on. In the former sense the Name is [essentially] the one Named, but other than He as representing some particular aspect.

If you have understood the elevation I have discussed, you will know that it is elevation neither of position nor of degree. As regards the latter, it is peculiar to persons in power, as sultans, governors, ministers, judges, and every holder of office, be they worthy of it or not. Self-sufficient elevation is not of this kind. It is quite possible for

---

93. Founder of a twelfth century Sufi movement. Ibn al-'Arabī wrote a commentary on this work, ms. Yusuf Agha 5624 [Eski], 109–338.

the most knowledgeable of men to be under the control of the most ignorant who happens to hold a powerful office. The elevation of the latter is entirely relative to the office he holds, while the former is elevated in himself. When the holder of office ceases to hold it, his elevation ceases also. This is not the case with a man of true knowledge.

CHAPTER V

THE WISDOM OF RAPTUROUS LOVE IN THE WORD OF ABRAHAM

INTRODUCTORY NOTE

The traditional title of the Patriarch Abraham is *al-Khalīl*, which is usually translated as "the friend." Ibn al-'Arabī, however, reads into the word one of the other derivative meanings of the root *khalla*, that of permeation or penetration. Thus, in this context, Abraham's title means, rather, "the permeated one," permeated, that is, by God. The friendship, therefore, is of the most intimate kind; indeed it is, as the title of the chapter suggests, more like rapturous love by which the lover is wholly permeated by the beloved. Our author goes on to use the example of Abraham to illustrate the principle of divine permeation in general. Thus, the Cosmos and each of its constituents, as being totally receptive to the divine Command, is wholly permeated by the divine agent as something implicit and not explicit, so that the manifest complexity and multiplicity of the Cosmos conceals the all-pervading reality of God. As usual, however, he insists on the mutuality of this principle of permeation, since, just as God is implicitly present in cosmic creation, so is creation implicitly and essentially present in God.

This leads Ibn al-'Arabī on to point out that the terms "God" and

"Cosmos" are interdependent, the notion of divinity being dependent on the notion of that which worships Him. Thus, neither God nor the Cosmos may be known, except in relation to each other. He is saying, therefore, that the Cosmos cannot be properly known or understood without reference to God, nor can the concept of divinity be comprehended without reference to creation. Proceeding to the subject of our essential latency *in divinis*, he concludes that, in knowing the Cosmos, God is knowing Himself, and that, in knowing God, we, as creatures, know ourselves in essence. Thus, *in aeternis*, we are the latent and essential content of His knowledge of Himself, while, in time and space, He is the all-permeating substance and reality of which we are but apparent facets. This prompts him to point out that, in view of this, we have no cause to blame God, since, in reality, as being nothing other than what He knows Himself to be, we determine what we experience ourselves to be, past, present, or future.

Ibn al-'Arabī goes on to reinforce the concept of mutual permeation between God and the Cosmos by comparing it with the process by which consumed food becomes one with the consumer by the assimilation of its particles and substances to the substance of the one who eats it. Thus, divinity is the existential nourishment of the Cosmos, while it, in turn, is the archetypal nourishment of the divine Self-awareness. Indeed, the two poems with which he concludes this chapter express his daring vision of mutuality very explicitly, and it was this kind of expression, on his part, of concepts shocking and unacceptable to less flexible minds, that earned Ibn al-'Arabī so much opprobrium among the religious scholars of his time.

THE WISDOM OF RAPTUROUS LOVE
IN THE WORD OF ABRAHAM

Abraham was called the Intimate [*khalīl*] [of God] because he had embraced [*takhallala*] and penetrated all the Attributes of the Divine Essence. The poet says,

> I have penetrated the course of the spirit within me,
> And thus was the Intimate [of God] so called.

In the same way, color permeates that which is colored, providing [it be understood] that the accident in relation to its substance is not as the thing and the space it occupies; or Abraham was so called because the Reality permeated his form. Either approach is valid, since every determination has an appropriate assignation beyond which it does not pass.

Do you not understand that the Reality is manifest through the attributes of relative beings, when He has informed us of that Himself, even through attributes of deficiency and blame? Do you not understand that the created being is manifest through the attributes of the Reality, from the first to the last, all of them being appropriate to it, even as the attributes of created beings are appropriate to the Reality? The words *Praise belongs to God*[94] mean that every instance of praise, as respecting the one who praises or the one praised, reverts to Him. *To Him the [whole] matter reverts*,[95] in which verse He embraces all [attributes] without reference to their praiseworthiness or blameworthiness, all being either the one or the other.

Know that whenever something permeates another it is assumed into the other. That which permeates, the agent, is disguised by that which is permeated, the object of permeation. Thus, the object in this case is the manifest, while the agent is the unmanifest, the hidden [reality]. The latter is as nourishment for the former, even as a piece of wool swells and expands because of the water that permeates it.

If, on the other hand, the Reality is considered as being the Manifest and the creature as being hidden within Him, the creature will assume all the Names of the Reality, His hearing, sight, all His relationships [modes], and His knowledge. If, however, the creature is considered the manifest and the Reality the Unmanifest within him, then the Reality is in the hearing of the creature, as also in his sight, hand, foot, and all his faculties, as declared in the [well-known] Holy Tradition of the Prophet.[96]

The Essence, as being beyond all these relationships, is not a divinity. Since all these relationships originate in our eternally unmanifested essences, it is we [in our eternal latency] who make Him a divinity by being that through which He knows Himself as Divine. Thus, He is not known [as "God"] until we are known.

Muḥammad said, "Who knows his [true] self, knows his Lord," being the creature who knows God best. Certain sages, among them

---

94. *Qur'an*, I:1.
95. Ibid., XI:123.
96. See above, p. 56. Bukhārī, LXXXI:38.

Abū Ḥāmid al-Ghazālī, have asserted that God can be known without any reference to the created Cosmos, but this is mistaken.⁹⁷ It is true that a primordial eternal essence can be known, but it cannot be known as a divinity unless knowledge of that to which it can be related is assumed, for it is the dependent who confirm the independence of the Independent.

However, a further spiritual intuition will reveal that that which was necessary to affirm His Divinity is none other than the Reality Himself, and that the Cosmos [of created beings] is nothing more than His Self-revelation [to Himself] in the forms [determined] by their eternally unmanifest essences, which could not possibly exist without Him. It will reveal also that He manifests Himself variously and formally according to the [inherent] realities and states of the essences, all of which is understood together with the knowledge that, in relation to us, He is the Divinity.

A final spiritual intuition will show you our forms manifest in Him, so that some of us are manifest to others in the Reality, know each other, and distinguish each other in Him. There are those of us who have spiritual knowledge of this mutual recognition in the Reality, while others have not experienced the plane on which this occurs. I seek refuge in God lest I be of the ignorant.

As a result of the last two intuitions it is known that we are determined only through ourselves [as essences]; indeed, it is we who determine ourselves through ourselves, which is the meaning of the words *God's is the conclusive argument*,⁹⁸ that is, against the veiled ones when they ask the Reality why He has done with them things contrary to their own aims. *And He made their affair difficult for them*,⁹⁹ and this is the truth revealed to the gnostics. For they see that it is not the Reality that has done with them what is claimed, and they see that what was done with them came from themselves, for His knowledge of them is according to what they are themselves [in their eternal essences]. Thus their complaint is nullified, the conclusive argument remaining with God.

If it be asked what is the point of His saying, *Had He wished He would have guided you all*,¹⁰⁰ we reply that the *Had He* in *Had He wished*

---

97. Cf. F. Shehadi, *Ghazali's Unique Unknowable God*, Leiden, 1964.
98. *Qur'an*, VI: 149.
99. Ibid., LXVIII:42.
100. Ibid., VI:149.

conveys the denial of a suggestion regarding the impossible, for He wills only that which is. However, according to rational principles the same contingency may admit of a thing or its opposite, but [in reality] whichever of the two [alternatives] occurs is the one assigned to the contingency in its eternal essence. The meaning of *He would have guided you* is that He would have made clear to you [your unmanifest realities]. However, it is not granted to everyone by God that his spiritual sight should be opened to perceive his essential reality [in its latency], for there are those who know and those who do not know. For this reason He did not will and did not guide them all, nor will He do so; the same applies to the words *If He wills*,[101] for how is He to will what is not?

His Will is self-dependent and is an [essential] attribution dependent on His Knowledge, which is [in turn] dependent on the object of His Knowledge, which is you and your essential status. Knowledge has no effect on the object of knowledge, while what is known has an effect on knowledge, bestowing on it of itself what it is.

The [scriptural] Revelations were formulated in accordance with what those addressed laid down [as regards the eternal measure of response eternally latent in their essences] and according to reason, which formulation does not [necessarily] conform to what [direct] spiritual intuition reveals. Thus, although believers are many, gnostics endowed with spiritual intuition are few. *There are none of us but have a known station*,[102] which is what you are in your eternal latency and in accordance with which you are manifest in existence, if, in truth, your reality includes the possibility of being manifested.

If it is agreed that existence may be attributed only to the Reality and not to you, you will [nevertheless, as essence] determine His existence. If it is agreed that you have existence, you are also a determinant. For, even though the Reality be the Determiner, it is for Him only to pour existence upon you, while you remain the determinant and the determined. Therefore praise none other than yourself and blame none other than yourself. Praise is due to the Reality only as pouring forth existence, which only He may do, not you.

You are His nourishment as bestowing the contents of His Self-Knowledge, while He is yours as bestowing existence, what is assigned to you being assigned also to Him. The order is from Him to

---

101. Ibid., IV:133.
102. Ibid., XXXVII:164.

you [*Be!*] and from you to [what you/He shall be]. However, you are called the one who is charged, but He charges you only in accordance with what your essential unmanifest reality bids Him. He is not so called, since He is not the object.

> He praises me and I praise Him,
>   He worships me and I worship Him.
> In my state of existence I confirm Him,
>   As unmanifest essence I deny Him.
> He knows me, while I know naught of Him,
>   I also know Him and perceive Him.
> Where then is His Self-sufficiency,
>   Since I help Him and grant Him Bliss?
> It is for this that the Reality created me,
>   For I give content to His Knowledge and manifest Him.
> Thus did the message come,
>   Its meaning fulfilled in me.

It was because Abraham attained to this rank by which he was called the Intimate [of God] that hospitality became a [sacred] act. Ibn Masarrah put him with Michael [the Archangel] as a source of provision, provisions being the food of those provided.[103] Food penetrates to the essence of the one fed, permeating every part. So also with God, although in His case there are no parts but only Divine Stations or Names through which His Essence is manifest.

> We are His as has been shown,
>   As also we belong to ourselves.
> He has no other becoming except mine,
>   We are His and we are through ourselves.
> I have two aspects, He and I,
>   But He is not I in my I.
> In me is His theater of manifestation,
>   And we are for Him as vessels.

---

103. Founder of a Sufi school, d. A.D. 931. Cf. A. Palacios, *Abenmasarrah y su escuela*, Madrid, 1914.

CHAPTER VI

THE WISDOM OF REALITY IN THE WORD OF ISAAC

INTRODUCTORY NOTE

Three very important aspects of Ibn al-'Arabī's thought are discussed in this relatively short chapter. The first of these is the subject of the Imagination, not so much in its macrocosmic and creative sense as an image of the divine Self-polarization, but rather in its microcosmic and recollective sense. The Imaginative faculty, whether macrocosmic or microcosmic, is seen as having two functions, the one creative and existential, the other recollective or recreational and spiritual. In the first case, the Imaginative process absorbs and involves consciousness, divine and human, in the creative urge of cosmic becoming in all its infinitely fascinating complexity. In the second case, by a process of interpretation and realization, consciousness rediscovers and reestablishes its ultimately inalienable and absolute integrity and unity. In the human individual sphere, the first is illustrated by the man whose consciousness is always being attracted outward to material objects, dissipated and absorbed by a multiplicity of "interests," while the second is illustrated by the person who abstracts the objects of sense around him to reinforce and confirm his own conscious identity.

The second process helps to illustrate the qur'anic view of the

Cosmos as being an infinite display of *āyāt* or signs, the intelligent interpretation and contemplation of which leads one, inevitably, back toward the absolute and unitive truth of God. The point being made in the first part of this chapter is that cosmic forms have two aspects, the existential and creative aspect of cosmic actuality, which seems always to alienate and dissipate integral consciousness, and the spiritual and symbolic aspect, which assists in refocusing the intellect on the archetypal and ideal. In other words, what one perceives with one's worldly and cosmic perception is an image that on the one hand conceals its essential truth, but on the other reveals that truth to spiritual perception. This latter perception requires the ability to leap, so to speak, from the outflowing to the inflowing current of the Imagination, which currents meet in the microcosmic synthesis of the human state, so that man alone is able to make this transition. This means that, in addition to being of both earth and Heaven, man also occupies a vital and important middle ground, the *'ālam al-mithāl* or world of likenesses in which archetypes mysteriously become translated into existent things, and through which cosmic forms are transformed into spiritual essences—a subtle, fluid realm in which the currents of cosmic becoming and spiritual reintegration meet and mingle. The leap, therefore, that man must make in order that he might use cosmic images as a means of realizing his eternal identity with God is precisely the act of *ta'wīl*, which means "going back to first principles," which means to perceive in cosmic forms that aspect which points, symbolically, to their creator, God. Thus, in short, cosmic forms are not what they seem, but rather what they mean, not what they have become, but what they are *in aeternis*. Although most cosmic forms are, potentially, diabolic in the sense that, in their existential aspect, they may encourage an apparent alienation and separation from the divine principle, that of Muḥammad, as a particular formal manifestation of the Perfect Man who unalterably symbolizes the wholeness of divine Reality, cannot be so.

The subject of the Perfect Man and his manifestation in the form of Muḥammad naturally leads on to the second of Ibn al-'Arabī's subjects in this chapter, that of the Heart. According to a Holy Tradition, the only thing that can contain God is the Heart of the gnostic. This is because the essential Heart, as opposed to the physical heart, is precisely that synthetic organ which, within the microcosmic context, symbolizes the unimaginable synthesis of the Reality Itself in Its undifferentiated wholeness. While, in his intellect and spirit, man is an aspect of God, in his body and life, an aspect of cosmic creation, and, in his soul, an aspect of the relationship between God and the Cosmos, it is in his Heart that man may fully realize his inexorable oneness with the Reality, which is the *coincidentia oppositorum*.

The third and last subject dealt with in this chapter is that of the *himmah* or creative force of the gnostic, that faculty which enables him to link his own particular power of creative imagination to the divine creative Imagination. As has been indicated elsewhere, unless this linking goes together with total self-effacement in the Self, it may lead to the illusion of self-deification, because of the seemingly miraculous powers attendant on the development of such power, albeit that the human *himmah* can never be anything but partial.

THE WISDOM OF REALITY IN THE WORD OF ISAAC

The ransom of a prophet is a beast slaughtered as a sacrificial offering,
But how can the bleating of a ram compare with the speech of Man?
God the Mighty made mighty the ram for our sake or its sake, I know not by what measure.
No doubt other sacrificial beasts fetch a higher price,
But they all are less than a ram slaughtered as an offering.
Would that I knew how a mere ram came to be a substitute for the Vice-Regent of the Merciful.
Do you not perceive a certain logic in the matter,
The realization of gains and the diminution of loss?
No creation is higher than the stone, and after it the plant,
In a certain sense and according to certain measures.
After the plant comes sentient being, all know their Creator by a direct knowledge and on clear evidence.
As for the one called Adam, he is bound by intelligence, thought, and the garland of faith.
Concerning this said Sahl, a gnostic like ourselves,[104]
Because we and they are at the degree of spiritual vision,
Whoso has contemplated what I have contemplated

---

104. Sahl al-Tustarī, d. A.H. 283. Cf. Hujwīrī, *Kashf*, pp. 139–140, 195–210.

Will say the same as I, whether in secret or openly.
Do not consider words contrary to ours, nor sow seed in blind soil.
For they are the deaf, the dumb of whom the sinless one spoke in the text of the Qur'an.

Know, may God strengthen us and you, that Abraham the Intimate said to his son, *I saw in sleep that I was killing you for sacrifice.*[105] The state of sleep is the plane of the Imagination and Abraham did not interpret [what he saw], for it was a ram that appeared in the form of Abraham's son in the dream, while Abraham believed what he saw [at face value]. So his Lord rescued his son from Abraham's misapprehension by the Great Sacrifice [of the ram], which was the true expression of his vision with God, of which Abraham was unaware.

The formal Self-revelation [of the Reality] on the plane of the Imagination requires an additional knowledge by which to apprehend what God intends by a particular form. Have you not considered what the Apostle of God said to Abu Bakr concerning the interpretation of visions when he said, "I was right in some cases and mistaken in others"? Abu Bakr asked him to acquaint him in which of them he had been right and in which wrong, but he did not tell him.

God says to Abraham, calling him *O Abraham, you believed what you saw,*[106] and He does not say, "You were right concerning what you saw," namely [in seeing] your son, because he did not interpret what he saw, but took it at its face value, although visions require interpretation. Thus Joseph's master says, *If you will interpret the vision.*[107] Interpretation means to pass from the form of what one sees to something beyond it.

Thus were the cattle [symbols] for years of scarcity and plenty.[108] Had he been true to the vision he would have killed his son, for he believed that it was his son he saw, although with God it was nothing other than the Great Sacrifice in the form of his son. Because of this He saved him, because of the mistaken notion that had entered Abraham's mind. In reality it was not a ransom in God's sight [but

---

105. *Qur'an*, XXXVII:102.
106. Ibid., XXXVII:105.
107. Ibid., XII:43.
108. Cf. ibid., XII:43.

the sacrifice itself]. The senses formulated the sacrifice and the Imagination produced the form of Abraham's son. Had it been a ram he saw in the Imagination he would have interpreted it as his son or as something else. Then God says, *This is indeed a clear test*,[109] that is, a test of his knowledge, whether he knew what interpretation was necessary in the context of vision or not. Abraham knew that the perspective of the Imagination required interpretation, but was heedless [on this occasion] and did not deal with the perspective in the proper way. Thus, he believed the vision as he saw it.

Taqī b. al-Mukhallad,[110] the Imam and author of the *Musnad*, heard that the Apostle had said, "Whoever sees me in sleep has seen me in waking, for the Devil cannot take my form upon himself."[111] Accordingly Taqī b. Mukhallad saw him [in sleep] and the Prophet was giving him milk to drink. He believed the vision superficially, and made himself vomit [to prove its truth]. Had he penetrated to the meaning of his vision, the milk would have been [what it represented] knowledge, but God denied him much knowledge because he had drunk it as milk.

Have you not considered that when the Prophet was brought a bowl of milk in a dream he said [of it], "I drank of it until I was completely satiated, and the rest I gave to 'Umar.'"[112] It was said to him, "What is your interpretation, O Apostle of God?" He said, "Knowledge," nor did he simply take it as milk according to the form he saw, because of his knowledge of the perspective of vision and the necessity to interpret [what is seen].

It is well known that the form of the Prophet perceived by the senses is buried in Madīnah and that the spiritual form and subtle essence have never been seen by anyone of anyone, nor yet his own, as is the case with every spirit. The spirit of the Prophet appears to one in the form of his body when he died, albeit unaffected by decay; indeed, it is Muḥammad appearing as spirit in a corporeal form resembling the buried body, which form Satan is unable to assume, as a protection from God for the recipient of the vision. Thus, whoever sees him in this way accepts from him all he commands or forbids and all he says, as he would accept his precepts in this world according to

---

109. Ibid., II:49.
110. An Andalusian Traditionist who died in A.H. 276. Cf. Hajjī Khalīfah, *Kashf al-zunūn* [1943], II, 1679.
111. Muslim, XLII:12.
112. Ḥanbal II:83, 154.

whether the sense of the words is explicit or implicit, or in whatever sense they are. If, on the other hand, he gives him something, its [form] is a matter for interpretation. If, however, that thing proves the same in the sensory world as in the imagination, the vision is one that does not require interpretation, which is how Abraham, the Intimate, and Taqī b. Mukhallad dealt with what they saw.

Since, then, the vision has these two aspects and since God has taught us by what he did with Abraham and what He said to him, which teaching is connected to the station of Prophecy, we know, in respect of any vision we may have of the Reality in a form unacceptable to the reason, that we must interpret that form in accordance with a doctrinal concept of the Reality, either from the standpoint of the recipient of the vision or the [cosmic] context [of the vision] or both. If, however, reason does not reject it, we accept it as we see it, even as we shall see the Reality in the Hereafter.

> In every abode [of being, becoming] the Unique, the Merciful has forms, whether hidden or manifest.
> If you say, "This is the Reality," you have spoken the truth,
> if "something other," you are interpreting.
> His determination applies in every abode equally,
> Indeed, He is [ever] unfolding His Reality to creation.
> When He manifests Himself to the sight, reason rushes to bring proof against it [Him].
> He is accepted as manifested on the intellectual plane as also in the imagination, but direct vision sees true.

Abū Yazīd al-Bisṭāmī said with respect to this station, "If the Throne and all that surrounds it, multiplied a hundred million times, were to be in one of the many corners of the Heart of the gnostic, he would not be aware of it."[113] This was the scope of Abū Yazīd in the realm of corporeal forms. I say, however, that, were limitless existence, if its limit could be imagined, together with the essence that brought it into existence, to be put into one of the corners of the Heart of the gnostic, he would have no consciousness of it. It is established that the Heart encompasses the Reality, but though it be filled,

---

113. Al-Bisṭāmī [d. A.D. 874] was a celebrated "ecstatic" mystic whose utterances often offended the religious establishment. Cf. R. C. Zaehner, *Hindu and Muslim Mysticism*, London, 1960, pp. 93–134, 198–218; also Hujwīrī, *Kashf,* pp. 106–108.

it thirsts on, as Abū Yazīd has said. We have alluded to this station as follows:

> O He Who creates things in Himself, You comprise all You create.
> Though You create beings without limit within Yourself,
> You are both the Restricted and the All-Encompassing.
> Were all the creation of God in my heart, its brilliant dawn would not shine there.
> Whoso embraces the Reality can contain all creatures,
> What then is the true situation, O Hearing One?

Every man creates by his fancy in the Imaginative faculty that which has existence nowhere else, this being a common facility. The gnostic, however, by his Concentration, creates that which has existence beyond the origin of the Concentration, indeed, the Concentration continues to maintain its existence, which depletes it in no way at all. Should the attention of the gnostic be deflected from the maintenance of what he has created, it will cease to exist, unless the gnostic commands all planes [of existence], in which case such deflection does not arise, since [at all times] he is present on some plane or another. When the gnostic who has such a command creates something by his Concentration, it is manifest in his form on every plane. In this case the forms [each on a different plane] maintain each other, so that if the gnostic is absent on a certain plane or planes, while present on another or others, all the forms [on all the planes] are maintained by the form on the plane to which his attention is given; lack of attention is never total, either with the generality of men or the elite.

Thus, I have expounded here a mystery that the Folk have always guarded from exposition, because it would seem to contradict their claim to be one with the Reality. The Reality is never unattentive, while the servant is always inattentive to something or other. With respect to the maintenance of something he has created, the gnostic may say, "I am the Reality,"[114] but his maintenance of that thing cannot be compared to the maintenance exercised by the Reality. The difference between the two we have already explained, since to the extent that he is inattentive to some form on its plane, he is a

---

114. This was perhaps the most famous utterance of al-Hallāj [d. A.D. 922], which brought about his execution. Cf. L. Massignon, *La Passion d'Al-Hallaj*, Paris, 1922.

servant as distinct from the Reality. The distinction remains even when we take account of the fact that attention to a single form on a particular plane assures the maintenance of all the other forms, for this is maintenance by implication. The maintenance by the Reality of His creation is of this kind, since He maintains each form Himself [at all times].

This whole question, as I have been told, has never previously been committed to writing, either by me or any other, until now. It is indeed unique and without precedent. Take care lest you forget this, for that plane in which you remain present with the form may be compared to the Book of which God said, *We have missed nothing in the Book*,[115] for it comprises all that has come to pass [into being] and all that has not come to pass. Only he will truly know what we have said whose essential self is a united totality [*qur'ān*]. For one who fears God, *He will make a discrimination for him*,[116] and he is as we have mentioned in discussing the distinction between servant and Lord. This discrimination is the loftiest discrimination.

> At the time the servant is a Lord, without a doubt,
> At the time the servant is a servant, most certainly.
> If servant, he encompasses the Reality,
> If Lord, he is in a lowly state.
> As servant he perceives the essential self
> And hopes range widely from him.
> As Lord he sees all creation, both lower and higher,
> Making demands on him.
> In himself he is quite unable to answer their demands,
> And for this reason you may see gnostics weeping.
> So be the servant of a Lord, not Lord of a servant,
> Lest you fall into Hell Fire.

---

115. *Qur'an*, VI:38.
116. Ibid., VIII:29.

CHAPTER VII

THE WISDOM OF SUBLIMITY IN THE WORD OF ISHMAEL

INTRODUCTORY NOTE

The main topic of this chapter is the relationship between the servant and Lord, which represents the particularization of universal relationship, previously discussed, between God and the Cosmos. Once again, as with the term "God," the term "Lord," in Ibn al-'Arabī's view, has meaning only within the context of its relationship with the concept of servant. That is to say, there can be no lordship or dominion without servitude. Thus, as was explained in the Introduction, this relationship denotes the polarity of servant, as the particular, individual created, existent thing, and the Lord, as the particular aspect of God that creates and determines the destiny of that thing according to its latent, essential reality in God. What follows from this is yet another of Ibn al-'Arabī's statements that instills horror into the mind of the religious establishment. He says that because each created being is and cannot be other than its Lord determines, as informed by its own eternal predisposition, each thing must therefore necessarily be, as the Qur'an puts it, "pleasing to its Lord," irrespective of whether that ontological approval appear, to the untutored view, as praise or blame, reward or punishment. The Lord cannot but approve of what He has willed should be, nor can the servant, in reality, disapprove of the Lord who, in effect, determines him only in accordance with what he himself inevitably is in essence.

Ibn al-'Arabī goes on to point out that Lordship is a concept that derives from the concept of the divine Names, which, as we have seen, denote the infinite complexity and multiplicity of particular relationships as aspects of the universal relationship between God and the Cosmos. Thus, in a certain sense, each lord is a particular divine Name defining the quality of a particular, aspectual relationship within the context of the universal relationship that is qualified by the universal Name, God. Once again, the Tradition of the Prophet is quoted, "Whoso knows himself knows his Lord," which is here interpreted in the light of his view of the relationship. That is to say, "Whoever knows himself as he is *in divinis*, knows his particular Lord as agent of his own release into existence."

Here again, Ibn al-'Arabī seeks to make clear the distinction between the term "God," which implies polarity and relationship, as also duality, triplicity, and multiplicity, and the term "Essence," which denotes the One in Itself, Alone and utterly unique, beyond the need for any polarizing otherness, no matter how contingent. Thus, the notions of God and Lord are not related to that of divine Essence.

Toward the end of this chapter, Ibn al-'Arabī, having stressed the mutuality of the terms servant and Lord and the essential oneness of all the divine Names, seeks also to correct any misapprehension in the reader that the principle of distinction and difference as between concepts and the realities they denote is redundant or unimportant. Always striving for as whole and balanced a view as possible, he is here maintaining that a whole and complete view of the Reality, of the way things really are, demands that both the truth of the oneness of universality and the truth of the oneness of singularity and uniqueness be grasped together in synthesis, each correcting and compensating the other as necessary aspects of the Reality's experience of Itself. Thus, although from one viewpoint the servant is the Lord is God is nothing other than the Reality, from the other standpoint the servant is not the Lord is not God is not the Reality, in the sense that each, while inwardly and essentially in a state of inexorable identity with every other, nevertheless reserves to itself, validly and legitimately within the context of Reality, its own special and peculiar characteristics. It is for the gnostic, therefore, as servant, to recognize not only his eternal identity with God, as latent essence, but also that he is not and can never be God as such; that it is for him to worship and for God to be worshiped, whatever his degree of attainment or gnosis.

Concluding the chapter, Ibn al-'Arabī explains that, in accordance with the qur'anic statement that the divine mercy is stronger than the divine wrath, the notion of punishment in Hell, which signifies a terrifying separation from God, cannot ultimately be more than a secondary consequence of ignorance, since all existent beings ultimately and finally share in the mercy of essential reality in Him.

THE WISDOM OF SUBLIMITY IN THE WORD OF ISHMAEL

Know that that which is termed "God" is One through the Essence and All through the Names. Each created being is related to God only as being its particular Lord, since its relationship to [God] as the All is impossible. As regards the divine Unity, there is no place in it for one as being one of many, nor does it admit of any differentiation or distinction. His Unity integrates all in potentiality.

Blessed is the one with whom his Lord is pleased, indeed, there is none but is pleasing in the sight of his Lord, since it is by him that the Lord maintains his Lordship so that he is pleasing in the sight of his Lord and is blessed. In this connection Sahl said, "In Lordship is a mystery, that mystery being you, which means every being, and were it to cease, the Lordship would cease."[117] Here he uses the words "were it to," which imply impossibility, since it will not cease, nor yet the Lordship, since the being exists only by its Lord. The being always exists and the Lordship never ceases.

One who is pleasing is loved so that all the loved one does is also loved, indeed, all is pleasing, since the individual being itself does not act, but its Lord in it. Thus the being is content that an action should be assigned to it and is pleased with that which is manifest in it and from it by its Lord. These actions are pleasing because every doer or maker is pleased with what he does or makes, and bestows on his action or work all that is necessary, as *He bestows on all He has created and*

---

117. Cf. H. Corbin's discussion of this saying in his *Creative Imagination*, pp. 121ff. and n. 40. See also A. A. Afifi's *Mystical Philosophy*, p. 90, n. 8.

then guides,[118] making clear that it is He Who bestows on all He has created, so that it is neither more nor less than it should be.

Ishmael was well pleasing to his Lord because he had come to know what we have mentioned, just as every created being is well pleasing. It does not follow, however, that because a created being is well pleasing to his Lord he is equally so to the Lord of some other servant, since he has his Lordship from a source embracing many, not only one. Thus, from the totality [of divine aspects] each being is assigned one particularly suited to it to be its Lord. This [Lord is assigned from God in His Names] not from [God] in His Unity.

For this reason the Folk are barred from a divine Self-revelation of His Unity. Were you to look on Him through Him, [you should know that] He is always looking on Himself by Himself. Were you to look on Him through you, His Unity would vanish in your being you. The same would be the case if you looked on Him through Him and through you. This is because by positing yourself in the pronoun *"you* look" you are positing something other than what is looked on, thus establishing a relation between two things, the observer and the thing observed, thereby nullifying the Unity [which admits of no other], although [in reality] only He sees Himself alone through Himself. Here also there would appear to be observer and observed [but both are He].

It is not usual for one who is pleasing to be absolutely so, unless all he manifests is from the action of the one pleased within him. Ishmael was more so than other beings in that the Reality describes him as being pleasing to his Lord. It is said, to every tranquil soul, *Return to your Lord*, that is to its own Lord, the one who summoned it, which it knows apart from all the others, *pleased and well pleasing*.[119] *Enter in among my servants*,[120] insofar as they have the same station.

The servants mentioned here are those who know their Lord, Most High, reserving themselves to Him and not to any other, despite the [essential] Unity [of all Being]. *And enter into my Paradise [jannah]*,[121] which is my covering. My Paradise is none other than you, for it is you who hide Me with your [individual] self, nor am I

---

118. *Qur'an*, XX:50.
119. Ibid., LXXXIX:28.
120. Ibid., LXXXIX:29.
121. Ibid., LXXXIX:30. He is here using the root *janna* with the meaning "to be hidden."

known except by you, as you have being only through Me. Who knows you knows Me, nor am I known [by another] as you also are not known. When you enter into His Paradise you enter into yourself. Then you will know yourself with a gnosis other than that by which you knew your Lord by knowing yourself. Thus, you will be possessed of two kinds of gnosis, first knowing Him as knowing yourself, second, knowing Him through you as Him, not as you.

> You are servant and you are Lord,
>   For One for Whom and in Whom you are servant,
> You are Lord and you are servant,
>   For One Who reminds of the covenant in His address.
> Every particular servant-Lord relationship
>   Is dissolved by every other such relationship.

God is pleased with His servants and they are well pleasing, and they are pleased with Him and He is pleasing. Thus the two planes [servants and Lords] are contrasted like similars that are [in a sense] opposed, since no two similar things can unite, otherwise there would be no distinction. There is [in fact] only He Who is distinct, nor is there any similarity [with Him]. In existence there is no similarity or dissimilarity, for there is but One Reality, and a thing is not the opposite of itself.

> Naught save the Reality remains, no being,
>   There is no arriving and no being afar,
> Spiritual vision confirms this, for I
>   Have not seen aught but Him, when I looked.

That is for one who fears His Lord,[122] meaning [who fears] that he "be" Him, since he knows the distinction [between servant and Lord]. This is further demonstrated to us by the fact that some beings are ignorant of what I [for example] know, for there are surely distinctions between servants, as also between Lords. Were it not for this distinction one divine Name would be interpreted, in every way, as another. The Name the Strengthener is not understood in the same way as the Name the Abaser, and so on. However, from the standpoint of the Unity, every Name evinces both the Essence and its own

---

122. Ibid., XCVIII:8.

reality, for the One named is One. Thus the Strengthener is the Abaser in respect of the named One, whereas the Strengthener is not the Abaser in respect of its own [relative] reality, the signification being different in both of them.

> Do not look upon the Reality, lest you abstract Him from creation.
> Do not look upon creation, lest you invest it with what is not the Reality.
> Know Him as both Comparable and Incomparable and so sit in the abode of truth.
> Be in [a state] if integration if you will, or be in [a state of] discrimination, if you will.
> Then you will, through the All, achieve the victor's Crown, if indeed a totality reveals itself [to you as combining both states].
> Do not pass away and do not subsist, nor yet annihilate or sustain.
> Thus revelation will not be granted you in respect of another, nor will you [as Lord] grant it [in respect of another].

Praise is not occasioned by His being true to His threat but by His being true to His promise [of Paradise]. Indeed the Plane of Divinity demands praise praised by Itself [the Essence]. Thus, It is praised through faithfulness to the promise [of Paradise] and not to the threat [of Hell], indeed, through His refraining from His threat. *Do not think that God will fail in His promise to His Apostles.*[123] He does not say "His threat," but says further, elsewhere, *We overlook their wrongdoings,*[124] despite His threat in this regard. He praises Ishmael for being *true to his promise.*[125] Thus possibility [contingency] ceases in respect of the Reality because of its [inherent] tendency to probability.

> Only He Who is true to His promise subsists,
> Nor does His threat have any true being.
> Even though they enter the abode of distress,

---

123. Ibid., XIV:47.
124. Ibid., XLVI:16.
125. Ibid., XIX:54.

IBN AL-'ARABĪ

    They have their pleasure in a delight,
Other than Heaven's delight, but they are One [in Him],
    The difference between the two being apparent in his Self-manifestation.
It is called an *'adhāb* because of its sweet taste,[126]
    Like a skin that preserves what is inside.

---

126. Here he is using the double meaning of the root, "torment" or "sweetness."

CHAPTER VIII

THE WISDOM OF SPIRIT IN THE WORD OF JACOB

INTRODUCTORY NOTE

Ibn al-'Arabī begins the chapter with a discussion of his view of the nature of religion. In doing so, he inevitably becomes involved once again in the related concepts of archetypal latency and the tension between the divine Will and the divine Wish. Although religious truth is dictated by God, the creature, according to his view, has an essential part in its determination and, although higher spiritual religion is primarily dedicated to the triumph of the divine Wish as expressed in God's revealed commands, the divine Will also produces religious forms, however heterodox they may seem from the orthodox viewpoint. Another point that emerges from his treatment of this subject is that religion, as such, is concerned almost entirely with the Reality as polarized in the relationship God-Cosmos.

He begins by dividing religion into two types, one that he calls the religion of God, and the other that he calls the religion of creatures. The former is indeed the religion of Islam as revealed in the Qur'an, which Ibn al-'Arabī regards, naturally enough, as the supreme expression of the divine Wish or the Obligating Command. As an example of the latter, he quotes the qur'anic reference to the Christian institution of monasticism, which implies that it is something the

IBN AL-'ARABĪ

Christians created by themselves. Indeed, Ibn al-'Arabī would include all non-Islamic religions under this heading, insofar as many of their doctrines and practices deviate, apparently, from the revealed qur-'anic norm. Not that such creature-originated religion could ever, really, be contrary to the divine Will, which is the creative origin of all things, whether they be regarded by what he calls divine religion as blameworthy or not. Furthermore, since the creatures, considered as the cosmic manifestations of eternal realities, are the very stuff of God's knowledge, they must be equally the determiners of religious forms and norms. Thus, whether a religion conforms, as it inevitably must, to the divine Will, or more specifically to the divine Wish, it is, unavoidably, of God and of us in God.

He further divides religion into outer and inner religion, the outer being concerned primarily to maintain the distinction and difference between the divine and cosmic poles in their creative and Self-realizing relationship, while the inner is concerned more with the original and ultimate oneness and identity of being, of God in the Cosmos, of the Cosmos in God, and of both in the Reality. Both types of religion, the exoteric and the esoteric, reflecting as they do fundamental polarities *in divinis*, are necessary manifestations of the Self-experience of the Reality. Both, however, are in a state of tension and conflict with each other at the verbal and formal levels, since the one would seem to contradict and threaten the other, which tension Ibn al-'Arabī experienced firsthand in Cairo.

There follows another discussion of the subject of sameness and uniqueness.

He brings this chapter to a conclusion with a fascinating insight into the nature of the relationship between the Will and the Wish or Command. He introduces the subject by pointing out that the physician can effect his cure of the patient only by working with and not against Nature, since, beyond the appraisal of human experience, sickness and health are both states of Nature. He then applies this illustration to the subject of the divine Will and Wish by comparing the Will to Nature, the Wish to the desire for good health, and the apostle to the physician. What he is saying is that the Will, like Nature, embraces equally, without distinction, what we call faith and infidelity, while the apostle is concerned to promote the state of faith in men. In order to do so, however, the apostle cannot do other than act in conformity not only with the divine Wish but also with the Will, which embraces also what is wished by God. When considering the question of the effects and result of the apostolic treatment, however, this is determined by the divine Will in accordance, once again, with the nature of the latent predisposition of the patient who may, accordingly, perish or be saved, indicating clearly the polar tension that can be resolved only in the inexpressible Oneness of Being.

THE WISDOM OF SPIRIT IN THE WORD OF JACOB

Religion is of two kinds, the religion of God and those whom God has taught His religion and those whom they have taught and, second, the religion of created beings, which God acknowledges. The religion of God is that chosen by Him and set by Him at a level far above the religion of creation. He says, *Abraham enjoined it upon his sons, as did Jacob his son [saying], "O my son, God has chosen for you the religion, so die not save as submitting yourselves to Him,"* which means following Him.[127] Religion [in this verse] has the definite article, namely, it is a known and established religion. He says, *The religion with God is Islam [submission],*[128] which means following and obeying [Him], religion meaning your yielding to and submitting [to Him].

That which comes from God is the Dispensation to which you submit yourself, which is religion, the Holy Writ being the Dispensation God has established. He who is marked by his submission to what God has laid down is the one who practices the religion and maintains its practice, who establishes its practice as he keeps up the [canonical] prayer.

It is the servant who establishes the practice of the religion and God Who determines its nature, for [your] submission is your action and the religion is from your act, since your being blessed may be only through that which derives from you yourself. Thus, just as your act establishes your blessedness, so also His acts establish the divine Names, which acts are you, being originated [relative], so that only in relation to His effects is He called a divinity and only in relation to your effects are you called blessed. Thus does God equate your

---
127. *Qur'an*, II:132.
128. Ibid., III:19.

position [in this respect] with His, when you maintain the practice of religion and submit to what He has established.

If God wills, we will elaborate on this point after we have explained religion as it is with creation, of which God takes due account. All religion is for God, from you not Him, except as being your Origin.

He, Most High, says, *Monasticism was introduced by them for the first time*,[129] which [incorporates] the revelations of Wisdom that were not brought by the Apostle as [generally] known in bringing [the Message] to the people from God in the customary fashion.[130] Since the Wisdom and good apparent in it are in harmony with the divine determination respecting the purpose of revealed Scripture, it is in God's sight as that which He laid down [in His Dispensation], although *He did not prescribe it for them*.[131] Thus, since God has, unknown to them, opened the door of His providence and Mercy to their hearts, He causes them to extol what they have established, apart from the more familiar way brought by the Prophet and recognized by divine revelation, seeking [by it] the pleasure of God. He says, *They do not observe it*,[132] that is, those who established it and for whom it was established, *as it should be observed, except to seek God's pleasure*.[133] Thus, they believe. *We brought those who believed*[134] in it *their reward, but many of them*,[135] that is, those among whom this way is practiced, *are astray*,[136] that is they have departed from submission to it and its proper practice. As for those who have departed in this way, God will not be well disposed toward them.

However, a command [divine] requires obedience. The one commanded either obeys willingly or opposes the command. As for the former, no more need be said; as for the latter, the opposition by which he is governed demands of God one of two courses, either indulgence and forgiveness, or censure. One of them must take place ac-

---

129. Ibid., LVII:27.
130. Throughout the *Qur'an*, the teaching of God is referred to as *the Book and the Wisdom* [II:188 *et passim*]. Ibn al-'Arabī sees in monasticism an expression of this Wisdom.
131. *Qur'an*, LVII:27.
132. Ibid.
133. Ibid.
134. Ibid.
135. Ibid.
136. Ibid.

cording as he requires it [deserves it] in himself, for the Reality always [acts] in accordance with the servant as regards his acts and state. Thus, it is the [essential] state that affects [the decision].

In this way religion [may be regarded as] a matter of requital and recompense for what pleases and what does not please. Concerning recompense for the former, He says, *God is pleased with them and they with Him*,[137] and concerning recompense for the latter, *Whosoever of you oppresses, We will cause him to experience a severe punishment.*[138] His saying, *We overlook their evil deeds*[139] is also a recompense. Thus religion is a form of recompense, for the religion is Islam, which means submission, so that one submits to what pleases and to what does not please, which [involves] recompense. This is, then, the outer aspect of the subject.

As for its inner and secret aspect, it is a [divine] Self-revelation in the mirror of the existence of the Reality. For the contingent beings receive from the Reality only as they themselves in their [essential] states dictate; they have a form for every state, the forms varying according to the variation of their states, as the Self-revelation [of the Reality] differs according to the state. Thus, the servant is affected in accordance with what he is in himself. Thus also, only he bestows good on himself and only he evil, being his own benefactor and chastiser. Therefore, let him not blame any but himself, nor praise any but himself.

God's is the conclusive argument,[140] through His Knowledge of them, since knowledge is dependent on that which is known. A deeper truth in this matter is that the contingent beings are, in the final analysis, nonexistent, since the only [true] existence is the existence of the Reality in the forms of the states in which the contingent beings are in themselves and in their [eternally latent] essences. So you should know [that it is none other than the Reality] Who undergoes pleasure and pain and that [it is the divine Self-revelation] that is the result of every state, which is called consequence and penalty. The same applies as a result of good or evil, except that convention calls the result reward in the case of good, and punishment in the case of

---

137. Ibid., V:119.
138. Ibid., XXV:19.
139. Ibid., XLVI:16.
140. Ibid., VI:149.

evil. In this sense the religion might be called or interpreted as a custom [*'ādah*], since there befalls [the servant] only that which his own state demands and necessitates.

The poet says: "As was your custom [*dīnika*] with Umm al-Huwairith before her."[141] That is to say, "your custom." The meaning of a custom is that something should revert to its original state, although custom in the sense of repetition is not appropriate to what we are concerned with. However, custom is an intelligible reality and a certain resemblance exists between the forms. For example, we know that Zaid is the same as 'Amr in respect to their humanity, although [in this instance] humanity does not occur twice for, if so, it would be a multiple thing and it is a single reality, not a multiplicity. We also know that Zaid is not the same as 'Amr in respect to their individuality. Thus, Zaid as Zaid is not 'Amr as 'Amr because of their individual identities. On the surface Zaid would appear to be a replica of 'Amr, but a true assessment shows this not to be true, there being from one standpoint no repetition, while from another there is [a certain] repetition. In the same way we may speak of recompense in one sense and deny it in another, since recompense is itself one of the states of contingent being. This is a question kept unexplained by those who know it as is proper, not because they are ignorant of it but because it is an aspect of the mystery of Premeasurement which governs created being.

Know that just as it may be said that the doctor is the servant of Nature, so might it also be said that the apostles and heirs are the servants of the divine Command in general and, at the same time, serving the states of contingent beings. Their service is one of their own states that they are in in their [eternal] essences. Consider what a wonderful thing this is! It must be understood, however, that the servant in this case limits his service to that which accords with the rules governing what he serves, with respect to state or speech.

The doctor may be called a servant of Nature only if he works in cooperation with her. Nature has established in the body of the patient a particular complex of conditions by which he is called sick. Were the doctor to assist her [in that particular manifestation] he would serve only to increase the sickness. Thus, he restrains her only in order to restore health [to his patient]. However, health is also

---

141. From the *Mu'allaqah* of Imru'l-Qais, line 7.

from Nature, which condition may be had by the setting up of another complex of conditions opposed to the existing one. Thus, the doctor is not [fully] the servant of Nature, being her servant only in the sense that he would be quite unable to cure the sick man and change his condition except by means of Nature. He serves her in a particular way, but not in a general way, which does not apply in this kind of question.

In this way the apostles and heirs are like the doctor who is at once both the servant and not the servant of Nature, as regards their serving the Reality. The Reality [manifests] two aspects in determining the states of those who receive the divine Command. The effect of the Command on the servant is as the Will of the Reality determines, which is itself determined by His Knowledge, which is determined in turn by that which the object of His Knowledge bestows of itself, which is not manifest except in its image [form].

Thus the apostle and the heir are servants of the divine Command through the Will, but are not servants of the Will, opposing it [the Will] with it [the Command] in order to secure the blessedness of the one charged to obey it. Were he the servant of the Will he would not seek to advise, or would advise only in accordance with it. The apostle, as also the heir, is a doctor of souls completely obedient to the Command of God. Considering both the Command of God and His Will, it may be seen that what is commanded may be contrary to His Will, since only what He wills takes place, which is the reason for the Command. If He wills what He commands, it takes place, and if He does not will what He commands, it does not. This is called [ordinarily] opposition and disobedience [sin].

The apostle is merely the transmitter [of the Command]. For this reason he [the Prophet] said, "The Chapter *Hūd*[142] and its kind caused me great anxiety, because of their oft-repeated saying, *Be upright as you have been commanded.*"[143] This caused him anxiety, namely the words *as you have been commanded,* for he did not know whether the Command was in accord with the Will and thus to be, or whether it conflicted with the Will, and thus would not be. None knows what the Will wills until what it has willed takes place, except one receive a spiritual intuition from God enabling one to perceive the essences of

---

142. Chapter XI.
143. *Qur'an,* XI:112. I have not been able to trace the source of this tradition.

contingent beings in their [eternal] latency, in which case he may act in accordance with what he sees. This may happen to a very few men in times of isolation from others. He says, *I know not what He will do with me or you*,[144] thus speaking openly of the veil [between God and us]. This is intended to convey that the Prophet has [unseen] knowledge of certain things.

---

144. Ibid., XLVI:9.

CHAPTER IX

THE WISDOM OF LIGHT IN THE WORD OF JOSEPH

INTRODUCTORY NOTE

Although the chapter begins with a discussion of the subject of the Imagination, with special reference to the dreams and visions of Joseph, the main theme of the chapter is, as the title suggests, the divine Light and the cosmic shadow.

Much of what he says here regarding symbols and the necessity for their interpretation is similar to material on the same subject in the chapter on Isaac [Chapter 6]. Ibn al-'Arabī does, however, introduce us here to another aspect of the subject of the Imagination, namely its twofold character in the human state. In other words, man, as the microcosmic image of the macrocosm, experiences the Imaginative process both as being part of the greater creative process and also as having within himself an imaginative faculty. Thus, as our author says, man experiences "an imagination within an Imagination," his own microcosmic "dream" being part of the greater macrocosmic "dream." Here we are introduced to Ibn al-'Arabī's view of the creative situation as a state of sleep in which the created Cosmos is seen as the divine dream, of which human experience is the microcosmic image. The whole creative situation, therefore, which requires the device of "the other" to effect its purpose, may be viewed as a kind of divine dreaming in which the illusion of something that is "not I" is presented to the divine consciousness as the reflection of

IBN AL-'ARABĪ

His own possibility. The waking state in this context is the inalienable state of the Oneness of Being.

The major theme of this chapter is that of the divine Light and the corresponding image of the cosmic shadow. Light is seen here as being yet another agency of creation, similar to the Breath of the Merciful, the Imagination, or the mirror. It is that power which illuminates or makes apparent the nonexistent and latent archetypes of God's knowledge, as created Cosmos. In a certain sense, however, it is also a symbol for the divinity Itself as Creator. The image of the cosmic shadow is rather more complicated, since Ibn al-'Arabī views its significance in two ways.

First, the shadow is seen as an image of the Cosmos itself, as being in a certain sense detached and apparently separate from God, while being ultimately an absurdity without His Light. Second, it is seen as an image of the unmanifested state of the latent essences of the Cosmos *in divinis*. In other words, he views the shadow's quality of darkness and obscurity both as an indication of the apparent distance of the Cosmos from God, as also its obscuring, by its formal complexity, of divine reality, and as a symbol of the occultation and nonexistence of the uncreated and unmanifested essences of the Cosmos in God. Thus, the shadow, whether as image of the created or, as yet, uncreated Cosmos is, in different ways, nothing other than God, either as reflecting image or as inherent content of knowledge. Another way in which he tries to explain the relationship in this chapter is to use the interaction of light and color, whether as potential and latent in its unillumined state or as illumined in all its variety of shades, so illustrating the mutual dependence of light and color, of light for its differentiation and of color for its manifestation.

Ibn al-'Arabī concludes the chapter with further discussion regarding the difference between the Reality as God in His relationship with created beings through His Names, and the Reality as Essence that transcends the whole creative process.

THE WISDOM OF LIGHT
IN THE WORD OF JOSEPH

The light of this luminous Wisdom extends over the plane of the Imagination, which is the first principle of revelation according to the people of Providence.

'Āishah [God be pleased with her] said, "Revelation began with the Apostle of God as the Verdicial Vision, which was [as clear] as the breaking of dawn every time he saw it, there being no obscurity."[145] 'Āishah's knowledge went no further than this. She added that he had been in this state for a period of six months after which the Angel [Gabriel] came to him. What she did not know was that the Apostle of God had said, "Men sleep and when they died they shall awake,"[146] all that is seen in sleep being of a similar nature, although the conditions are different. She stated a period of six months, whereas [in truth] his whole earthly life was after this fashion, [earthly existence] being a dream within a dream.

All things of this kind come within the realm of the Imagination, because of which they are interpreted. That means that something that of itself has a certain form appears in another form, so that the interpreter proceeds from the form seen by the dreamer to the form of the thing in itself, if he is successful, as for example the appearance of knowledge in the form of milk. Thus, he [the Apostle] proceeded in his interpretation from the form of milk to the form of knowledge, thus transposing [the real meaning of both] from one plane to another, the proper transposition of the milk form being to the form of knowledge.

When the Apostle used to receive a revelation he was withdrawn from all usual sensations, covered with a cloak, and [in all but his body] absent from all present. When the revelation ceased he was restored [to the sensory world]. What he perceived [in this state] he perceived only in the plane of the Imagination, except that he was not considered to be sleeping. In the same way the appearance of the Angel to him as a man was also from the plane of the Imagination, since he [Gabriel] is not a man but an angel who took on himself human form. This [form] was transposed by the beholder with gnosis to its own true form. He said, "It is Gabriel who has come to teach you your religion"; he had also said, "Return the man's greeting," calling him a man because of the form in which he appeared to them. Then he said, "This is Gabriel,"[147] [this time] taking into account the original form of the imaginative human form. He was right in both cases,

---

145. Bukhārī, I:3.
146. I have not been able to trace the source of this tradition, although it is frequently quoted by Sufi authors.
147. Muslim, I:1.

right from the viewpoint of the physical eye and right also in that it was, without doubt, Gabriel.

Joseph said, *I saw eleven stars and the sun and moon prostrating before me.*[148] He saw his brothers in the form of stars and saw his father and aunt as the sun and the moon. This is the viewpoint of Joseph. However, had it been so from the standpoint of those seen, the manifestation of his brothers as stars and his father and aunt as the sun and the moon would have been according to their wishes. Thus, since they had no knowledge of what Joseph saw, Joseph's perception [of what he saw] took place through his own imaginative faculty. When Joseph told Jacob of his vision, Jacob knew the situation and said, *My son, do not relate your vision to your brothers, lest they conspire against you.*[149] Then he goes on to absolve his sons of conspiracy and to lay it at Satan's door, who is the very essence of conspiracy, saying, *Surely Satan is Man's certain foe,*[150] which is outwardly so.

Much later on Joseph said, *This is the original meaning of my vision, which my Lord has made true,*[151] that is, He has made it manifest to the senses, being previously in a form from the Imagination. Concerning this, the Prophet Muḥammad said, "Men sleep," while Joseph said, *My Lord has made it true,*[152] since he [in relation to what the Prophet said] is in the position of one who dreams that he has waked from a dream and proceeds to interpret it. Such a one does not know that he is still asleep and dreaming, but when he does wake, he says, "I saw such and such, which, dreaming that I had waked, I interpreted." Joseph's situation is similar to this.

Consider then the difference between the perception of Muḥammad and that of Joseph when he said, *This is the real meaning of my vision, which my Lord has made true,*[153] by which he means sensible. It could not be other than sensible, since the Imagination deals only in what is sensible. Consider also how lofty is the knowledge of Muḥammad's heirs! We will elaborate further on this plane, if God will, through Joseph's words conceived in the spirit of Muḥammad's insight.

---

148. *Qur'an*, XII:4.
149. Ibid., XII:5.
150. Ibid.
151. Ibid., XII:100.
152. Ibid.
153. Ibid.

THE BEZELS OF WISDOM

Know that what is "other than the Reality," which is called the Cosmos, is, in relation to the Reality, as a shadow is to that which casts the shadow, for it is the shadow of God, this being the same as the relation between Being and the Cosmos, since the shadow is, without doubt, something sensible. What is provided there is that on which the shadow may appear, since if it were possible that that whereon it appears should cease to be, the shadow would be an intelligible and not something sensible, and would exist potentially in the very thing that casts the shadow.

The thing on which this divine shadow, called the Cosmos, appears is the [eternally latent] essences of contingent beings. The shadow is spread out over them, and the [identity of] the shadow is known to the extent that the Being of the [original] Essence is extended upon it. It is by His Name, the Light that it is perceived. This shadow extends over the essences of contingent beings in the form of the unknown Unseen. Have you not observed that shadows tend to be black, which indicates their imperceptibility [as regards content] by reason of the remote relationship between them and their origins? If the source of the shadow is white, the shadow itself is still so [i.e., black].

Do you not also observe that mountains distant from the observer appear to be black, while being in themselves other than the color seen? The cause is only the distance. The same is the case with the blueness of the sky, which is also the effect of distance on the senses with respect to nonluminous bodies. In the same way the essences of contingent beings are not luminous, being nonexistent, albeit latent. They may not be described as existing because existence is light. Furthermore, even luminous bodies are rendered, by distance, small to the senses, which is another effect of distance. Such bodies are perceived by the senses as small, while being in themselves large. For example, the evidence is that the sun is 160 times the size of the Earth, while, to the eye, it is no larger than a shield. This is also the effect of distance.

No more is known of the Cosmos than is known from a shadow, and no more is known of the Reality than one knows of the origin of a shadow. Insofar as He has a shadow, He is known, but insofar as the form of the one casting the shadow is not perceived in the shadow, the Reality is not known. For this reason we say that the Reality is known to us in one sense and unknown in another.

IBN AL-'ARABĪ

Have you not seen how your Lord extends the shade; if He so willed He would make it stay,[154] that is, it would be in Him potentially, which is to say that the Reality does not reveal Himself to the contingent beings before He manifests His shadow, the shadow being [as yet] as those beings that have not been manifested in existence. *Then We made the sun as an indication of it,*[155] which is His Name, the Light of which we have already spoken and by which the senses perceive; for shadows have no [separate] existence without light.

Then We take it back to Ourselves easily,[156] only because it is His shadow, since from Him it is manifest and to Him the whole manifestation returns, for the shadow is none other than He. All we perceive is nothing other than the being of the Reality in the essences of contingent beings. With reference to the Identity of the Reality, it is Its Being, whereas, with reference to the variety of its forms, it is the essences of contingent beings. Just as it is always called a shadow by reason of the variety of forms, so is it always called the Cosmos and "other than the Reality." In respect of its unity as the shadow [of God], it is the Reality, being the One, the Unique, but in respect of the multiplicity of its forms it is the Cosmos; therefore understand and realize what I have elucidated for you.

If what we say is true, the Cosmos is but a fantasy without any real existence, which is another meaning of the Imagination. That is to say, you imagine that it [the Cosmos] is something separate and self-sufficient, outside the Reality, while in truth it is not so. Have you not observed [in the case of the shadow] that it is connected to the one who casts it, and would not its becoming disconnected be absurd, since nothing can be disconnected from itself? Therefore know [truly] your own self [essence], who you are, what is your identity and what your relationship with the Reality. Consider well in what way you are real and in what way [part of] the Cosmos, as being separate, other, and so on. It is in this respect that the sages are better than one another; so heed and learn!

The Reality is, in relation to a particular shadow, small or large, pure or purer, as light in relation to the glass that separates it from the beholder to whom the light has the color of the glass, while the

---

154. Ibid., XXV:45.
155. Ibid.
156. Ibid., XXV:46.

light itself has no [particular] color. This is the relationship between your reality and your Lord; for, if you were to say the light is green because of the green glass, you would be right as viewing the situation through your senses, and if you were to say that it is not green, indeed it is colorless, by deduction, you would also be right as viewing the situation through sound intellectual reasoning. That which is seen may be said to be a light projected from a shadow, which is the glass, or a luminous shadow, according to its purity. Thus, he of us who has realized in himself the Reality manifests the form of the Reality to a greater extent than he who has not. There are those of us in whom the Reality has become their hearing, sight, and all their faculties and limbs, according to signs taught us by revealed Law that tells us of God.[157]

Despite this, the shadow [the individual] still exists essentially, for the pronoun used [in the words of the Tradition] "his hearing," refers to him [as shadow] particularly, since other servants are not of this attainment. Such a servant is more closely attached to the being of the Reality than others.

If things are as we have decided, know that you are an imagination, as is all that you regard as other than yourself an imagination. All [relative] existence is an imagination within an imagination, the only Reality being God, as Self and the Essence, not in respect of His Names. This is because the Names have two connotations: The first connotation is God Himself Who is what is named, the second that by which one Name is distinguished from another. Thus the Forgiving is not [in this sense] the Manifest or the Unmanifest, nor is the First the Last. You are already aware in what sense each Name is essentially every other Name and in what sense it is not any other Name. As being essentially the other, the Name is the Reality, while as being not the other, it is the imagined Reality with which we are here concerned.

Glory be to Him Who Alone is evidence of Himself Alone, and Who is Self-subsisting. There is naught in Being but is implicit in the divine Unity, and there is naught in the Imagination but is implicit in [Cosmic] multiplicity. Whoever holds to multiplicity is [involved] with the Cosmos, the divine Names [in their distinctions], and the

---

157. Bukhārī, LXXXI:38.

cosmic names. Whoever holds to the Unity is with the Reality in His Essence as Self-sufficient beyond all worlds. Being Self-sufficient beyond all worlds, He is independent of and beyond all nominal relationships, since the Names, while implying Him [as the Essence], also imply the realities named, whose effects they manifest.

Say: He God is One,[158] in His [Unique] Self; *God the Eternal Refuge,* in respect of our dependence on Him; *He begets not,* in His Identity or in relation to us; *nor is He begotten,* as for the preceding verse; *He has no equal,* as for the preceding verse. Thus does He describe Himself and isolates His Essence in the words *God is One,* although the multiplicity manifest through His Attributes is well known among us. We, for our part, beget and are begotten, we depend on Him and we compete one with another. However, the Unique One transcends all these attributes, having no need of them or of us. Indeed, the Reality has no [true] description better than this chapter, *al-Ikhlās,*[159] which was revealed precisely for this reason.

God's Unity, in respect of the divine Names that require our existence, is a unity of many, while in respect of His complete independence of the Names and us, it is unity of Essence, for both of which the Name the One is used, so take note.

God created shadows lying prostrate to right and left only as clues for you in knowing yourself and Him, that you might know who you are, your relationship with Him, and His with you, and so that you might understand how or according to which divine truth all that is other than God is described as being completely dependent on Him, as being [also] mutually interdependent. Also that you might know how and by what truth God is described as utterly independent of men and all worlds, and how the Cosmos is described as both mutually independent with respect to its parts and mutually dependent.

Without any doubt, the Cosmos is fundamentally dependent on causes, the greatest of which enjoys the causality of the Reality. The divine causality on which the Cosmos depends is the Divine Names, which are every Name on which the Cosmos depends, whether on [a Name manifested in] a cosmos or the divine Essence. Whichever it be, it is [essentially] God, no other. Thus, He says, *O Men, your need of God*

---

158. This and the subsequent verses quoted here make up Chapter CXII of the Qur'an.
159. Qur'an, CXII.

is total, while He is the Self-sufficient, the Praised.[160] Besides this it is well known that we are also mutually dependent. Therefore, our [true] names are God's Names, since all depends on Him. At the same time our essential selves are His shadow. He is at once our identity and not our identity. We have paved the way for you, so consider!

---

160. Ibid., XXXV:15.

CHAPTER X

THE WISDOM OF UNITY IN THE WORD OF HŪD

INTRODUCTORY NOTE

Although the main subject of the chapter on Hūd is the concept, qur'anic in origin, of the Straight Path, the underlying theme is, as the title suggests, the original and ultimate mutuality in oneness that is the essential nature of reality.

Ibn al-'Arabī uses the subject of the Straight Path to introduce this principal theme. Although the most obvious meaning of the words Straight Path in the Qur'an is as the path to salvation, he characteristically uses this idea to support his own mystical thesis of the Oneness of Being. This Path is, for him, nothing other than the way of inexorable return to the original and undifferentiated state of Oneness that is the Reality Itself. It is in fact Ibn al-'Arabī's explanation of another qur'anic quotation, "And to Him is the eventual becoming," which means that all the infinite possibility of becoming unavoidably returns to its source in pure, unitary Being, and that the whole creative device of polarity and otherness must inevitably melt away to reveal the unaltered and unalterable face of the Reality. As Ibn al-'Arabī says, at the very beginning of the chapter, all things are, without exception, on this Path toward the ultimate realization, not only because all things are inescapably of the Reality, but also because the factor of the divine Wrath, which would seem always to be condemning created beings to perdition and exile, is subordinate and accidental to the all-prevailing Mercy, which ultimately guarantees their essential reality *in aeternis*. Thus, the dazzling and fascinating panorama of cosmic forms in all their contradictions and multiplicity, which at once manifest and obscure the Truth, is always within the embrace of the divine Mercy, however negative and therefore wrathful the secondary and accidental effects may seem.

Perhaps in this chapter more than in any other, Ibn al-'Arabī drives home, over and over again, using various analogies, the relentless logic of his fundamental thesis of the Oneness of Being, that nothing can ever be other than It. Consequently, in other places, he is swift to point out that the concept of the Straight Path itself is deceptive insofar as it suggests the possibility of distance and separation, which is itself no more than a device the purpose of which is to create the polarity by which alone the divine might "enjoy Himself." Indeed, the whole exercise is, as Rūmī suggests, "like flying birds looking for air." In a letter to the celebrated theologian al-Rāzī [Hyderabad, 1948] Ibn al-'Arabī goes so far as to say that the very differentiation between God and creation, so necessary to exoteric faith, is, in fact, infidelity, since it posits two entities, Him and us. This underlying Oneness is succinctly expressed in this chapter when he says that God is our outer form [the Outer] and also the inner spirit of that form [the Inner], so that nothing remains of us as something other than He. Although he has a great deal to say on this subject, both here and elsewhere, Ibn al-'Arabī would have been the first to admit that it is a subject that is, essentially, inexpressible, since human language, being human and formal, cannot by its very nature adequately describe what transcends form, nor can human reason be expected to cope properly with experiences and realities that pertain to realms beyond the human. Much of what he says on this particular subject is therefore necessarily approximate and inadequate to the reality and experience he is trying to describe.

THE WISDOM OF UNITY
IN THE WORD OF HŪD

The Straight Path of God is not hidden,
  But manifest universally.

> He is essentially in all things great or small,
>> Ignorant of truth or aware.
> Thus does His Mercy embrace all things,
>> Be they mean or mighty.

No living being is there but He will seize it by its forelock. Surely my Lord is on a straight path.[161] All things walk on the Straight Path of their Lord and, in this sense, they do not incur the divine Wrath nor are they astray. This is because the divine Wrath, like error, is an accidental [nonessential], all things stemming ultimately from the Mercy, which embraces all things and which has precedence. All that is other than the Reality is a being walking [*dābbah*] [on the Path], since each has a spirit and none proceeds [on the Path] by itself but by another [God]. It proceeds [along the path] following, according to a [certain] determination, Him Who is on the Path [the Lord]. It would not be a path but for the procession along it.

> If the creature submits to you,
>> It is [in truth] the Reality Who submits.
> And if the Reality submits to you,
>> The created may not follow Him in that.
> Therefore realize what we say,
>> For all I say is true.
> There is no created being
>> But is endowed with speech [expression].
> Nor is there aught created, seen by the eye,
>> But is essentially the Reality.
> Indeed, He is hidden therein,
>> Its forms being merely containers.

Know that the divine and gnostic sciences possessed by the Folk vary according to the variety of spiritual capacities, although they all stem [ultimately] from one source. God, Most High, says, "I am his hearing by which he hears and his sight by which he perceives, his hand with which he takes and his foot by which he moves along."[162] He states that He is, in His Identity, the limbs themselves that are the servant himself, even though the Identity is One and the limbs many.

---

161. *Qur'an*, XI:56.
162. Bukhārī, LXXXI:38.

THE BEZELS OF WISDOM

For each limb or organ there is a particular kind of spiritual knowledge stemming from the one source, which is manifold in respect of the many limbs and organs, even as water, although a single reality, varies in taste according to its location, some being sweet and pleasant, some being salty and brackish. In spite of this it remains unalterably water in all conditions, with all the varieties of taste.

This wisdom is concerned with the knowledge related to the "feet" referred to in what the Most High says concerning the spiritual nourishment bestowed on those who properly uphold the Scriptures: [*And if they had observed the Torah and the Gospel and that which is revealed to them from their Lord, they would certainly have eaten from above them*] *and from beneath their feet.*[163] For the way, which is the [Straight] Path, is there to be traveled along and walked on, which is not accomplished except by the feet. It is only this particular kind of esoteric knowledge that results in this particular insight into the leading by Him Who is on the Path by the forelocks with His Hand.

And He drives the wrongdoers,[164] who merit the station to which He drives them, by means of the westerly wind by which He purges them of their [separatist] selves. He draws them along by their forelocks, while the wind drives them [from behind] to Hell, [the driver] being none other than their own desires and inclinations, and Hell the distance they imagined [to be between them and the Reality].

Since it is He [their Lord] Who drives them to this abode, they [in truth] attain nearness [to Him], all distance and notion of Hell ceasing for them. Thus they attain [in reality] the blessing of nearness [to Him] in respect of what they have merited [in their eternal essences], being [eternally] wrongdoers; nor does He grant them this pleasurable station as a freely given gift, since it is they themselves who adopt it according as their essential realities have merited eternally by their deeds [thus determined]. Indeed, in performing their deeds they are, nevertheless, on the Path of their Lord, their forelocks being in the hand of the One thus qualified; thus, they do not walk [on their Path] by themselves, but under compulsion till they reach [their] nearness [to Him].

And We are nearer to him [*the dying*] *than you, but you do not see* [*Us*],[165] the dying man having sight because the covering has been

---

163. *Qur'an*, V:66.
164. Cf. ibid., XIX:86.
165. Ibid., LVI:85.

IBN AL-'ARABĪ

drawn back, and his sight is sharp.¹⁶⁶ In this verse He does not specify a particular kind of person, one who is blessed rather than one who is damned. Again, *We are nearer to him than his jugular vein,*¹⁶⁷ where no particular man is specified. The divine proximity is clearly stated in His Revelation. No proximity is closer than that His Identity should be the very limbs and faculties of the servant, which are the servant himself. For the servant is an attested reality in an illusory creation.

For the believers and men of spiritual vision it is the creation that is surmised and the Reality that is seen and perceived, while in the case of those not in these two categories, it is the Reality Who is surmised and the creation that is seen and perceived by the senses. The latter are as the salty, bitter water, while the former are as the sweet, pleasant water, fit to drink.

Men may be divided into two groups. The first travel a way they know and whose destination they know, which is their Straight Path. The second group travel a way they do not know and of whose destination they are unaware, which is equally the Straight Path. The gnostic calls on God with spiritual perception, while he who is not a gnostic calls on Him in ignorance and bound by a tradition.

Such a knowledge is a special one stemming from *the lowest of the low,*¹⁶⁸ since the feet are the lowest part of the person, what is lower than that being the way beneath them. He who knows that the Reality is the way knows the truth, for it in none other than He that you progress and travel, since there is naught to be known save He, since He is Being Itself and therefore also the traveler himself. Further, there is no Knower save He; so who are you? Therefore, know your true reality and your way, for the truth has been made clear to you on the tongue of the Interpreter [Muḥammad], if you will only understand. His is a true word that none understands, save that his understanding be true; the Reality has many relations and many aspects.

Have you not considered 'Ād, the people of Hūd, how they said, *This is a cloud come to rain upon us,*¹⁶⁹ thinking well of God Who is present in what His servant thinks of Him. But God detached Himself from what they said and told them of that which is more com-

---

166. Cf. ibid., L:22.
167. Ibid., L:16.
168. Ibid., XCV:5.
169. Ibid., XLVI:24.

plete and lofty in proximity. For, when He caused the rain to fall on them it proved a boon to the earth and a draught for the seed, while they enjoyed the fruits of that rain only from afar [beyond the grave]; He said to them, *This is what you have sought to hasten on, a wind in which is a painful punishment,*[170] making the wind [*rīḥ*] an indication of what it contained by way of respite [*rāḥah*], since by it He delivered them from the darkness of their bodies, the roughness of their paths, and their [spiritual] blackness. In this wind there was an *'adhāb* [punishment or sweetness], that is something they would delight in when they experienced it, even though it caused them pain by separating them from what was [previously] familiar to them.

He brought them the punishment [inherent in their own eternal essences] and it was nearer to them [their realities] than they imagined. All was destroyed by the command of its Lord; *and they were not to be seen in the morning, except their dwellings,*[171] that is, their bodies in which their essential spirits had dwelt. In other words the particular relationship of spirit with body ceased and the bodies continued living [the spiritless life of material being] the life accorded them by the Reality, that life of which the skin, the hands, the feet give evidence, as also the the tips of the lashes and the thighs. All this is contained in Holy Writ.

God, Most High, has described Himself as Jealous [that aught should exist but Himself], and it is because of this that He "forbade excesses,"[172] which means that which is manifest and apparent. As for that which is unmanifest, it is [excessive] for him to whom it is apparent [in himself]. Thus, He forbade excesses [relative existence], that is, He prevented the real secret from being known, namely that He is the essential Self of things. He conceals it by otherness, which is you [as being not He]. Otherness asserts that the hearing [referred to in the Tradition] is Zaid's hearing, while the gnostic [who sees beyond that to the Oneness of Being] asserts that it is the Reality Himself, and similarly with the other organs and faculties. Not every one knows the Reality, some men excelling others according to [known] spiritual ranks, so that it is plain who is superior [in this respect] and who is not.

Know that when the Reality revealed to me and caused me to

---

170. Ibid.
171. Ibid., XLVI:25.
172. Cf. ibid., VII:33.

witness the essential realities of His apostles [on whom be peace] and prophets of humanity from Adam to Muhammad [peace and blessings be on all of them] at an assembly in Cordova in the year 586,[173] none addressed me from among them save Hūd, who informed me of the reason for their gathering together. I saw him as a stout man, fair of form, subtle of converse, a gnostic, a discloser of the realities. What proved this to me was the verse, *There is no walking being but He draws it by its forelock. Surely my Lord is on the Straight Path.*[174] What greater tidings could there be for creation? Indeed, God reminds us of His favor on us in bringing this [verse] to us in the Qur'ān. Then Muhammad, who integrates the whole, completes the tidings in transmitting to us the Tradition in which it is said that the Reality is [essentially] the hearing [of the servant, the gnostic], the sight, the hand, the foot and the tongue, indeed, all the senses.[175] Further, although the spiritual faculties are nearer than the [outer] senses, He contented Himself with what was more distant but known, instead of what was closer but unknown.

God interprets as tidings for us the words of His Prophet Hūd to his people, and the Apostle of God interprets for us God's words [in the Tradition].

Thus, knowledge is perfected in the hearts of those who have been granted knowledge, *and none deny Our signs save the concealers [kāfirūna]*.[176] For there are those who would conceal them [God's signs], even though they themselves possess knowledge of them, out of envy, rivalry, and injustice. For our part, whenever God has revealed or informed us [through Holy Traditions] concerning Himself, whether it assert His transcendence or comparability, we always see it in terms of limitation.

The first limitation [to which He subjects Himself] is "The Dark Cloud having no air above or beneath it."[177] The Reality was in it before He created His creation. Then He says, *He established Himself on the Throne,*[178] which also represents a Self-limitation. He then says that He descended to the lower heaven, also a limitation. He says further that he is in the Heaven and on the Earth, that He is with us

---

173. Cf. *Sufis of Andalusia*, p. 124.
174. *Qur'an*, XI:56.
175. Bukhārī, LXXXI:38.
176. *Qur'an*, XXIX:47.
177. Cf. *Futūhāt*, II, p. 310, Hanbal, IV:11, 12.
178. *Qur'an*, VII:54.

wherever we are, and finally that He is, in essence, us. We are limited beings, and thus He describes Himself always by ways that represent a limitation on Himself. Even the verse *There is none like unto Him*[179] constitutes a limitation if we regard the *kāf* as simply emphatic, since one who is distinguished from what is limited is himself limited because he is not that thing; to deny all [possibility of] limitation is itself a limitation, the Absolute being [in a sense] limited by His Own Absoluteness.

If we regard the *kāf* as a second qualification, we limit Him. If we take the verse *There is none like unto Him*[180] as denying similarity, we have realized the true sense and the intended meaning, that He *is* essentially all things. Created things are limited, even though their limitations are various. Thus, He is limited by the limitation of every limited thing, each limitation being a limitation of the Reality. He permeates through all beings called created and originated, and were it not the case, [relative] existence would not have any meaning.

He is Being Itself, the Essence of Being, *He is the Preserver of all*[181] by His Essence, nor does this preservation *weary Him*.[182] In preserving all things, He is preserving His Form, lest aught assume a form other than His Form, which is not possible. He is the observer in the observer and the observed in the observed; the Cosmos is His Form and He is the governing Spirit of the Cosmos, which is the Great Man [Macrocosm].

> He is all Becoming and He is the One by Whose
> Becoming I become, therefore I say He feeds
> On my being, so we are modeled in His Image.
> As also, from a certain aspect, I seek refuge in Him from Him.

It was because of the bursting fullness [of the essential realities in the undifferentiated Essence] that He breathed forth [the primordial creative Word *kun*]. He relates the Breath to the Merciful, because by it He had mercy [assented] on the demand of the divine Modes for the creation of the forms of the Cosmos, which are the manifest Reality, He being the Manifest. He is also their inner Essence, being also the Unmanifest. He is the First, since He was when they were not, and

---

179. Ibid., XLII:11.
180. Ibid.
181. Ibid., XI:57.
182. Ibid., II:255.

also the Last, since in their manifestation He is their Essence; the Last is the Manifest and the First is the Unmanifest. Thus, *He knows all things*,[183] as knowing Himself.

Since He created the forms in the Breath, and there became manifest the dominion of the relations, called the Names, the divine connection with the Cosmos is established, all beings deriving from Him. He says, "This day have I reduced your relationship and raised My connection," that is, I have taken away your relationship to yourselves and have returned you to your [proper] relationship with Me.

Where are the righteous? They are those who take God as their protection, He being their manifest form, as being the inner reality of their manifested forms. Such a one is the mightiest and strongest of men in the eyes of all men. The righteous one is also he who makes himself a protection for God, as being His form, since the Identity of God is, in essence, the faculties of the servant. He makes what is termed the servant a protection for what is called the Reality, though perceiving [the truth, namely that both are one], so that the knower is clearly distinguished from the ignorant.

Say: Are those who know the same as those who do not know, only those with true insight reflect,[184] that is, those who look on the inner reality of a thing, which is the real object of knowledge regarding a thing. For one who is negligent is not superior to one who is diligent, nor is a hireling to be compared with the servant. If, then, God is a protection for the servant, from one aspect, and the servant for God in another, you may say of Being what you will; either that it is the creation or that it is the Reality, or that it is at once the creation and the Reality. It might also be said that there is neither creation nor the Reality, as one might admit to perplexity in the matter, since by assigning degrees the difficulties appear. But for the [principle of] limitation [in defining the Reality], the apostles would not have taught that the Reality transforms Himself in cosmic forms nor would they have described Him [at the same time] as abstracting Himself from all forms.

    The eye perceives naught but Him
        Only He is determined [by Himself].

---

183. Ibid., VI:101.
184. Ibid., XXXIX:9.

THE BEZELS OF WISDOM

We are His, by Him we exist and by Him we are governed,
And we are in His Presence at all times, in all states.

Because of this [inevitable limitation by definition] He is both denied and known, called incomparable and compared. He who sees the Reality from His standpoint, in Him by Him is a gnostic. He who sees the Reality from His standpoint, in Him, but with himself as the seer, is not a gnostic. He who does not see the Reality in this way, but expects to see Him by himself, is ignorant.

In general, most men have, perforce, an individual concept [belief] of their Lord, which they ascribe to Him and in which they seek Him. So long as the Reality is presented to them according to it they recognize Him and affirm Him, whereas if presented in any other form, they deny Him, flee from Him and treat Him improperly, while at the same time imagining that they are acting toward Him fittingly. One who believes [in the ordinary way] believes only in a deity he has created in himself, since a deity in "beliefs" is a [mental] construction. They see [in what they believe] only themselves [as relative beings] and their own constructions within themselves.

Consider this matter, for, as men know God [in this world], so will they see Him on the Day of Resurrection, the reason for which I have informed you of. So, beware lest you restrict yourself to a particular tenet [concerning the Reality] and so deny any other tenet [equally reflecting Him], for you would forfeit much good, indeed you would forfeit the true knowledge of what is [the Reality]. Therefore, be completely and utterly receptive to all doctrinal forms, for God, Most High, is too All-embracing and Great to be confined within one creed rather than another, for He has said, *Whereosever you turn, there is the face of God*,[185] without mentioning any particular direction. He states that there is the face of God, the face of a thing being its reality.

By this He [intends] to keep alert [spiritually] the Hearts of the gnostics, lest the transient things of this world deflect them from [constant] reflection on this [truth]; for no servant knows in which breath he will be taken [from this life], and it may be that he be taken in a moment of heedlessness, so that he will not be equal [in the Hereafter] to one taken in a moment of attentiveness. The perfect servant,

---

185. Ibid., II:115.

despite his knowledge of this [truth concerning God's omnipresence], nevertheless maintains himself, in his outer and limited form, in [constant] prayer, his face turned toward the Sacred Mosque, believing God to be in that direction when he prays; the Sacred Mosque is, in truth, representative of a facet of the Reality, as in the verse, *Wheresoever you turn, there is the face of God*,[186] and [in facing it] one is face to face with God in it. However, do not tell yourself that He is in that direction only, but rather maintain both your [particular] attitude [of worship] in facing the Sacred Mosque and your [more universal] attitude [of knowledge] to the impossibility of confining His face to that particular direction, it being merely one of many points toward which men turn.

God has made it clear that He is in every direction turned to, each of which represents a particular doctrinal perspective regarding Him. All are [in some sense] right [in their approach]; everyone who is right receives his reward, everyone who receives his reward is blessed, and everyone who is blessed is well pleasing [to his Lord], even though he may be damned for a time in the Final Abode. For [even] the people of Providence are sick and suffer pain in this world, though we know them to be blessed among the Folk of God. Thus, there are those servants of God who are afflicted with sufferings in the afterlife in a place called Hell. Despite this, those who possess knowledge and have spiritual insight into what really is do not deny that they will enjoy their own delight in that place, whether by a relief from the pain they suffer, which will be their delight, or [perhaps] a separate delight similar to that enjoyed by the people of Paradise; but God knows best.

---

186. Ibid.

CHAPTER XI

THE WISDOM OF OPENING IN THE WORD OF ṢĀLIḤ

INTRODUCTORY NOTE

Two subjects are dealt with in this rather short chapter. The first is the concept of triplicity, which Ibn al-'Arabī sees as the basis of the creative process. The second concerns certain symbols associated with salvation and damnation on the Last Day.

In this chapter Ibn al-'Arabī returns to the subject of number, being here concerned not with the relationship between unity and multiplicity but rather with the process by which singular unity projects itself into the many, so that the many may exist as the infinite diversification of the One. Unity alone is not creative, but sufficient to itself, not requiring anything beyond itself to preserve its absolute integrity. The One simply is, there being in it no implication of becoming or development. Similarly with duality, unless there is a working relationship between the two entities, there are merely two singulars in sterile and contradictory isolation from each other. If there is a relationship, it is the connecting principle that relates the two entities, bringing their separate qualities together to form a third entity, born, so to speak, of their union. Put another way, this is the familiar triplicity of knower-knowledge-known in which the term "knowledge" as relationship brings together the receptive objectivity of the known and the active subjectivity of the knower to produce the principle of knowledge itself. Although not specifically stated here, it is man him-

IBN AL-'ARABĪ

self who is precisely the third and relating entity in the duality God-Cosmos, being at once the meeting point of Heaven and Earth and also that entity which symbolizes their union, potentially.

In this chapter, Ibn al-'Arabī describes the concept of triplicity somewhat differently. Indeed, as one might expect, he describes a double or bipolar triplicity that, on the side of the divine pole, consists of the singular Essence Itself, the Will or the urge to Self-alteration, and the verbal creative command "Become!" On the side of the cosmic pole the triplicity consists of the latent essence, the "hearing" or readiness to be created, and the coming into existence in obedience to the creative command. Here the former triplicity is mirrored by the latter, together forming the complete triplicity of the Reality Itself, which consists of Essential Oneness, the urge to polarity, and the actual experience of bipolarity, which itself is eternally being resolved back into the Essence. Once again he is describing in terms of triplicity the process *in divinis* that he has elsewhere described in terms of the Breath of the Merciful, the Creative Imagination, the Mirror, and the Light-shadow relationship. In all of this the difficulty of adequate expression conceals what is really an attempt to describe a bipolarity within a greater bipolarity. That is to say, the creative bipolarity that creates the "otherness" necessary for the Self-realization of infinite possibility eternally inherent in absolute unity is itself, so to speak, one pole of the polarity Essential Unity-bipolarity, both elements of which relate and unite to constitute the Reality in Itself. Ibn al-'Arabī returns to this theme in the last chapter of this work.

Ibn al-'Arabī concludes this chapter with a discussion of the manifestation of the inner in the outer, illustrating this from the qur'anic description of the effects on the righteous and the sinners of the promise of Paradise and the threat of Hell. He seeks to link this section to the first by pointing out that these effects take place in three stages. At the end of the chapter he reminds the reader, yet again, that the outer manifestation of man's cosmic existence derives only from his own inner and essential predisposed determination.

THE WISDOM OF OPENING
IN THE WORD OF ṢĀLIḤ

Among His signs are the riding beasts,
Because of the variety of the paths.

Some follow the true course,
  While others traverse trackless wastes.
The former are possessed of true vision,
  The latter have missed the way.
To both there come from God
  Revelations of inner realities from every side.

Know, may God prosper you, that the [Creative] Command is essentially based on unevenness in which triplicity is implicit, since three is the first of the uneven numbers. It is from this divine plane that the Cosmos is created; He says, *When We wish a thing, We only say to it, "Be," and it is*,[187] there being the Essence, the Will, and the Word. Were it not for the Essence, the Will, which denotes the particular tendency to bring something into being, and the Word *Be* accompanying that tendency, that thing would not be. Furthermore, the triple unevenness is manifest in that thing by which its being brought into being and its being said to exist may be said to be true. This [principle] of unevenness constitutes its thingness, its "hearing," and its obeying of its Creator's command to come into being. These three [aspects of the creature] correspond to three [in the Creator]. Its latent essence in its state of nonexistence corresponds to the Essence of its Creator, its "hearing" [receptivity] to the Will of its Creator, and its compliance with the Creative Command to His saying [Word] *Be*. It is He, and [as obeying the Command] the becoming is attributed to it. Indeed, were it not able to come into being of itself, on receiving the Command [Word], it would not come to be. In truth, it was none other than the thing itself that brought itself into being from nonexistence when the Command was given.

Thus, the Reality establishes that the coming into being stems from the thing itself and not from the Reality Who is the origin of the Command. Thus He says of Himself, *When We wish a thing [to be], Our Command is only that We say "Be" and it is.*[188] Here He attributes the becoming of the thing itself, at the Command of God, and God speaks true, this being understood in the Command, just as when one who is feared and obeyed commands his servant to stand, the servant stands obediently. With respect to the standing of the servant, only the com-

---

187. *Qur'an*, XVI:40.
188. Ibid.

mand to do so belongs to the master, the standing being the servant's action and not that of the master.

Thus, bringing or coming into being is based on a triplicity, or rather a bipolar triplicity, one being of the Reality, the other of the creature. This [principle of triplicity] pervades to the existence of ideas arrived at by logical proofs. Thus, a proof arrived at by syllogism is made up of three parts in a particular way that inevitably yields a result. First of all the person establishes two premises, both of which include two terms so that there are four terms. However, one of the terms is present in both premises, to link the two together, so that there are [really] three parts because of the repetition of one term in both premises. The proof comes into being when this particular arrangement occurs, which is the binding of the two premises together by the repetition of one term, producing a triplicity. The special condition attendant on this is that the major should be more general than the middle term, or at least similar, if the result is to be true, otherwise it will be untrue. This kind of thing occurs in creation, as when acts are attributed solely to the servant without reference to God, or when coming into being, with which we are concerned, is ascribed solely to God, while the Reality ascribes it to that to which *Be* is addressed.

For example, if we wished to prove that the Cosmos is caused, we would say, "Every originated thing has a cause," in which we have the two terms "originated" and "cause." In the second premise we would say, "The Cosmos is originated," the term "originated" being repeated in both premises. The third term is therefore "Cosmos," the conclusion being that the Cosmos has a cause. The same term, namely "cause," appears both in the first premise and in the conclusion. The special point is the repetition of the word "originated." The special condition is the generality of the [occasioning] principle, which is, in the case of the existence of the originated [being], the cause that, as the major term, is general with respect to the originating of the Cosmos from God. We have decided that every originated being has a cause, whether the middle term is similar to the major term or whether the latter is more general than it and coming within its provenance; and the conclusion is true. The principle of triplicity is thus apparent also in the creation of concepts arrived at by [syllogistic] proofs.

The origin of all becoming is thus triplicity. For this reason the Wisdom of Ṣāliḥ, which God manifested in delaying the destruction of his people for three days, was no vain promise since it came true in the cry by which God destroyed them, so that *they became stricken down in their tents.*[189] On the first of the three days the faces of the people changed color to yellow, on the second to red, and on the third to black. On the completion of the third day, [their essential] natures were ready to receive the manifestation of wickedness within them, which manifestation is called destruction.

The yellowing of the faces of the damned corresponds to the shining of the faces of the blessed, as in His saying, *Faces on that day will be shining,*[190] [stemming] from [the word] unveiled, which means manifested. In this way the yellowness of their faces on the first day signals the manifestation of damnation in the people of Ṣāliḥ. Corresponding to the redness is what He says concerning the blessed, *laughing,*[191] since laughter is a cause of redness in the face, being, in the case of the blessed, a rosiness of the cheeks. Corresponding to the blackening of the skins of the damned is what He says [of the blessed] that they are *joyful,*[192] being the effect of joy on their complexions, as the blackness in the case of the damned. Thus He uses the term *tidings* [*bushrā*][193] for both parties [the blessed and the damned]; that is, He tells them things that affect their complexions, causing them to change to a color other than the one they had before. In the case of the blessed, He says, *Their Lord brings them glad tidings of mercy from Him and His good pleasure,*[194] while in the case of the damned, *Bring them tidings of a painful punishment,*[195] each party showing outwardly the effects of this address on their souls. This is because what is outwardly manifest only accords with the inner effect of the sense [of these words].

In truth, they themselves affect themselves even as they themselves come into being of themselves [in obedience to the divine Command]. *God's is the final argument.*[196]

Whoever [truly] understands this Wisdom and establishes it in

---

189. Ibid., XI:57.
190. Ibid., LXXX:38.
191. Ibid., LXXX:39.
192. Ibid.
193. Here he is using both meanings of the root *bashara*, "to give tidings" and "skin."
194. *Qur'an*, IX:21.
195. Ibid., III:21.
196. Ibid., VI:149.

himself and realizes it releases himself from dependence on others and knows that good and evil come to him only from himself. By good I mean what is in consonance with his aim, in harmony with his nature and disposition, and by evil what is contrary to his aim and in conflict with his nature and disposition. He who has such a knowledge [vision] excuses all creatures regarding what they manifest, even though they themselves make no excuse, knowing as he does that all he undergoes is from himself, as we have mentioned previously to the effect that knowledge depends on what is known. Thus, he says to himself when something contrary to his aim befalls him, "Your two hands cast the dye and your own mouth breathed the breath [of your life]." God speaks true and guides aright.

CHAPTER XII

THE WISDOM OF THE HEART IN THE WORD OF SHU'AIB

INTRODUCTORY NOTE

As the title suggests, Ibn al-'Arabī returns, in this chapter, to the subject of the Heart, particularly the Heart of the gnostic. This concept of the Heart is perhaps, in the human context, the most important of his concepts insofar as it corresponds, in man, as already mentioned, to the concept of the Reality Itself. If, in a general way, the Perfect Man symbolizes the synthesis of all aspects of being, it is the Heart of the Perfect Man that particularly symbolizes this synthesis. He dramatically illustrates the wholeness of the Heart in saying that it is capable of embracing the Reality, while the Mercy is not, even though he elsewhere accords to the principle of Mercy a seemingly similar capacity. The reason for the greater capacity of the Heart is that, whereas the Mercy is exclusively concerned with the complementary processes of creative manifestation and its resolution into unity, the Heart symbolizes the whole experience of the Oneness of Being, as including not only the creative process and its resolution, but also that inalienable and unalterable aspect of the Reality which knows nothing of cosmic becoming. This synthetic wholeness of the Heart, however, is realized fully only in the Perfect Man, remaining potential and latent in most human beings. For them the Heart is able to contain usually no more than the particular Lord as essential determiner of their particular existence according to the predisposition of their own latent essences. It is only by gnosis, or the gradual seeing beyond formal multiplicity, that the Heart is enabled to fulfill its true function. In other words, for most men, the function of the Heart remains confined to the context of creative bipolarity.

This leads Ibn al-'Arabī on to discuss one of the most interesting of his ideas, the "god created in belief," which of course brings in the question of the diversity of approaches to truth and salvation. This subject enables him, in his characteristic way, to relate his discussion to the prophet Shu'aib, after whom the chapter is named, since the root from which this name is derived is *sha'aba*, which means "to diverge." Thus, since the Reality as God, the Supreme Name, transcends all its Names or aspects, the Heart of the ordinary man cannot see God or know God as such, but only the God of his credal belief, which conforms to the Self-manifestation of "his Lord" to him, which of course in turn conforms to what his own latent essence determines should be the content of his belief. In this way each man's belief regarding the nature of God not only differs from the particular belief of other men, but is also, inevitably, but a minute facet of what God is in Himself. Each belief, determined as it is by essential predisposition, cannot be other than what God is, but neither, paradoxically, can it be wholly faithful to the divine Truth. It is only through the acquiring of gnosis that the Heart can be made receptive, not only to the particular Lord, but also to the universality of "God," and ultimately to the Reality Itself. Since, however, knowledge of one's Lord, as reflected in one's particular belief, is part of knowledge of God and ultimately of the Reality, and since no man ever ceases to be the particular existing creature of his Lord according to essential predetermination, the gnostic, in experiencing the greater vision of universal divinity, may not deny his creatureliness nor refuse the obligations of his particular determination, since true gnosis reveals to the gnostic the ontological necessity of particular servanthood as part of the nature of things. For the gnostic, the only alternative to creatureliness, however enlightened, is precisely annihilation in God, not some false personal inflation.

Ibn al-'Arabī concludes the chapter by dealing with another of the concepts for which he is famous, that of "the renewal of creation by Breaths." He views the creation of the Cosmos neither as a once-and-for-all act, nor as a continuous and developing process, but rather as constantly recurring acts of creation and resolution from instant to instant. The human symbol here is the process of breathing, consisting of an inhalation followed by exhalation. On a divine scale, in the case of the Breath of the Merciful, each inhalation represents the resolution of the Cosmos into the Essence, while each exhalation represents the creation of the Cosmos, representing the two currents of the divine Mercy, the one releasing the archetypal desire for existence, the other reaffirming the exclusive integrity of the Absolute One. In reality, however, there is no temporal sequence here, but an eternal simultaneity, since at each instant the Cosmos is and is not, is manifest and latent, created and uncreated, is other and non-other in a timeless divine pulse, at once creative and noncreating. In other words the whole becoming of the Cosmos through the breathing out of the divine Mercy is not seen by Ibn al-'Arabī as a long creative exhalation in time, followed by a corresponding resolving inhalation, but rather as a situation in which each instantaneous exhalation heralds and includes inhalation and vice versa.

As Ibn Al-'Arabī points out in this chapter, the Ash'arite theologians also had a theory of instant creation and re-creation, while maintaining, unlike Ibn Al-'Arabī, an absolute discontinuity between God and creation. The main purpose behind the Ash'arite theory seems to have been the removal of any constraint whatsoever on God's ability to do whatever He wishes, as also to undermine the structure of cause and effect without which reason and logic cannot function. The important difference between the Ash'arites and Ibn al-'Arabī is that the latter insists that the Cosmos, however apparently other than God, cannot, in reality, be other than He, and that, as essentially latent *in divinis,* mysteriously is none other than its own Creator.

THE WISDOM OF THE HEART IN THE WORD OF SHU'AIB

Know that the Heart, by which I mean the Heart of the gnostic, derives from the Divine Mercy, while being more embracing than it, since the Heart encompasses the Reality, exalted be He, and the Mercy does not. This is alluded to and supported in Tradition.

The Reality is the subject and not the object of the Mercy, so that the latter has no determining power with respect to the Reality. In a more particular way, one might say that God has described Himself as the Breath [*nafas*], from *tanfīs*, which means to cause respite or relief. It is also true that the divine Names are [in a certain sense] the thing named, which is none other than He. [At the same time] they require the very realities they bestow, which are the Cosmos. For Divinity [*ulūhiyyah*] implies and requires that which depends on it, just as Lordship requires servanthood, since neither would have any existence or meaning otherwise.

The Reality, in Its Essence, is beyond all need of the Cosmos. Lordship, on the other hand, does not enjoy such a position. The truth [in this matter] lies between the mutual dependency [implicit] in Lordship and the Self-sufficiency of the Essence. Indeed, the Lord is, in its reality and qualification, none other than this Essence.

When, however, differentiation and opposition arise by virtue of the various relationships, the Reality begins to describe Itself as the bestower of compassion on His servants.

The Reality first expressed the Breath, which is called the Breath of the Merciful, from Lordship by creating the Cosmos, which both Lordship and all the Names require by their very nature. From this standpoint it is clear that the Mercy embraces all things including the Reality Himself, being more or less as encompassing as the Heart in this respect. So much for that.

Know that the Reality, as is confirmed by Tradition, in His Self-manifestation, transmutes Himself in the forms; know also that when the Heart embraces the Reality, it embraces none other than He, since it is as if the Reality fills the Heart. By this is meant that when the Heart contemplates the Reality in Its Self-manifestation to it, it is unable to contemplate anything else whatever. The heart of the gnostic is, in respect of its compass, as Abū Yazīd al-Bistāmī has said, "Were the Throne and all it comprises to be placed one hundred million times in the corner of the gnostic's Heart, he would not be aware of it."[197] On this question Junayd said, "When the contingent is linked with the eternal there is nothing left of it."[198] Thus, when the heart embraces the Eternal One, how can it possibly be aware of what is contingent and created?

Since the Self-manifestation of the Reality is variable according to the variety of the forms, the Heart is necessarily wide or restricted

---

197. See above, p. 101.
198. Cf. A. Abdel-Kader, *Al-Junayd, His Life, Personality and Writings*, London, 1962, Epistle VI.

according to the form in which God manifests Himself. The heart can comprise no more than the form in which the Self-manifestation occurs; for the Heart of the gnostic or the Perfect Man is as the setting of the stone of the ring, conforming to it in every way, being circular, square, or any other shape according to the shape of the stone itself, for the setting conforms to the stone and not otherwise. This is opposed by those who maintain that the Reality manifests Himself in accordance with the predisposition of the servant. This is, however, not the case, since the servant is manifest to the Reality according to the form in which the Reality manifests Himself to him.

The solution of this question rests on the fact that God manifests Himself in two ways: an unseen manifestation and a sensible manifestation. It is from the former type that the predisposition of the Heart is bestowed, being the essential Self-manifestation, the very nature of which is to be unseen. This is the divine Identity in accordance with which He calls Himself [in the Qur'ān] *He*.[199] This Identity is His alone in all and from all eternity.

When the predisposition comes to the Heart there is then manifest to it the sensible Self-manifestation in the sensible world, so that it sees Him manifest in the form in which He manifests Himself to it, as we have said. It is none other than God Who bestows on the Heart its predisposition in accordance with His saying, *He bestows upon everything He has created*.[200] Then He raises the veil between Himself and the servant and the servant sees Him in the form of his belief; indeed, He is the very content of the belief. Thus, neither the Heart nor the eye [of the Heart] sees anything but the form of its belief concerning the Reality. It is the Reality contained in the belief whose form the Heart encompasses. It is this Reality that manifests itself to the Heart so that it recognizes it. Thus the eye sees only the credal Reality, and there are a great many beliefs.

He who restricts the Reality [to his own belief] denies Him [when manifested] in other beliefs, affirming Him only when He is manifest in his own belief. He who does not restrict Him thus does not deny Him, but affirms His Reality in every formal transformation, worshiping Him in His infinite forms, since there is no limit to the forms in which He manifests Himself. The same is the case with the gnosis of God, there being no limit for the gnostic in this respect.

---

199. *Qur'an*, passim.
200. Ibid., XX:50.

IBN AL-'ARABĪ

Always the gnostic is seeking more knowledge of Him, saying, *O Lord, increase me in knowledge.*[201] The possibilities are without end on both sides, that of the Absolute and that of relative being.

When you consider His saying, "I am his foot with which he walks, his hand with which he strikes, and his tongue with which he speaks,"[202] and all the other faculties and members in which they are situated, why do you make the distinction by saying it is all the Reality, or it is all created? It is all created in a certain sense, but it is also the Reality in another sense, the Essence being one. After all, in essence, the form of a Self-manifestation and that of the one who perceives it are the same, for He is [at once] the Self-manifesting subject and the object of that manifestation. Consider then how wonderful is God in His Identity and in His relation to the Cosmos in the realities [inherent] in His Beautiful Names.

> Who is here and what there?
>   Who is here is what is there.
> He who is universal is particular,
>   And He Who is particular is universal.
> There is but one Essence,
>   The light of the Essence being also darkness.
> He who heeds these words will not
>   Fall into confusion.
> In truth, only he knows what we say
>   Who is possessed of spiritual power [*himmah*].

Surely in that is a reminder for him who has a heart,[203] by reason of His [constant] transformation through all the varieties of forms and attributes; nor does He say, "for him who has an intellect." This is because the intellect restricts and seeks to define the truth within a particular qualification, while in fact the Reality does not admit of such limitation. It is not a reminder to the intellectuals and mongers of doctrinal formulations who contradict one another and denounce each other, . . . *and they have no helpers.*[204]

The god of one believer has no validity in respect to the god of

---
201. Ibid., XX:114.
202. Bukhārī, LXXXI:38.
203. *Qur'an*, L:37.
204. Ibid., III:91.

one who believes something else. The supporter of a particular belief defends what he believes and champions it, while that which he believes in does not support him. It is because of this that he has no effect on his opponent's belief. Thus, also, his opponent derives no assistance from the god formulated in his own belief. . . . *they have no helpers.*[205] This is because the Reality has denied to the gods of credal formulations any possibility of rendering assistance, since each one is restricted to itself. Both the one assisted and the one who assists are [in truth] the Totality [*majmū'*] [of the Divine Names].

For the gnostic, the Reality is [always] known and not [ever] denied. Those who know in this world will know in the Hereafter. For this reason He says, *for one who is possessed of a heart,*[206] namely, one who understands the formal transformations of the Reality by adapting himself formally, so that from [or by] himself he knows the Self. [In truth], his self is not other than the divine Identity Itself, as also no [determined] being, now or in the future, is other than His Identity; He is the Identity Itself.

He [God] is the one who knows, the one who understands and affirms in this particular form, just as He is also the ignorant one, the uncomprehending, the unknown in that [particular] form. This, then, is the lot of one who knows the Reality through His Self-manifestation and witnessing Him in the totality of formal possibilities. This is what is meant by the saying, *for one possessed of a heart,*[207] that is, one who turns [toward the Reality] [*taqlīb*] in all the diversity of the forms [in which He manifests Himself].[208]

As for the people of faith who follow blindly the utterances of the prophets and apostles concerning the Reality, not those who slavishly follow thinkers and those who derive their knowledge from intellectual processes, they are referred to in His saying *or gives ear*[209] to what God has said through the lips of the prophets. By this is meant one who gives ear in witness, indicating the plane of the Imagination and its use, alluded to in the saying of the Prophet, "that you should worship God as if you saw Him,"[210] for *God is in the qiblah of*

---

205. Ibid.
206. Ibid., L:37.
207. Ibid.
208. Here he uses the root meaning of the word for "heart" [*qalb*], which is "to turn."
209. *Qur'an*, L:37.
210. Bukhārī, II:37.

IBN AL-'ARABĪ

*the one who prays.*²¹¹ Because of this he is a witness [to God]. It cannot be said of one who follows the thinker and is bound by his thoughts that he is one *who gives ear,*²¹² since one who gives ear is also a witness to what we have mentioned. And since, as we have mentioned, such a one is not a witness, the verse quoted does not refer to him; they are referred to in God's saying, *when those who are followed will be acquitted of [any association with] those who follow them.*²¹³ The same may not be said of the apostles with respect to those who follow them. Therefore, O Friend, realize the truth of this Wisdom of the Heart that I have set forth for you.

As for its special connection with Shu'aib, it is because of its [innumerable] ramifications [*tasha"ub*], since each and every creed is a [particular] path. Thus, when the covering [of this earthly life] is drawn back, everyone will see what is disclosed according to his belief—or he might see what is contrary to his belief regarding the [divine] determination; as He says, *And there is manifest to them of God what they had not expected to see.*²¹⁴ Such cases usually concern [divine] determination. Such a one is the Mu'tazilite, who believes that God will carry out His threat [to punish] the sinner who dies unrepentant. When he dies and is in fact granted mercy with God, since [divine] providence has already decreed that he should not be punished, the Mu'tazilite finds that God is Forgiving and Merciful, so there is manifest to him of God that which he had not considered in his belief.²¹⁵

As regards God in His Identity, certain of His servants have judged in their belief that God is such and such, so that when the covering is removed, they see the form of their belief, which is true, and they believe in it. When however the knot [of belief] is loosened, belief ceases [to bind his heart] and he knows once more by [direct] contemplation. After his sight has been sharpened, his weak-sightedness does not recur. Some servants [then] have God disclosed to them in various forms, other than those first seen, since [a particular] Self-manifestation is never repeated. He then holds this to be true with respect to His Identity, so that *there is manifest to them of God,* in His

---

211. The *qiblah* is the direction toward which the Muslim turns in prayer.
212. *Qur'an*, L:37.
213. Ibid., II:166.
214. Ibid., XXXIX:47.
215. As part of their doctrine of the divine Justice, the Mu'tazilites believed that God acts in a logical way, which notion Ibn al-'Arabī seeks to refute here.

Identity, *what they had not considered*,[216] before the drawing back of the veil.

We have discussed advancement in the divine sciences in our *Book of Theophanies*,[217] where we talk of those of the Order we have met with in vision [*kashf*] and what we imparted to them on this question that they did not know already. The amazing thing is that such a one is always advancing, although he is not aware of it, by reason of the subtlety and fineness of the veil and the ambiguity of forms; as He says, *It is brought to them in an ambiguous way*.[218] It [the veil] is not the same as the other, for similars in the sight of the gnostic, though similars, are also different from each other. That is because he who has attained to realization sees multiplicity in the One, just as he knows that essential oneness is implicit in the divine Names, even though their [individual] realities are various and multiple. It is a multiplicity intelligible in the One in His Essence. In manifestation it is a discernible multiplicity in a single essence, just as the Primal Substance is assumed in the case of every form, which, despite the multiplicity and variety of forms, springs in reality from a single substance, its primal substance.

He, therefore, who knows himself in this way knows his Lord, for He created him in His image, indeed, He is his very identity and reality. It is because of this that none of the scholars have attained to knowledge of the self and its reality except those theosophists among the messengers and the Sufis.

As for the theorists and thinkers among the ancients, as also the scholastic theologians, in their talk about the soul and its quiddity, none of them have grasped its true reality, and speculation will never grasp it. He who seeks to know it by theoretical speculation is flogging a dead horse. Such are certainly of those *whose endeavor is awry in this world, but who consider that they do well*.[219] He who seeks to know this matter other than by its proper course will never grasp its truth.

How wonderful are the words of God concerning the Cosmos and its transformation according to the Breaths "in a new creation" in a single essence. He said concerning a portion, nay most of the

---

216. *Qur'an*, XXXIX:47.
217. Written at Aleppo prior to A.D. 1209. Published in *Rasa'il Ibnul 'Arabi*, Hyderabad-Deccan, 1948, No. XXIII.
218. *Qur'an*, II:25.
219. Ibid., XVIII:104.

Cosmos, *Nay, they are in the guise of a new creation.*[220] They do not understand the renewal of the Creative Command according to the Breaths.

The Ash'arites did indeed discover it for certain things, namely accidents, as did also the Sophists for the Cosmos as a whole.[221] However the speculative thinkers dismissed them all as ignorant.

In fact, both the Ash'arites and the Sophists were mistaken.

As for the latter, although they speak of the transformation of the Cosmos, they fail to grasp the Unity of the Essence of the substance that assumes this form, that it cannot be created without it [form], while it [form] cannot be comprehended without it [substance]. Had they made that clear they would have realized the truth of the matter.

As for the Ash'arites, they did not realize that the whole Cosmos is a sum of accidents, so that it is transformed in every duration, since the accident does not last for more than one duration. This is manifest in the defining of things, since when they define a thing its being accidental is evident in their doing so. Also that the accidents implicit in its definition are nothing other than the substance and its reality, which subsists of itself. As accident, it does not subsist of itself, whereas the sum of what does not subsist of itself is that which subsists of itself, just as the position taken in defining the substance that subsists of itself, as also its assuming accidents, is an essential definition. There is no doubt that the assuming [of accidents] is itself an accident, since it cannot occur except in the case of a recipient, because it does not subsist of itself. It is essential to the substance. Having a position is also an accident that can only occur in respect of that which takes a position; it does not subsist of itself.

Neither the taking of a position nor the assumption [of accidents] constitutes anything additional to the essence [*'ain*] of the defined substance, because the essential limits are nothing other than the thing defined and its identity. Thus, that which does not last for two durations becomes [in sum] a thing that lasts for two, indeed many durations, and that which was not self-subsistent becomes once again self-subsistent.

They are not aware of what they are about, while they are in the

---

220. Ibid., L:15.
221. The Ash'arite doctrine of Atomism states that God creates and destroys from instant to instant and that there is no obligation on God to follow any causal sequence or any logical connection between one act of creation and another. Cf. H. A. Wolfson, *The Philosophy of Kalam*, Harvard, 1976, chap. 6.

guise of a new creation. As for those to whom the higher worlds are disclosed, they see that God is manifest in every Breath and that no [particular] Self-manifestation is repeated. They also see that every Self-manifestation at once provides a [new] creation and annihilates another. Its annihilation is extinction at the [new] Self-manifestation, subsistence being what is given by the following [other] Self-manifestation; so understand.

CHAPTER XIII

THE WISDOM OF MASTERY IN THE WORD OF LOT

INTRODUCTORY NOTE

According to the title, this chapter is concerned with the subject of "mastery," which term in the original Arabic implies possession and control. It becomes evident, however, early in the chapter, that what Ibn al-'Arabī means by mastery is not physical or vital power, but rather spiritual power, since such power is usually acquired, as he points out, not in the physical vigor of youth, but at a more advanced age when physical power is declining. His discussion of the question of mastery, as illustrated by the situation of the prophet Lot, leads Ibn al-'Arabī on to yet another exposition on the subject of the spiritual power of Concentration or *himmah*. In this chapter he is particularly concerned with the relationship between this power and gnosis [*ma'rifah*] and how the attainment of the latter severely restricts and limits the exercise of the former.

In a certain sense, the two are aspects of spiritual attainment, the one dynamic, the other static. Gnosis, however, being recollective and centripetal, is superior to spiritual concentration, which is creative and cosmically oriented. He illustrates this by explaining that the prophets were reluctant to exercise their *himmah* to produce miracles with a view to convincing the unbelievers to accept the faith because their gnosis made them aware that, in reality, it is only God

Who guides men to the Truth and, furthermore, that He does so according to His knowledge of the realities, which is itself eternally informed by the latent archetypes of created beings. This is indeed the realization by the gnostic that not only the creative power itself, but also the principle of conscious identity that exercises it, is in reality God's power and His identity, which means that any notion of individual or personal autonomy in the exercise of such power is inevitably illusory both in its conception and its result.

He concludes the chapter by reminding his reader once again that, in reality, it is we ourselves, as being nothing other, *in divinis*, than that which God Himself knows Himself to be, who determine the nature of our created experience in the Cosmos and the course of our destiny.

THE WISDOM OF MASTERY IN THE WORD OF LOT

Mastery implies force, and the master [of a thing] is one who is forceful and firm. One says, "I mastered the dough" when one makes it firm. Qais b. al-Khaṭīm says, describing a thrust:

> My hand so mastered it that I made the gaping wound pour forth,
> So that one in front of it could see through to the other side.[222]

That is to say, "My hand made a good job of it," namely the wound.

This brings to mind God's saying concerning Lot, *If only I had some power over you, or had recourse to some firm support.*[223] The Apostle of God said, "May God have mercy upon my brother Lot, seeing that he had recourse to a firm support."[224] By this he means that he was with God, Who is Forceful. By the words *firm support* Lot meant his tribe, and by the words, *Would that I had some power* he meant resistance, which here means that power of concentration peculiar to man. The Apostle of God said, "Since that time," that is, from the

---

222. Marzūkī, *Sharḥ ʿalā dīwān al-ḥamāsah*, ed. A. Amīn and A. Harūn, Cairo, 1951, p. 184, 1.2.
223. *Qurʾan*, XI:80.
224. Bukhārī, LX:11.
225. *Qurʾan*, XI:80.

time when Lot said, *or had recourse to some firm support,*[225] every prophet sent forth has encountered the opposition of his people and has been protected by his own tribe,"[226] as in the case of 'Alī and the Apostle of God.

Lot said, *If only I had some power over you,*[227] because he had heard the saying of God, *It is God Who created you in weakness,* as a fundamental characteristic, *then He brought about strength after weakness.* The strength occurs by the [divine] bringing about, being an accidental strength. *Then He brought about, after strength, weakness and white hair.*[228] Now the white hair pertains to the bringing about, while the weakness is a regression to the original nature of His creation, as He says, *Who created you in weakness.*[229] Thus does He return him to the state in which He created him, as He says, *Then he is returned to a most ignoble state, so that, having enjoyed knowledge, he now knows nothing anymore.*[230] Here He indicates that he is restored to the original weakness, since, with respect to weakness, the old man is much like a child.

No prophet has ever been sent until he has completed his fortieth year, at which time decrease and weakness begin to set in. Because of this he said, *If only I had power over you,*[231] which requires an effective power of concentration. Should you ask what prevented him from exercising such power effectively, seeing that it is evident in those of the followers who are actively on the Way, and that the prophets are most entitled to it, I would reply that while you are right [in one sense], you are mistaken [in another]. That is because gnosis allows such a power no room for maneuver, his power of concentration decreasing as his gnosis grew stronger. There are two reasons for this. The first is his confirmation of the status of servanthood and his awareness of the original characteristic of his natural creation. The second is [the truth of the essential] unity of the One Who acts and that which is acted upon. Thus he could not see anything [other] at which to direct his power of concentration, which prevented him from exerting it. In such a state of perception he realized that his opponent had in no way deviated from his reality as it was in its state of essential latency and nonexistence. The opponent was there-

---

226. Bukhārī, LX:19.
227. *Qur'an,* XI:80.
228. Ibid., XXX:54.
229. Ibid.
230. Ibid., XVI:70.
231. Ibid., XI:80.

fore manifest in existence just as he was in his state of latency and nonexistence. In no way was he transgressing the limits of his [essential] reality, nor had he failed to fulfill his [eternally appointed] role. Calling his behavior "opposition" is merely of accidental import, seen thus only because of the veil that obscures the eyes of men; as God says of them *Most of them know not. They know the externals of this world's life, but are heedless of the Hereafter.*[232] This is an inversion and relates to their saying, *Our hearts are enveloped;*[233] that is to say by a covering that prevents them from grasping the matter as it is in reality. These and similar things restrain the gnostic from acting freely in the world.

The Shaikh Abū 'Abdallāh b. Qā'id asked Shaikh Abū al-Su'ūd b. al-Shibl,[234] "Why do you not exert your power?" To which he replied, "I leave God to act for me as He wills," having in mind His saying, *Let Him be your agent,*[235] and the agent is the one who acts; for he knew God's saying, *Spend of that with which We have encharged you.*[236] Now Abū Su'ūd and other gnostics knew that the matter in hand was not his to dispose of as he willed, but that it had only been entrusted to him. God was saying to him [in effect], "With regard to this matter that I have put into your charge and control, make Me your agent therein." So did Abū Su'ūd obey the command of God and yielded the initiative to Him. How then could any power of concentration remain to be exerted by one who [truly] contemplates on this matter, seeing that such power is effective only by total concentration, which itself is not within the scope of the one exerting it, except with regard to that particular thing on which his concentration is fixed? Indeed it is precisely this gnosis that prevents him from reaching such total concentration, since the true gnostic manifests his gnosis by weakness and lack of power.

One of the Substitutes[237] said to Shaikh 'Abd al-Razzāq,[238] "When you have greeted Shaikh Abū Madyan,[239] ask him how it is

---

232. Ibid., XXX:7.
233. Ibid., II:88.
234. A disciple of the celebrated Al-Jīlānī [d. A.D. 1166].
235. *Qur'an*, LXXIII:9.
236. Ibid., LVII:7.
237. A Substitute is a member of that spiritual heirarchy of saints considered necessary to maintain cosmic order.
238. A Tunisian disciple of Abū Madyan; cf. *Sufis of Andalusia*, p. 101.
239. Perhaps one of the most influential spiritual masters of his time. He died in A.D. 1197. Cf. J. J. Bargès, *Vie du célèbre marabout Cidi Abou Medien*, Paris, 1884.

that while nothing is impossible for us and many things are impossible for him, it is we who aspire to his station, while he does not aspire to ours?" This was how it was with Abū Madyan, having attained to that station and others. We, however, have attained to that station of incapacity and weakness more completely. Nevertheless, that is what the Substitute said to him. This matter is related to the same subject.

The Prophet, speaking of God's decree for him, said of this station, *I know not what will be done with me or with you. I follow only that which is revealed to me.*[240] In this station the Apostle is governed by what is revealed to him, having nothing more than that. If it was revealed to him unequivocally that he should act, he acted, but if he was restrained, he held back. If he was given the choice, then he chose not to act, unless his gnosis was deficient. Abū al-Su'ūd said to a trusty disciple, "Fifteen years ago, God granted me the freedom to act, but I have not used it, thinking that it would seem an affectation."[241] This is pompous talk. We ourselves did not leave it aside for such a reason, which implies choice in the matter, but only because of perfect gnosis; for gnosis does not leave the matter to choice, since, when the gnostic acts in the world through his power of concentration, he does so only by divine command and compulsion, not by his own choice. We have no doubt, however, but that the rank of Apostleship requires freedom of action in order to effect the acceptance of its mission. Thus there is evident in the apostle that which would confirm his veracity with his community and people, so that God's dispensation might become manifest. The same is not the case with the saint. The apostle, however, does not require it outwardly, but out of consideration for his people and not wishing to expose them too much to the Irrefutable Arguement (of God),[242] which would destroy them, preferring to preserve them.

The apostle realizes that when something miraculous is shown to a group of people, some will believe what they see; others, realizing what was happening, would reject it; while others would connect it with magic and trickery, so that it would not result in the desired confirmation [of his mission]. When, therefore, the apostles grasped this and realized that only he would believe whose heart had been il-

---

240. *Qur'an*, XLVI:9.
241. I have not been able to trace this quotation.
242. Cf. *Qur'an*, VI:149.

lumined by God with the light of faith, and that certain people would not see by the light called faith, it became obvious that miraculous activity was useless. For this reason the power of concentration was kept from seeking miracles, seeing that their effect was not universal in the hearts of those who witnessed them. In the case of the most perfect of apostles, the wisest of creation, the truest in state, God says, *You will not guide those whom you wish to guide; rather it is God Who guides whom he wishes.*[243] Had the power been effective, which it usually is without doubt, then none would have used it to more effect than the Apostle of God, since none enjoyed a greater and more potent power than he, although it could not effect the conversion of his uncle Abū Ṭālib concerning whom the verses we have mentioned were revealed. This is why He says of the Apostle that it is for him only to proclaim the message. He says, *It is not your task to guide them; rather God guides whom He pleases.*[244] In the *Surat al-Qaṣaṣ* He adds, *He knows best those that are rightly guided,*[245] that is, those who have given Him the knowledge of their guidance in their state of nonexistence through their latent essences.

This confirms the fact that knowledge is dependent on what is known, since he who is a believer in his latent essentiality and in his state of nonexistence becomes manifest in that form in the state of existence. God has learned from him the fact that he would be thus. He says, *He knows best those that are rightly guided.*[246] In saying this He is really saying, *It is not by Me that the word is changed,*[247] because what I say is determined by what I know of My creation, and, *I do not wrong My servants,*[248] that is, I do not decree for them the infidelity that will damn them and then require of them what is not in their power to achieve. Indeed, We treat them only in accordance with what We know of them [in their latent essentiality], and what We know of them is what they give Me of themselves as they are [in eternity]. If there is any question of wrong, it is they who are the wrongdoers." Thus He says, *It is they who wrong themselves.*[249] It is not God Who has wronged them. "We only say to them what Our Essence has

---

243. Ibid., XXVIII:56.
244. Ibid., II:272.
245. Ibid., XXVIII:56.
246. Ibid., XVI:125.
247. Ibid., L:29.
248. Ibid.
249. Ibid., II:57.

given us to say to them, and Our Essence is too well known to Us in its reality to say one thing rather than another. We say only what We know We say, for the utterance is to Ourselves from Ourselves, and it is for them to comply or not once they have heard Us."

> All is from Us and from them,
> > It is learned from Us and from them.
> Even if they are not of Us,
> > Most surely We are of them.

So realize, O friend, this Wisdom of mastery concerning the Word of Lot, for it is part of gnosis.

> The mystery is now clear to you,
> > And the matter is well explained.
> For that which is called odd
> > Is enshrined within the even.

CHAPTER XIV

THE WISDOM OF DESTINY IN THE WORD OF EZRA

INTRODUCTORY NOTE

Continuing from the end of the last chapter, Ibn al-'Arabī here develops further the theme of human and cosmic destiny. Indeed, it is in this chapter in particular that he treats, more fully than elsewhere in this work, his theory of divine creative determination. As was suggested in the Introduction to this translation, the two concepts of Decree [*qaḍā'*] and Destiny [*qadar*] by which Ibn al-'Arabī seeks to explain the way in which created being is determined are very closely related to the concepts of the divine Will [*mashī'ah*] and Wish [*irādah*], all these concepts being themselves dependent on the underlying concept of the eternal predisposition of the latent essences.

The term "Decree" [*qaḍā'*] derives from the Arabic root *qaḍā*, which means "to carry out," "to execute," that is, the carrying out of the divine Creative Command [*amr*], which is itself the result of the divine decision to create [*ḥukm*], which is prompted by the inherent urge of the preexistent and latent essences to cosmic actualization. Thus, the Decree is another way of expressing the creative process itself, the releasing of the Breath of the Merciful, the projection of the reflecting image, but with the extra dimension of inevitability and *fait accompli*. This concept is not so much concerned with the will or the urge to create stemming from the divine inner desire for Self-awareness, but rather with the fact of existence itself and the inescapable consequence of becoming. The Decree is what is willed, the execution of the Will together with all the consequences that flow from that execution, which consequences are none other than the infinite elaboration and manifestation in existence of what creation is in its latency.

Destiny [*qadar*] is, so to speak, a modification of the Decree in that it determines the mode and measure of its becoming, again as essential realities dictate. Being concerned with measure and proportion, it determines the when, where, and how of creation, the particular instant of its manifestation, the context and nature of its existence. Thus Destiny is concerned not so much with the universal outpouring of the creative act, but rather with the allotment to individual created beings of the limits of their existence, thus checking and individually defining the creative act. In a certain sense, therefore, Destiny reverses the current of the Decree and renders the Cosmos back to God Who has the measure of all things and thus knows and has power over all things. According to Ibn Al-'Arabī, the mystery of Destiny is one only God knows properly, although mortal men may be granted some insight into their own destiny, which knowledge itself is dependent on a predisposition to know it. Such knowledge, as he says, produces a perplexity of conflicting feelings, of calm, total resignation on the one hand, and of painful anxiety on the other; calm resignation to what is, ultimately, one's own self-determined destiny, and anxiety at the apparent otherness of cosmic existence.

The other major subject of this chapter is Sainthood [*walāyah*]. Here, Ibn al-'Arabī points out that the name "the friend" [*al-walī*] is the only one God shares with man, so that the saint is one who has realized a state of intimacy with God, who has seen through the veil of cosmic otherness to the essential identity, who knows himself, like Abraham, to be permeated by the divine Reality. As already mentioned, this is the universal state that underlies the more limited functions of the prophet and the apostle. Thus, each prophet and apostle, while being the bringer of formal revelation, expressing the Wish of God, is also the repository of an inner wisdom that expresses more esoteric and paradoxical insights.

THE BEZELS OF WISDOM

THE WISDOM OF DESTINY IN THE WORD OF EZRA

Know that the Decree [*qaḍā'*] is God's determination of things, which is limited to what He knows of them, in them, since His knowledge of things is dependent on what that which may be known gives to Him from what they are [eternally] in themselves [essentially].

Destiny [*qadar*] is the precise timing of [the manifestation and annihilation of] things as they are essentially. This then is the very mystery of Destiny itself *for him who has a heart, who hearkens and bears witness*,[250] *for God has the last word*,[251] for the Determiner, in actualizing His determination, complies with the essence of the object of His determination in accordance with the requirements of its essential nature. The thing determined, in strict accordance with its essential state, itself determines the Determiner to determine concerning it by that [which it is essentially], since every governor is itself governed by that in accordance with which it governs or determines, whoever or whatever the one governing may be. Therefore grasp this point, for Destiny is unknown only because of the intensity [immediacy] of its manifestation and, although greatly sought after and urgently pursued, it is seldom recognized [for what it is].

Know that the apostles, as apostles and not as saints or gnostics, conform to the [spiritual] level of their communities. The knowledge with which they have been sent is according to the needs of their communities, no more nor less, since communities vary, some needing more than others. Thus, in the same way, do apostles vary in the knowledge they are sent with according to the variety of communities. He says, *We have given some of these apostles more than others.*[252] Just as the doctrines and regulations deriving from their essences are various according to their [eternal] predispositions, so He says, *We have favored some of the prophets over others.*[253] Of creation, God says, *God has favored some of you over others in the matter of provisions.*[254] Provisions may be either spiritual, like learning, or sensible, like food, and the

---

250. *Qur'an*, L:37.
251. Ibid., VI:149.
252. Ibid., II:253.
253. Ibid., XVII:55.
254. Ibid., XVI:71.

IBN AL-'ARABĪ

Reality sends it down only according to a known measure, to which a creature is entitled, since *God has given to everything He has created,*[255] and *He sends down as He wills,*[256] and He wills only in accordance with what He knows and by what He determines. As we have already said, He knows only what is given to Him to know by what is known. Thus the timing [of Destiny] ultimately belongs to that which is known, while the Decree, knowledge, Will and Wish depend on Destiny.

The mystery of Destiny is one of the most glorious kinds of knowledge, and God grants insight into it only to one whom He has selected for perfect gnosis. Knowledge of this mystery brings both perfect repose and terrible torment, for it brings the opposites by which God has described Himself as Wrathful and Approving. It is by this mystery that the divine Names polarize. Its truth holds sway over both the Absolute and the contingent, and nothing is more perfect, powerful, and mighty by reason of the totality of its dominion, whether direct or indirect.

Since, therefore, the prophets derive their knowledge only from a particular divine revelation, their Hearts are simple from the intellectual point of view, knowing as they do the deficiency of the intellect, in its discursive aspect, when it comes to the understanding of things as they really are [essentially]. Similarly, [verbal] communication is also deficient in conveying what is only accessible to direct experience. Thus, perfect knowledge is to be had only through a divine Self-revelation or when God draws back the veils from Hearts and eyes so that they might perceive things, eternal and ephemeral, nonexistent and existent, impossible, necessary, or permissible, as they are in their eternal reality and essentiality.

It was because Ezra sought the special way that he incurred the condemnation related of him. Had he sought rather the divine inspiration we have mentioned, he would not have been condemned. His simplicity of heart is shown by his saying, in another connection, *How can God revive it [Jerusalem] after its oblivion?*[257] His character is summed up in this saying even as Abraham's character is summed up in his saying, *Show me how you revive the dead.*[258] Such a request de-

---

255. Ibid., XX:50.
256. Ibid., XLII:27.
257. Ibid., II:259.
258. Ibid., II:260.

manded an active response, which the Reality accordingly made evident in him when He says, *God caused him to die for a hundred years and then brought him forth alive.*[259] He said to him, *Behold the bones, how We have joined them together and then clothed them in flesh.*[260] In this way he perceived directly how bodies grow forth, with immediate perception. Thus, He showed him how it was done. He, however, had asked about Destiny, which can be known only by a revelation of things in their latent state and in their nonexistence. It was not accorded him, since such knowledge is the prerogative of divine awareness. It is surely absurd that any other than He should know such things, seeing that it concerns the primordial keys, that is the keys of the Unseen, which none knows save He.[261] God does, however, inform those whom He wishes of His servants about some of these things.

Know that they are called keys to indicate a state of opening, which is the state in which the process of bringing into existence affects things, or, if you prefer, the state in which the capacity to come into existence attaches to what is destined to exist, a state of which only God may have any real experience. That is because the keys of the Unseen are never manifested or unveiled, since all capability and activity are God's particularly, Who has absolute being, unrestricted in any way.

When we learn that the Reality rebuked Ezra for his request concerning Destiny,[262] we may realize that it was a request for this kind of awareness in particular, seeking as he was a capability regarding what is destined, which capability is reserved only to Him Who has absolute being. He sought that which no creature may experience, nor may the modalities [of things] be known except by direct experience.

When God said to him, "Unless you desist, I will surely erase your name from the register of prophets," He meant, "I will deprive you of the means to [divine] communication and present things to you as they are manifested, which will occur only in accordance with your own [eternal] predisposition, which is the means by which direct perception is experienced. Know, O Ezra, that you may perceive only what you seek to perceive as your [eternal] predisposition per-

---

259. Ibid., II:259.
260. Ibid.
261. Ibid., VI:59.
262. Ibid., II:259.

IBN AL-'ARABĪ

mits. If you do not, then you will know that your predisposition does not permit that you should and that it is something reserved to God. Although God has given to everything He has created, He has nevertheless not bestowed on you this particular predisposition. It is not inherent in your creation; had it been so, He Who said *He gives to everything He has created*[263] would have given it to you. You should have refrained from such a request of yourself, without needing a divine refusal." Such was God's concern with Ezra, who knew [the truth of the matter] in one way but was ignorant of it in another.

Know that Saintship is an all-inclusive and universal function that never comes to an end, dedicated as it is to the universal communication [of divine truth]. As for the legislative function of Prophecy and Apostleship, it came to an end in Muhammad. After him there will no longer be any law-bringing prophet or community to receive such, nor any apostle bringing divine law. This statement is a terrible blow to the friends of God because it implies the cessation of the experience of total and perfect servanthood. The special name of "friend" [of God] is not widely used of the servant in that he does not presume to share a name with his Lord, Who is God. God Himself is not called by the names "prophet" or "apostle," but He does call Himself "friend," and is so described. He says, *God is the friend of those who believe,*[264] and, *He is the Friend, the Praiseworthy.*[265] The name is also often applied to God's servants, alive and dead. With the coming to an end of the Prophecy and Apostleship, however, the servant no longer has another name not applicable also to the Reality.

God, however, is kind to His servants and has left for them the universal Prophecy, which brings no law with it. He has also left to them the power of legislation through the exercise of individual judgement [*ijtihād*] concerning rules and regulations. In addition, he has bequeathed to them the heritage of legislation in the tradition, "The learned are the heirs of the prophets."[266] This inheritance involves the use of individual judgment in certain rulings, which is a form of legislation.

When the prophet speaks on matters that lie outside the scope of

---

263. Ibid., XX:50.
264. Ibid., II:257.
265. Ibid., XLII:28.
266. Bukhārī, III:10.

law, he is then speaking as a saint and a gnostic, so that his station as a knower [of truth] is more complete and perfect than that as an apostle or lawgiver. If you hear any of the Folk saying or transmitting sayings from him to the effect that Saintship is higher than Prophecy, he means only what we have just said. Likewise, if he says that the saint is superior to the prophet and the apostle, he means only that this is so within one person. This is because the apostle, in his Saintship, is more perfect than he is as a prophet or an apostle. It does not mean that any saint coming after him is higher than he, since one who follows cannot attain to the one who is followed, as regards that which he follows in him. Were he indeed to affect such a position, he would no longer be a follower; so understand. The Apostleship and Prophecy stem from Saintship and learning. Consider how God commands him to seek an increase in knowledge, rather than anything else, saying, *Say: O my Lord, increase me in knowledge.*[267]

Now the law imposes certain obligations to perform some things and forbids certain other things, all of which apply to this world, which will come to an end. Saintship, on the other hand, is not of that kind, since, were it to come to an end, it would end as such, as does the Apostleship. Indeed, were it to end in this way it would cease to have a name. The friend [saint] is a name that is God's eternally, as also one that attaches to, is characteristic of, and is realized in His servants. Related to this is His saying to Ezra that unless he desisted from asking about the nature of Destiny, He would erase his name from the register of Prophecy, that the command would come to him as a manifested revelation, that he might no longer be called a prophet or an apostle, but that he would continue in his Saintship. When, however, the attendant circumstances of his state indicated to him that the [divine] address to him was in the form of a warning, he, experiencing that state and heeding the warning, realized that it was a threat to deprive him of certain degrees of Saintship in this world, since Prophecy and Apostleship constitute certain degrees of Saintship. Thus, he might know that he was superior to the saint who has no legislating Prophecy or Apostleship. In the case of someone associated with some other state also requiring the rank of prophecy, it would have come as a promise and not a threat.

---

267. *Qur'an*, XX:114.

IBN AL-'ARABĪ

His request is in fact acceptable since the prophet is a special kind of saint who knows by the circumstances of his state that it would be absurd for a prophet, having this special degree of Saintship, to approach what he knows God would not approve of, or to address himself to something impossible to attain. In the case of one associated with such states and in whom they are well established, His words, "I will surely erase your name from the register of prophecy," come forth as a threat that clearly indicates the sublimity of an eternal degree [of Saintship], which is that degree which remains to the prophets and apostles in the Hereafter where there is no occasion for lawgiving to any of God's creation once they have entered either into Paradise, or into the Fire. I have restricted discussion on this point to entry into the two states of Paradise and the Fire because of what He has ordained, on the Day of Resurrection, for those who lived between periods of revelation, for young children and the insane, all of whom He will gather in a particular place, there to do justice, to punish wrongdoing and to reward the good deeds of the people of Paradise. When they have been gathered, apart from other men, into that place, He will send the best one of them as a prophet to the others to present a fire to them and say, "I am the messenger of the Reality to you." Some of them will then believe in him, while others will reject him. Then he will say to them, "Cast yourselves into this fire, for whichever of you obeys me will be saved and will enter the Garden, but whoever disobeys me and opposes my command will perish and become dwellers in the Fire." Then, those who obey him and throw themselves into the fire will be blessed and gain their reward, finding the fire cool and safe, while those who disobey him will be worthy of punishment and will enter the fire, descending into it with their contentious deeds, so that justice might be done by God upon His servants.

Thus He says, *On the day when the leg will be uncovered,*[268] which indicates an important matter concerning the Hereafter, *they will be summoned to prostrate themselves,*[269] which denotes obligation and legislation. Some of them will be able to do it, while others will not. Of the latter God has said, *They will be summoned to prostrate themselves,*

---

268. Ibid., LXVIII:42.
269. Ibid.

and they will not be able to do it,[270] just as certain servants found themselves unable to comply with God's command, like Abū Jahl and others.[271] This much legislation will remain in the Hereafter on the Day of Resurrection before the entry into Paradise and the Fire. We have therefore restricted our treatment of this subject. Praise be to God.

---

270. Ibid.
271. Cf. ibid., XXVIII:56. Abū Jahl was one of the Prophet's most persistent opponents.

CHAPTER XV

THE WISDOM OF PROPHECY IN THE WORD OF JESUS

INTRODUCTORY NOTE

The greater part of this chapter is concerned with the various modes and manifestations of the Spirit [*rūḥ*] and the way it is imparted to matter and form. In particular, it is concerned with the role of the Spirit in the creation of Jesus and also his powers of revival.

So far, in this work, Ibn al-'Arabī has spoken in terms of the Breath of the Merciful when discussing the creative act, described as a movement of relief from inner pressure within the Reality, the expression of which brings about the existence of the created Cosmos. However, in discussing the nature and activity of the Spirit here, he is concerned with more particular aspects of that spontaneous act of creative expiration. The two most important words he uses in this context are *rūḥ* [spirit] and *nafakha* [to blow]. In relation to the primordial Breath [*nafas*], the former is its content, while the latter describes a mode of its operation. The Spirit, the root meaning of which, in Arabic, is closely related in meaning to the root *nafasa*, clearly denotes the living reality of God, His living consciousness, which as the active pole inflates, inseminates, irradiates, and informs the dark passivity of primal substance, of original Nature. Thus, it is also clear from Ibn al-'Arabī's treatment of the subject that the concepts of breath-blowing, seed-impregnation, light-radiation, and word-enunciation are very closely related in his mind, as they are in the spiritual lore of most religious traditions. It is probably the last of these related concepts, word-inform, that provides a clue to the title of this chapter, since the word for Prophecy in Arabic [*nubuwwah*] comes from the root *naba'a*, which means "to inform," a prophet [*nabī*] being a particular and special receptacle for the divine Word, just as, in a more universal sense, the whole Cosmos [*'ālam*] is "informed" [created] by the divine Spirit, its multiple forms constituting clues [*a'lām*] from which the "intelligent ones" might learn [*'ilm*] the truth.

The concept of Spirit—like its other complement, the soul, which is its passive and experiential pole—is complicated by the fact that its manifestation differs according to the existential level at which it is being considered. Thus, the Spirit, at its source, is thought of as pure light, while at the physical level it is manifest as the fire and heat of cosmic life, representing, as it does, the pulse of life-reality, the expression of Being, at every level of the divine creation–Self-manifestation. At source, it is pure Identity-consciousness, but as it reaches out further and further it is experienced as commanding Word and impregnating seed.

As elsewhere in this work, Ibn al-'Arabī speaks of the relationship between the Spirit and Nature as being, so to speak, a parental relationship on a macrocosmic scale in which the Spirit is the Father and Nature the Mother. While the former is viewed as active, luminous, and commanding, the latter is thought of as passive, dark, and receptive, that primordial matrix which is ever ready to receive the determining impress of the Spirit. Sometimes this relationship is expressed in terms of the Universal Intellect and the Universal Soul or, in more qur'anic terms, the Pen and the Tablet. Perhaps the best way to explain the difference between Nature and the Soul on the one hand and between Spirit and the Intellect on the other is that the first term in both cases is ontological, while the second term is experiential. Thus, while Nature may be said to be the reality of passive receptivity, the Soul denotes rather the experience of that reality; similarly, while the Spirit denotes the reality of active truth, the Intellect may be seen as the consciousness of being that reality. Thus, within the context of creation and Self-manifestation, we have yet another expression of the polarity subject-object, and their mutual dependence.

In the human or microcosmic context, Ibn al-'Arabī illustrates a particular and special instance of this relationship in the case of Jesus, who is the product of both Mary, who personifies the "water" of Nature, and Gabriel, who represents by his blowing the seed-word of the Spirit. The creation of Jesus is a special case in that, unlike most men, the Spirit impregnated Mary not through the loins of a mortal man but directly by the angelic instrument, as in the case of revelation to Jesus himself as a prophet of God. His Prophecy, however, or "being informed" by the divine Word, was not only verbal but also vital, in that the spiritual "blowing" of which he was a channel transmits the divine Command in all its modes. Thus, by virtue of the direct means of his being begotten, Jesus was able to communicate the divine Spirit not only verbally, but also vitally, since the Spirit enlivens at every level.

Thus, Jesus was, in a special way, what every man is potentially, that is to say, a spirit enshrined within natural form, which is nothing other than the Spirit enshrined within His Nature. Throughout the chapter, Ibn al-'Arabī is concerned, as always, to explain the paradox of "He" and "other than He," to try to make clear in what sense Jesus, or for that matter anything, is himself rather than Himself, or to what extent it is Jesus himself or God Himself who speaks and revives. This, of course, is the question of the underlying and constantly recurring theme of the Oneness of Being, the essence of which the author finds himself unable to explain satisfactorily because of the inherent polarization of language.

THE WISDOM OF PROPHECY
IN THE WORD OF JESUS

From the water of Mary or from the breath of Gabriel,
  In the form of a mortal fashioned of clay,
The Spirit came into existence in an essence
  Purged of Nature's taint, which is called *Sijjīn*.[272]
Because of this, his sojourn was prolonged,
  Enduring, by decree, more than a thousand years.
A spirit from none other than God,
  So that he might raise the dead and bring forth birds from clay.

---

272. Another name for Hell; cf. *Qur'an*, LXXXIII:7.

And became worthy to be associated with his Lord,
  By which he exerted great influence, both high and low.
God purified him in body and made him transcendent
  In the Spirit, making him like Himself in creating.

Know that it is a particular characteristic of the spirits that everything on which they descend becomes alive, and life begins to pervade it. Thus did al-Sāmirī arrogate [to himself] some of the influence of the messenger Gabriel, who is a spirit.[273] When he realized that it was Gabriel, and knowing that all he touched would come alive, al-Sāmirī snatched some of it (his power), either with his hand or with his fingertips. Then he transferred it to the [golden] calf, so that it bellowed, which is the sound cattle make. Had he fashioned it in some other form, it would have made the appropriate sound, such as the grumbling of the camel, the bleating of lambs and sheep, or the articulate speech of man.

Now the measure of life that pervades a creature is called divine, humanity being [preeminently] the locus in which the Spirit inheres. Thus humanity is called a spirit by virtue of that which inheres in it.

When the trusty spirit, which was Gabriel, presented itself to Mary as a perfectly formed human, she imagined that he was some ordinary man who desired to lie with her. Accordingly, she sought refuge from him in God, totally, so that He might rid her of his attentions, knowing that to be forbidden.[274] Thus she attained to perfect presence with God, which is the [pervasion of] the unseen spirit. Had he blown [his spirit] into her at that moment, Jesus would have turned out too surly for any to bear, because of his mother's state. When he said to her, *I am only a messenger of your Lord, come to give you a pure boy*,[275] her anxiety subsided and she relaxed. It was at that moment that he blew Jesus into her.

Gabriel was, in fact, transmitting God's word to Mary, just as an apostle transmits His word to his community. God says, *He is His word deposited with Mary, and a spirit from Himself.*[276]

Thus did desire pervade Mary. The body of Jesus was created

---

273. Cf. ibid., XX:86–89.
274. Cf. ibid., XIX:17–21.
275. Ibid., XIX:19.
276. Ibid., IV:171.

from the actual water of Mary and the notional water [seed] of Gabriel inherent in the moisture of that blowing, since breath from the vital body is moist owing to the element of water in it. In this way the body of Jesus was brought into being from a notional and an actual water, appearing in mortal form because of his mother's [being human] and the appearance of Gabriel in human form, since all creation in this human species occurs in the usual way.

Jesus came forth raising the dead because he was a divine spirit. In this the quickening was of God, while the blowing itself came from Jesus, just as the blowing was from Gabriel, while the Word was of God. As regards what was made apparent by his blowing, Jesus' raising of the dead was an actual bringing to life, just as he himself became manifest from the form of his mother. His raising of the dead, however, was also notional, as coming from him, since, in truth, it came from God. Thus he combines both [the notional and the actual] by the reality according to which he was created, seeing, as we have said, that he was created of notional and actual water. Thus, bringing the dead to life was attributed to him both actually and notionally. Concerning the former, it is said of him, *And He revives the dead*,[277] while of the latter, *You will breathe into it [the clay] and it will become a bird by God's leave*.[278] Now that which relates to the words *by God's leave* is *it will become* and not *you will breathe*. The words *you will blow* may be considered to relate to them [*by God's leave*] if it means that it will become a bird in a sensible, corporeal form. The same is the case with His saying, *You will cure the blind and the leprous*, and everything else attributed to him and to God's permission, as also by allusion, such as His saying *By My permission*,[279] and *By God's permission*.[280] If the word *permission* is connected with *You will blow into*,[281] then the one who blows is permitted to blow, so that the bird comes into being through the one blowing, but by God's permission. If the one blowing does so without permission, then the coming into being of the bird is by His permission, in which case the word *per-*

---

277. Ibid., XLII:9.
278. Ibid., V:110. Ibn al-'Arabī has here misquoted the verse, which should read *by My permission*. The words *by God's leave* appear in III:49 where Jesus relates the same event in the first person.
279. Ibid., V:110.
280. Ibid., III:49.
281. Ibid., V:110.

mission is related to the words *it will become.*[282] Were it not for the fact that actuality and hypothesis are both present in the matter, the [resulting] form would not possess these two aspects, which it has because the makeup of Jesus effects it.

The humility of Jesus was such that his community was commanded *that they should pay the poll-tax completely, humbling themselves,*[283] that if any one of them were struck on one cheek, he should offer also the other, and that he should not hit back or seek retribution. This aspect [of his teaching] derives from his mother, since woman is lowly and humble, being under the man, both theoretically and physically. His powers of revival, on the other hand, derive from the blowing of Gabriel in human form, since Jesus revived the dead in human form. Had Gabriel not come in human form, but in some other, whether animal, plant or mineral, Jesus would have been able to quicken the dead only by taking that form to himself and appearing in it. Similarly, had Gabriel appeared in a luminous, incorporeal form, not going beyond his nature, Jesus would not have been able to revive the dead without first appearing in that luminous natural form, and not in the elemental human form deriving from his mother.

It used to be said of him, when he revived the dead, "It is he and yet not he." Both the sight of the observer and the mind of the intelligent man were confused at seeing a mortal man bring the dead to life, rationally as well as physically, which is a divine prerogative. The spectator would be utterly bewildered to see a mortal man performing divine acts.

This matter has led certain people to speak of incarnation and to say that, in reviving the dead, he is God. Therefore, they are called unbelievers [concealers], being a form of concealment, since they conceal God, Who in reality revives the dead, in the human form of Jesus. He has said, *They are concealers [unbelievers] who say that God is the Messiah, son of Mary.* The real error and unbelief in the full sense of the word is not in their saying "He is God" nor "the son of Mary," but in their having turned aside from God by including [God in human form] in the matter of reviving the dead, in favor of a merely mortal form in their saying [He is] *the son of Mary,* albeit that he is the son

---

282. Ibid.
283. Ibid., IX:29.

of Mary without doubt. Hearing them, one might think that they attributed divinity to the form, making it the form itself, but that is not the case, having in fact asserted that the divine Identity is the subject in the human form, which was the son of Mary, Thus they distinguished between the form and its determination, but did not make the form the same as the determining principle. In the same way, Gabriel was in mortal form [at first] without blowing [into Mary]; then he blew [into her]. Thus the blowing is distinguished from the form, since, although it derives from the form, it is not of its essence. So do the various sects quarrel concerning the nature of Jesus.

Considered in his [particular] mortal form, one might say that he is the son of Mary. Considered in his form of humanity, one might say that he is of Gabriel, while considered with respect to the revival of the dead, one might say that he is of God as Spirit. Thus one might call him the Spirit of God, which is to say that life is manifest into whomsoever he blows. Sometimes it might be imagined, using the passive participle, that God is in him, sometimes that an angel is in him, and at other times mortality and humanity. He is indeed according to that aspect [of his reality] which predominates in the one who considers him.

Thus he is [at once] the Word of God, the Spirit of God, and the slave of God, and such a [triple] manifestation in sensible form belongs to no other. Every other man is attributed to his formal father, not to the one who blows His Spirit into human form. God, when He perfected the human body, as He says, *When I perfected him*,[284] blew into him of His spirit, attributing all spirit in man's being and essence to Himself. The case of Jesus is otherwise, since the perfection of his body and human form was included in the blowing of the spirit [by Gabriel into Mary], which is not so of other men. All creatures are indeed words of God, which are inexhaustible, stemming as they do from [the command] *Be*, which is the Word of God.[285] Now, can the Word be attributed to God as He is in Himself, so that its nature may never be known, or can God descend to the form of him who says *Be*, so that the word *Be* may be said to be the reality of the form to which He descends and in which He is manifest? Some gnostics support the former, some the latter, while others are confused and do not know what is the truth of the matter.

---

284. Ibid., XV:29.
285. Ibid., II:117.

This matter is one that can be known only by direct experience, as with Abū Yazīd al-Bisṭāmī when he blew on an ant he had killed and it came alive again.[286] At that very moment he knew Who it was that blew, so he blew [into it]. In that respect he was like Jesus.

As for revival by knowledge from spiritual death, it is that eternal, sublime, and luminous divine life of which God says, *Who was dead and We made him alive again, and for whom We made a light wherewith to walk among men.*[287] Anyone who revives a dead soul with the life of knowledge relating to some truth about God has thereby brought him to life, so that he has a light by which to walk among men; that is to say those that are formed like him.

> But for Him and but for us,
>   That which has become would not be.
> We are servants in very truth,
>   And it is God Who is our master.
> But we are of His very essence, so understand,
>   When I say "man"
> And do not be deceived by (the term) "man,"
>   For He has given you a proof.
> Be divine (in essence) and be a creature (in form),
>   And you will be, by God, a compassionate one.
> We have given Him what is manifest in us through Him,
>   As He has given to us also.
> The whole affair is shared, divided,
>   Between Him and us.
> He Who knows by my heart
>   Revived it when He gave us life.
> In Him we were existences, essences,
>   And instances of time.
> In us it is not permanent,
>   But only intermittent. (But it gives us life).

A corroboration of what we have said regarding the coming together of the spiritual blowing with the elemental mortal form is that the Reality describes Himself as the Merciful Breath, and that all that attaches to an attribute, in the case of something described, should ad-

---

286. Cf. n. 113.
287. *Qur'an*, VI:122.

here to that attribute. You know that the breath in one breathing is all that it needs to be. Therefore, the Divine Breath is receptive to cosmic forms, in relation to which it is like the Primordial Substance, being very Nature Herself.

The elements are a form of Nature, just as that which is above them and what they generate, which is the sublime spirits that are above the seven heavens.

As for the spirits of the seven heavens and their essences, deriving as they do from the *smoke*[288] they [the elements] generate, they, as also the angels, which come into being from each heaven, are elemental. These angels are elemental, while the ones above them are of Nature. It is for this reason that God has described them, that is the heavenly host, as being in conflict, Nature itself being self-contradictory. Indeed it is the Breath that has brought about the mutual conflict among the divine Names, which are relationships. Consider, however, how the divine Essence, which is beyond this regime [of conflict], is characterized by [utter] Self-sufficiency, beyond all need of the Cosmos. Because of this the Cosmos has been set forth in the form of its Creator, which is nothing other than the divine Breath. To the extent that it is hot, it is high, while to the extent that it is cold and moist, it is low. According as it is dry, it is fixed and does not move, since precipitation relates to cold and moisture. Consider how the physician, when he wishes to prescribe a potion for a patient, looks first at the sedentation of the urine. When he sees that it is precipitating he knows maturation is complete and prescribes the medicine to accelerate the cure. It only precipitates because of its natural moisture and coldness.

God kneads this human clay in His two hands, which, although both are right hands, are nevertheless in opposition. There is no concealing the difference between them, even if it be only that they are two [separate] hands, since naught influences Nature except what conforms to her, and she is polarized; so He came forth with two hands. When He created him [Adam] with two hands He called him *bashar* [mortal, human] because of the direct connection [*mubāsharah*] suggested by the two hands ascribed to Him.[289] This He did out of concern for this humankind, saying to the one who refused to prostrate himself before him, *What restrains you from prostrating before him*

---

288. Cf. ibid., XLIV:10.
289. Cf. ibid., V:18.

whom I have created with My two hands; are you too proud [to do so]—that is, before one who is elemental like yourself, *or are you one of the sublime ones?*[290] By the epithet sublime He means one who, in his luminous makeup, is beyond the elements, although he is natural. Man's only superiority over other creatures is in his being a *bashar* [mortal, human], for [in this respect] he is superior to all things created without that direct connection [*mubāsharah*] [with the Divine Presence]. Thus man ranks above the terrestrial and celestial angels, while God has stipulated that the sublime (higher) angels are superior to mankind.

Whoever wishes to know the divine Breath, then let him [first] know the Cosmos, for "Who knows himself, knows his Lord," Who is manifest in him. In other words, the Cosmos is manifested in the divine Breath by which God relieved the divine Names from the distress they experienced by the nonmanifestation of their effects. Thus He bestows favor on Himself by what He creates in His breath. Indeed, the first effect of the Breath is experienced only in the divine Presence, after which it continues its descent by a universal [process of] release, down to the last thing to be created.

> All is essentially in the Breath,
>   As light is, in essence, in the dark before dawn.
> Knowledge [of this] by [intellectual] proof
>   Is like the emergence of daylight to one half asleep.
> He perceives what we speak of,
>   In a way that gives him a clue to the Breath.
> What I say relieves him of anxiety,
>   As he recites the chapter, *He Frowned.*[291]
> It manifests itself to him who
>   Comes seeking a coal [from its fire].
> He sees it as fire, but it is
>   A light to kings and nightfarers.
> When you understand what I am saying,
>   You will know that you are indigent.
> Had he [Moses] sought other than that [a fire],
>   He would have seen it in it, and not inversely.

---

290. Ibid., XXXVIII:75.
291. Ibid., LXXX.

IBN AL-'ARABĪ

When the Reality addressed Himself to this Word of Jesus in the station of *until We know*,[292] although He knows [well], He asked him whether it was true or not that certain things had been attributed to Him, knowing full well what had transpired, saying, *Did you say to the people, "Take me and my mother as gods rather than God?"*[293] Now courtesy requires that the questioner be given an answer, since when He reveals Himself to him in this station and this form, wisdom dictates that the answer be given from the standpoint of distinction [between speaker and the one spoken to], but with the reality of synthesis clearly in view. Jesus replied, emphasizing the divine transcendence, *May You be exalted*,[294] stressing the *You*, a word that implies encounter and dialogue. *It is not for me*, that is, for me rather than You, *to say what I have no right to say*, that is, what my identity [might] require, but not my [latent] essence. *If, indeed, I said such a thing, You know of it*, because You are the [true] speaker, and one who utters a statement knows what he is saying. You, therefore, are the tongue by which I speak; as the Apostle has told us of his Lord, with respect to divine communication, "I am his tongue by which he speaks."[295] Thus does He make His Identity the same as the tongue of the speaker, attributing the speech to the servant. Then His devoted servant completes the reply, saying, *You know what is in my soul*,[296] the speaker being [in essence] God, *but I do not know what is in it [as form]*.[297] He denies knowledge to Jesus in his own identity, but not as speaker or as possessor of [creative] effect. Then he says *Surely You*,[298] using a reinforcing pronoun to emphasize and confirm the following declaration, seeing that none knows the Unseen except God.

Thus [in his reply] he distinguishes and synthesizes, singularizes and pluralizes, broadens and narrows. Then he says, completing the answer, *I told them only what You commanded me to say*,[299] so indicating by denial that it was he [who said it]. The uttering [of the reply] requires a certain courtesy toward the enquirer. Had he not answered

---

292. Ibid., XLVII:31.
293. Ibid., V:116.
294. Ibid., as also the following quotations.
295. Bukhārī, LXXXI:38.
296. *Qur'an*, V:116.
297. Ibid.
298. Ibid.
299. Ibid., V:117.

at all, he would have been considered devoid of all knowledge of the realities, which is, of course, quite untrue of him. His saying *only what You commanded me to say*[300] is as if to say, "You are the speaker on my tongue, and you are [in truth] my very tongue." Consider then how precise and subtle is this divine and spiritual intimation.

[So I said], *Worship God.*[301] He uses the name *Allāh* because of the variety of worshipers in their acts of worship and the different religious traditions. He does not use one of the particular names, but rather that Name which includes them all. Then he goes on to say, *My Lord and your Lord,*[302] since it is certain that His relationship with one creature, as Lord, is not the same as with another. For that reason he makes the distinction between *My Lord and your Lord,* referring separately to the speaker and the one spoken to.

When he says, *only what You commanded me to say,*[303] he lays the stress on himself as being commanded, which is his servanthood, since a command is only given to one who, it is supposed, will comply, whether he does so or not. Since the command descends according to the regime of ranks, everything manifested in a particular rank is affected by what is afforded it by the reality of that rank. The rank of the "ordered" has a regimen that is apparent in everything ordered, just as the rank of commanding has a regimen apparent in everyone who commands. When God says, *Establish prayer,*[304] He is [at once] the Commander, the one who obliges, and the commanded. When the servant prays, *O my Lord, forgive me!*[305] he is the commander, while the Reality is the commanded, for what God requires of His servant by His command is the same as that which the servant requires of the Reality by his command. For this reason [one might say] that every supplication is inevitably responded to, even if it be delayed. For instance, certain people under obligation, when commanded to pray, might not pray at that time, but postpone compliance by praying at another time, although they are quite capable of praying at the time. Thus, response is inevitable, even if only by intention. Then he says, *I am, concerning them,*[306] not concerning myself together

---

300. Ibid.
301. Ibid.
302. Ibid.
303. Ibid.
304. Ibid., II:43.
305. Ibid., XXIII:118.
306. Ibid., V:117, as also the following quotations.

with them, as when he said, *My Lord and your Lord, a witness so long as I remain with them.* This is because the prophets bear witness concerning their communities while they are with them.

He continued, *And when You caused me to die,* that is, when You raised me to Yourself, hiding them from me and me from them, *You were the watcher over them,* not in my material substance, but in theirs, since You were their sight, which required supervision. Man's consciousness of himself is indeed God's consciousness of him, but he [Jesus] has attributed this consciousness to the name, the Watcher, referring the consciousness to Him. He wishes thereby to distinguish between himself and his Lord, so that he may know that he is himself a servant, and that God is Himself as his Lord, considering himself as witness and God as the Watcher. Thus, in relation to himself, Jesus puts his people first, saying, *concerning them a witness, while I am with them,*[307] preferring them out of courtesy. He places them last, however, when speaking of God in saying, *the Watcher over them,* since the Lord is deserving of precedence.

Then he shows that God, the Watcher, bears also the name that he used of himself when he said *concerning them a witness.* He says, *You are the Witness of every thing,* the word "every" denoting generality and the word "thing" being the most unspecific of words. That is because He is the witness of everything that is witnessed, according as the reality of that thing dictates, so showing that it is, in fact, God Who is the witness concerning the people of Jesus in his saying, *I was a witness concerning them while I was with them.* This is the witnessing of God in the substance of Jesus, having confirmed that He was his tongue, hearing, and sight.[308]

God speaks of a word of Jesus and a word of Muḥammad. As for it being of Jesus, it is because it is the utterance by Jesus of God's communication concerning him in His Book. As for its being of Muḥammad, it is because it happened to Muḥammad in a particular place. He spent a whole night repeating it and nothing else, until the breaking of dawn.

If You chastise them, then they are Your servants, but if You forgive them, then You are the Mighty, the Wise.[309] The word "them," as also the

---

307. Ibid., V:117, as also the following quotations.
308. Bukhārī, LXXXI:38.
309. Qur'an, V:118.

word "he," is a pronoun of absence. He also says, *It is they who disbelieve*,³¹⁰ using the third person pronoun, the absence veiling them from what is meant [by the gnostics] by "the witnessed One Who is present." He says, *If You chastise them*,³¹¹ with the pronoun of absence, which is naught but the veil that hides them from God. He therefore reminds them of God before their presence [on the Last Day], so that when they are present, the leaven may gain control in the dough and make it like Itself. *For they are Your servants*,³¹² using the singular pronoun because of the unity by which they exist.

There is no abasement greater than that of slaves, seeing they have no freedom of action with respect to themselves. Their lot is determined by what their Master wants with them, and He has no associate in what concerns them; as He says, *Your servants*, with the singular pronoun. By chastisement is meant their abasement, and there is none more abased than they because they are slaves. That they are abased is determined by their essences.

He means "You do not abase them any more than their state of servitude requires." *If You forgive them*,³¹³ that is, if you shield them from the befalling of punishment they deserve by their contention, or make a covering for them to shield them from it and avert it from them, *You are the Mighty*,³¹⁴ the Averter, the Protector. When God bestows this name on one of His servants, He Himself is called the Strengthener [*al-muʿizz*], while the recipient is called the mighty [*al-ʿazīz*]. Thus God, as Protector, guards against the wishes of God the Avenger, the Chastiser. Here also He uses a reinforcing pronoun to make things clear, the verse being of the same kind as His saying, *Surely You are the knower of the unseen things*,³¹⁵ and *Surely You were the Watcher over them*.³¹⁶ He also says, *Surely You are the Mighty, the Wise*.³¹⁷

The words [*if You chastise them . . . if You forgive them*] became an urgent question for the Prophet Muḥammad, which he repeated all

---

310. Ibid., XLVIII:25.
311. Ibid., V:118.
312. Ibid.
313. Ibid.
314. Ibid.
315. Ibid., V:109.
316. Ibid., V:117.
317. Ibid., V:118.

night until daybreak, seeking an answer. Had he received the answer immediately, he would not have gone on repeating the question. God, for His part, set out for him, in detail, all the reasons for their being punished, and at each one he would say to God, *If You chastise them, then they are Your servants, but if You forgive them, then surely You are the Mighty, the Wise.*[318] Had he perceived, in what was set forth to him, any reason to take God's side, he would have pleaded against them rather than for them. God set forth to him what they deserved, to emphasize the submission to God and the exposure to His forgiveness set out in this verse.

It is said that when God likes the voice of His servant in his supplication to Him, He postpones the response, so that he might repeat it, not out of any aversion, but out of love for him. So He is called the Wise, and the Wise One is He Who apportions things to their proper places and does not deviate, concerning them, from what their realities, through their attributes, dictate and require, Thus the phrase, *the Wise, the Knowing,*[319] is in the proper order, which the Prophet reiterates in accordance with a profound knowledge from God, Most High. Whoever recites it should do so in this manner, or remain appropriately silent.

When God befits a servant to give expression to some matter, He does so only that He might respond to him and fulfill his need. Therefore let no one think that what he has been made fit for is late in coming. Let him rather emulate the zeal of God's Apostle, in respect of this verse, in all his states, so that he may hear with his inner or outer hearing, or in whatever way God may cause him to hear His response. If God blesses you with a physically expressed request, He will cause you to hear His response with the physical ear, but if He blesses you with an inner request, then He will cause you to hear His response inwardly.

---

318. Ibid., V:118.
319. Ibid.

CHAPTER XVI

THE WISDOM OF COMPASSION IN THE WORD OF SOLOMON

INTRODUCTORY NOTE

Once again, in this chapter, Ibn al-'Arabī returns to one of his favorite subjects, that of the divine Mercy. Generally speaking, when he talks of the divine Mercy, he means the creative Mercy that generously and infinitely bestows existence on the latent essences in answer to the desire for divine Self-consciousness. Here, however, he points out that Mercy is implicit not only in the act of cosmic creation but also in the annihilating reversal of that act, which would restore all being to God alone. The first Mercy directs God's attention [*himmah*] to the creation and maintenance of His cosmic image, while the second Mercy refocuses all that attention on Himself, alone, in His perfect uniqueness and Self-sufficiency. By the first He freely gives of His power and consciousness in response to the urge of the latent essences to realize in existence what they are eternally predisposed to become. By the second He rigorously obliges the Cosmos to recognize that, in itself, it is nothing other than He and to yield its being back to its sources in Him. Thus, the second kind of Mercy is essentially synonymous with the divine Wrath, while the first is essentially the same as the divine Good Pleasure. It is wrathful in the sense that it seeks to annihilate the existence of creatures and inflict on them the pain of being, after all, "nothing worth mentioning."

IBN AL-'ARABĪ

From another standpoint, the first Mercy is related to the concept of the divine Will, while the second is related to the divine Wish, the former being concerned purely with existential becoming, while the latter seeks to encourage the reawakening from the dream of cosmic existence to a clearer consciousness of His sole right to be. However, in keeping with the Qur'an [VII:156] and Tradition, Ibn al-'Arabī points out that the second Mercy is contained within and subordinate to the first, so confirming the continuance of the polarity God-Cosmos, but only within the context of the Oneness of the Reality, since the Cosmos is but Its form.

The other major subject discussed here is that of dominion or mastery. We have seen that each prophet is seen as a particular channel for the transmission of the divine Spirit, which initiates, enlivens, and determines. Thus, just as Jesus was favored with the spiritual power to revive, so was Solomon favored with the spiritual power to effect changes in the way physical and elemental things behaved, in addition to the usual verbal revelation. Many of the prophets, therefore, transmit not only the Word of God as usually understood but also some other aspect or mode of the creative and determining power of the Spirit. In the case of Solomon, Ibn al-'Arabī is saying that he was granted, without the need for special disciplines, and particularly for himself, the power to master and direct physical and elemental forms.

The other important subject dealt with in this chapter is that of the concept of creation from instant to instant, which we have discussed in the note to Chapter 12.

THE WISDOM OF COMPASSION IN THE WORD OF SOLOMON

It, meaning the letter, *is from Solomon,* ... *and it,* that is, the contents of the letter, are *in the name of God, the Compassionate, the Merciful.*[320] Some have supposed that the name of Solomon is here given precedence over the name of God, but this is not so. They speak of it in a way that is not consonant with Solomon's gnosis of his Lord. Indeed, how could what they say be appropriate in view of what

---

320. *Qur'an,* XXVII:30. The story of Solomon and Bilqīs, or the Queen of Sheba, discussed here is told in chapter 17 of the *Qur'an,* vv. 15–44 incl.

Bilqīs says of it, *I have been sent a respectful letter*,³²¹ that is, respectful to her. Perhaps they are prompted to say such things because Chosroes tore up the letter of the Apostle of God, although he did not do so until he had read the letter and acquainted himself with its contents. Indeed Bilqīs would have done the same, had she not been fitted for grace as she was, nor would the placing of his name before or after the name of God have saved the letter from destruction.

Solomon mentions two kinds of Mercy, the mercy of unobligating giving and the mercy of binding obligation, which are the Compassionate and the Merciful. As the Compassionate He gives freely, while as the Merciful He binds by obligation, although the latter proceeds from the former, the Merciful being implicit within the Compassionate. God has prescribed Mercy on Himself for his servant in return for the acts performed by the servant, which are mentioned by God, as a right God has imposed on Himself, so that by those acts the servant might be deserving of His Mercy, that is the mercy of obligation. Servants of this kind know well what part of themselves is the doer of the action, since human action is divided among eight members. Now God has shown that He is [in reality] the identity of each of the members, so that He is the only true agent, the form alone belonging to the servant. This identity is implicit in him, that is in his name [of servant] alone, since God is the essence of what is manifest and what is called creature, by which the names the Outer and the Last may accrue to the servant, seeing that he was not and then existed. Similarly, the names the Inner and the First are His because his being manifest and his acting are dependent on Him. Thus, when you see a creature, you are seeing the First and the Last, the Outer and the Inner.

Solomon was by no means unaware of this knowledge, which was indeed an integral part of that "dominion" accorded to no one after him, at least in its sensory manifestation.³²² Muḥammad was granted what was granted to Solomon, but it was not outwardly manifest. God gave Muḥammad power over a demon that came to him by night to destroy him. He siezed it and tied it to a pillar of the mosque until morning, when the children of Madīnah played with it.³²³ He had remembered the supplication of Solomon, and God had cast it

---

321. Ibid., XXVII:29.
322. Cf. ibid., XXXVIII:35.
323. Bukhārī, VIII:75.

IBN AL-'ARABĪ

out, but whereas Solomon exercised that power outwardly, Muḥammad did not.

Solomon spoke of "a dominion" and not dominion as such, and we know that he wished for some dominion. We also know that others shared with him in every aspect of the dominion God granted to him, as we know that he was especially privileged in that he enjoyed that dominion in its totality and, as shown by the tradition concerning the demon, that he alone exercised it outwardly.

Had Muḥammad not said of the demon, "God caused me to get the better of it,"[324] we would have said that when he went to sieze it, God caused him to remember the prayer of Solomon, so that he might know that God was not giving him the power to sieze it, since it was God Who cast it away. When he said that God had caused him to get the better of it, we conclude that, having granted him a certain freedom of action with it, God reminded him and he remembered the prayer of Solomon, aquitting himself in a similar manner. From this we may learn that what was denied to creatures after Solomon was the manifestation [of the dominion] in a universal way. Our only aim in discussing this point is to expound on the two kinds of Mercy that Solomon mentioned in the two words, which in Arabic are *al-raḥmān* and *al-raḥīm*.

God binds [restricts] the Mercy of obligation and unleashes the Mercy of giving in His saying, *My Mercy encompasses every thing*,[325] even the divine Names, which are the real relationships. Indeed He bestows on them by us, since we are the result of the Mercy of giving on the divine Names and dominical relationships. Then He made it binding on Himself for us by our manifestation, and made us know that He is our identity, from which we might know that [in truth] He imposed it on Himself only for Himself, since the Mercy is never outside Him. On whom, therefore, does He bestow, seeing that there is only He? Despite the oneness of the [original] Essence, one must, when speaking of the various capacities of creatures in the sciences, express things in various details, so that one says that such a one is more learned than another.

This means that the scope of the divine Wish [*irādah*] falls short of the scope of the divine knowledge, which shows the comparative nature of the divine Attributes, as with the superiority of the scope

---
324. Ibid.
325. *Qur'an*, VII:156.

of his Wish over His power; similarly with His hearing and sight. Thus all the divine Names are graded according to their relative merits, one with another, as is also the case with what is manifest in creation, so that one may say that such a one is more learned than another, despite the oneness of the Essence. Just as, in emphasizing a particular Name, one names it and describes it by all the Names, such is also the case of a particular creature, in that it may be qualified by all the qualities with which it is normally compared. This is because every part of the Cosmos is the totality of the Cosmos in that it is receptive to the realities of the disparate aspects of the Cosmos. Thus the fact that the Identity of God is the essence of Zaid and 'Amr does not contradict our saying that Zaid is less learned than 'Amr, since the Identity is more perfect and knowing in 'Amr than in Zaid, the divine Names being nothing other than the Reality, however much they may vary in merit. Thus, God as the Knower is more universal in His scope than as He Who wishes or as the Powerful, albeit He is Himself and none other.

So, O friend, do not know Him in one context and be ignorant of Him in another, nor affirm Him in one situation and deny Him in another, unless you affirm Him in an aspect in which He affirms Himself and deny Him in an aspect in which He denies Himself, as in the verse in which denial and affirmation of Himself are brought together. He says, *There is nothing like unto Him,*[326] which is a denial, *And He is the Hearer, the Seer,*[327] which is an affirmation of Himself with attributes attributable to all living creatures that hear and see. There is always some living creature in the world hidden from the awareness of some men, which will be manifest in the Hereafter to all men, it being the Abode of the Living,[328] as is also this lower world, although its life is hidden from certain servants, so that the distinction and variety of degrees among God's servants concerning what they grasp of the realities of the Cosmos may be demonstrated.

The Reality is more evident in one whose awareness is universal than in one who lacks such universality, so do not be deceived by the manifest disparity [of created things] into gainsaying the one who asserts that creation is [none other than] the Identity of the Reality. I have just demonstrated the disparity among the Names of God,

---

326. Ibid., XLII:11.
327. Ibid.
328. Cf. ibid., XXIX:64.

which you do not doubt are the Reality, their significance being in the One named by them, which is none other than God, Most High.

How then may Solomon give precedence to his name over the Name of God, as they say he did, seeing that he is but a part of the whole created by the divine Mercy? Surely *The Compassionate, the Merciful* should have been put first to confirm the dependence of the one who receives the Mercy. Indeed, the putting first of one who should be last and the putting last of one who should be first in the position he merits runs counter to all accepted realities.

In her wisdom and sublime knowledge, Bilqīs does not mention the person who sent her the letter, so that her advisers might know that she was in touch with things the course of which they did not perceive. This is the way of God in the matter of dominion, since if the means of information coming to a ruler remain unknown to others, the people of the kingdom are very cautious in exercising their free will and do not do so except in matters that have first been considered for them by their ruler, thus being safe from the possible evil consequences of such free action. Were it to be accorded to them by the one by whom the ruler is informed, they would treat with him and honor him until they could do what they wanted, and the ruler would not hear of it.

She said *A letter has been sent to me*,[329] without naming the sender, as a matter of policy. She had inherited the awe of her people and close advisors, and so merited precedence over them. As for the superiority of human over demonic [*jinn*] learning concerning the mysteries of disposition and the special nature of things, it may be known from the measure of time, since the *perception of the eye*[330] is quicker than the action of one rising from his seat, the movement of the eye in perceiving its object being more rapid than that of the body in moving from its place. That is because the time it takes for perception to take place is the same as it takes to reach its object, no matter what the distance is between the perceiver and perceived, since it takes no more time for the eye to open than for its sight to reach the fixed stars, just as the closing of the eye takes no longer than the ceasing of perception. The rising of a person is not the same and is not as rapid. Thus Asaf Ibn Barkhiyah proved better in this respect than the Jinn, since his utterance and his action took place in a single moment.

---

329. Ibid., XXVII:29.
330. Ibid., XXVII:40.

In that moment Solomon saw with his eye the throne of Bilqīs firmly set before him, lest he should imagine that he was seeing it while it remained in its own place without being moved. We do not know of instantaneous transference. Indeed the causing not to be and to be [of the throne] happened in a way unknown to any but He Who apprised us of it in His saying, *Nay, they are confusion regarding a new creation*,[331] although there was no lapse of time in which they did not see what they were looking at. If it is as we have said, then the moment of its disappearance from its place is the same as its presence with Solomon, by virtue of the renewal of creation by breaths. No one has any knowledge of this decree, indeed no one is aware of the fact in himself that, with each breath, he is not and yet comes into being again.

Therefore, do not say "then," which implies a lapse of time, for the word *thumma* in Arabic implies a process of cause and effect in specific situations, as the poet says,

   Like the quivering of the spear, then it shook.[332]

Now the time of its quivering is the same as that of its shaking. He says "then," although there is no lapse of time. Similarly with the renewal of creation by breaths, the moment of the nonexistence of a thing is the very moment of the existence of its like, as with the renewal of accidents according to the Ashʿarites.

The matter of the obtaining of the throne of Bilqīs is no different from most other [theological] questions, except for those who have inner knowledge of what we have said about it. Asaf's only merit in the matter was that he effected the renewal in the court of Solomon. One who truly understands what we have said will realize that the throne covered no distance, that no land was folded up for it, nor was it penetrated. It happened by means of a follower of Solomon so that it should be something greater for Solomon in the hearts of those present, than for Bilqīs and her associates.

That was because Solomon was a gift from God to David, and He says, *And We gave to David Solomon.*[333] A gift is the bestowal of something as a favor by the giver, not a token of agreement or reward. Such a [divine] gift is the complete favor, the irrefutable argument, and the unmistakeable stamp. Concerning his knowledge, He says,

---

331. Ibid., L:15.
332. I have not been able to trace this line of poetry.
333. *Qurʾan*, XXXVIII:30.

*And We caused Solomon to understand it,*³³⁴ despite the contrary judgment [of David], although God granted them both judgment and knowledge.³³⁵ David's knowledge was an acquired knowledge granted him [indirectly] by God, while Solomon's knowledge was God's own knowledge on the matter, He being the judge [in the matter] without intermediary, since Solomon was himself the exposition of God, of perfect veracity. Likewise, one who strives and makes a right decision in a matter in which God has ruled, whether it be by his own effort or according to what God has inspired His Apostle, has two rewards, while one who makes a mistaken decision has only one, the former having used learning and judgment. Now this Community of Muḥammad has been granted the rank of both Solomon and David in the matter of judgment. How fine a Community it is!

When Bilqīs saw her throne, knowing the great distance involved and the impossibility, in her view, of its being moved in such a short time, she said, *It is as if it were it,*³³⁶ so confirming what we have said concerning the renewal of creation by similars. It is it, and so confirms the [divine] command, since you are, in the moment of recreation, [essentially] the same as you were before it.

Solomon's direction concerning the palace was characteristic of the perfection of his knowledge. She was told, *Enter the palace,*³³⁷ which was paved in perfectly smooth glass. When she saw it she thought it was a deep lake, so *she bared her legs,*³³⁸ so that the water should not reach her gown. He then explained to her that the seeing of her throne was after the same manner, which did more than justice to the matter. By that he showed her how right she had been in saying, *It is as if it were it.*³³⁹ Then she said, *O my Lord, surely I have wronged my own soul, so I submit with Solomon,* that is, the submission of Solomon, *to God, Lord of the worlds.*³⁴⁰ She was yielding to God, the Lord of the worlds, and not to Solomon himself, who is of the worlds.

She was not restricted in her yielding, no more than are the apostles in their belief in God, unlike Pharaoh who said, *The Lord of Moses*

---

334. Ibid., XXI:79.
335. Cf. ibid., XXI:78–79.
336. Ibid., XXVII:42.
337. Ibid., XXVII:44.
338. Ibid.
339. Ibid., XXVII:42.
340. Ibid., XXVII:44.

and Aaron.[341] Although Pharaoh shares to some extent in this yielding of Bilqīs, his power was weak, and she had a greater understanding than he in her yielding to God. That is because Pharaoh was subject to the pressure of the moment in saying, *I believe in what the Children of Israel believe in,*[342] so specifying his belief. He did so only because he heard the magicians say, concerning their faith in God, *The Lord of Moses and Aaron.*[343]

The submission of Bilqīs was the same as that of Solomon, seeing that she said *with Solomon,*[344] following him in all the teachings he believed in. In the same way, we are on the same Straight Path our Lord is on, our forelocks being in His grasp, nor is it possible that we should be separated from Him. We are with Him by implication and He is with us by declaration, since He has said, *He is with you wherever you are.*[345] We are with him by the fact that He has us by the forelock, and He is with Himself wherever He may take us on His path, everything in the Cosmos being on a straight path, which is the path of the Lord. Thus Bilqīs learned from Solomon and said *to God, the Lord of the worlds,*[346] without specifying any particular world.

As for the Power of subjugation by which Solomon was favored and made superior to others, and the dominion God granted to him and to none after him, [its significance lies in the fact] that it proceeded from him, as He says, *We subjected to him the wind, so that it blew at his command.*[347] The matter of subjection alone is not the point, since God has said, *And He has subjected to you all that is in the Heaven and the Earth,*[348] and He has mentioned the subjection of wind, stones, and other things. The point is that these things occur not by our command but by God's. What singles Solomon out [from the rest of us], if you will only understand, is that he could effect such things by personal command alone, without the need for spiritual concentration or the exertion of spiritual power. We say this because we know that cosmic bodies are susceptible to the powers of souls raised to the sta-

---

341. Ibid., VII:122.
342. Ibid., X:90.
343. Ibid., VII:122.
344. Ibid., XXVII:44.
345. Ibid., LVII:4.
346. Ibid., XVII:44.
347. Ibid., XXXVIII:36.
348. Ibid., XLV:13.

tion of spiritual synthesis, having observed such things along the Way. Solomon, however, had only to utter the command to whatever he wished to subject, without the need for special states.

Know, may God assist both you and us with his Spirit, that such a favor conferred on a servant does not affect any dominion he might enjoy in the Hereafter, nor is it counted against him, although Solomon asked for it from His Lord. Experience of the Way requires that Solomon should be given in advance what is held in store for others, who would be taken to task if they presumed to wish for it in the Hereafter. God said to him, *This is our favor*,[349] without saying "upon you" or any other, going on to say, *So give or withhold, without reckoning.*[350] From spiritual experience on the Way we learn that his request [for that] was made at the command of his Lord. Now when a request is made by divine command, the one who requests is fully rewarded for his request.

The Creator fulfills the need implicit in what is requested, if He so wills, or withholds it, since the servant has performed what God obliged him to do in obeying His command regarding that which he requested from his Lord. Had he made the request on his own initiative rather than at his Lord's command, He would have called him to account for it. This is the case in everything requested of God, as He said to our Prophet Muhammad, *Say, O my Lord, increase me in knowledge.*[351] Accordingly, he obeyed his Lord's command and was ever seeking more knowledge, so that when he was brought milk, he would regard it as a symbol of knowledge. He once dreamed that he had been given a bowl of milk, which he drank, giving what was left to 'Umar b. al-Khaṭṭāb. On being asked how he interpreted it, he said that he saw it as knowledge.[352] Similarly, when he was taken on the Night Journey, the angel brought him a vessel containing milk and another wine. He drank the milk and the angel said to him, "You have attained to the primordial state [of innate spirituality]; may God bless your Community by you."[353] Thus, whenever milk appears [in a vision], it is an image of knowledge, just as Gabriel presented himself to Mary in the guise of a well-made man.

When Muḥammad said, "All men are asleep and when they die

---

349. Ibid., XXXVIII:39.
350. Ibid.
351. Ibid., XX:114.
352. Hanbal, II:83,154.
353. Bukhārī, LX:24,48.

they will awake,"³⁵⁴ he meant that everything a man sees in this life is of the same kind as that which one sleeping sees; in other words an apparition that requires interpretation.

> All becoming is an imagination,
>   And in truth also a reality.
> Who truly comprehends this,
>   Has attained the mysteries of the Way.

Thus, when milk was offered to him he said, "God bless us by it and give us increase of it!" because he saw it as an image of knowledge, increase in which he had been commanded to seek. When something other than milk was offered, he would say, "O God, bless us by it and feed us with what is better than it."³⁵⁵ God, therefore, does not call anyone to account in the Hereafter for what He has bestowed in answer to a commanded request. When, however, God bestows something in answer to a request not commanded by Him, it is then for God to call that servant to account or not, as He wishes. I particularly hope, and especially concerning knowledge, that He will not call to account, since His command to His Prophet to seek an increase in knowledge applies equally to his Community. God has said, *You have in the Apostle of God an excellent exemplar*,³⁵⁶ and what finer example is there for one who learns of God than this following by Muḥammad [of God's command]?

Had we expounded the station of Solomon completely you would have encountered something awesome, for most of the learned of this Order are ignorant of the station of Solomon, nor is the matter as they claim it to be.

---

354. I have not been able to trace this tradition.
355. Da'ūd, XXV:21.
356. *Qur'an*, XXXIII:21.

CHAPTER XVII

THE WISDOM OF BEING IN THE WORD OF DAVID

INTRODUCTORY NOTE

The prophet David, like all the prophets who feature in this work, was the special and particular human context for some particular aspect of divine Wisdom. In his case, it was the personal appointment to the office of vicegerent, which function is, in a general sense, shared potentially by all humankind. Man, for Islam in general and Sufism in particular, is, as has already been mentioned in the Introduction, at once the slave and the appointed representative of God, that unique microcosmic creation who reflects in his makeup both the createdness of the Cosmos and the creativity of God, being of both, yet being neither of them completely.

Man, as *khalīfah* [vicegerent], must not fail in his divine stewardship to remember [*dhikr*] always in Whose Name he acts and commands, being always in danger of the sin of self-deification or the association of himself [*shirk*] with God, as a separate identity. As is clear from this chapter, the office of vicegerent is of two kinds, the one concerned with matters spiritual and divine, the other directed to the ordering of the Cosmos, the one inner and universal, the other outer and restricted to a particular religious heritage. The first kind relates to that inner Wisdom, mentioned in the Qur'an, which impels man to reaffirm his commitment to the uniqueness of the divine Identity and to efface his own in the divine Oneness of Being. The second is related to the revelation of Scripture that urges man to govern and order the many and complex concerns of this world, which is the kind with which David was personally invested, according to the Qur'an [XXXVIII:26], not indirectly by some human authority, as is generally the case, but directly by God Himself.

The outer Vicegerency is granted only to certain prophets and apostles or to their successors, whether by appointment, election, or providence, apart from the general vicegerency implicit in all human power and activity. The inner office is granted, often in a more direct way, to certain saints who are appointed to be special transmitters of spiritual power and authority. There is no doubt that, for Ibn al-'Arabī, the inner Vicegerency was the greater office and, in view of his own special sense of spiritual mission, he probably considered that he himself enjoyed this privilege. He is quick to point out, however, that such a person would always, outwardly, conform to and pay allegiance to the Tradition of the prophet or apostle under whose dispensation he was living.

David, however, is the only individual appointed by name to this office, and thus he enshrines in his life and person that particular Wisdom of governance which is itself a mode of the revelation of the Spirit in man.

The chapter ends with yet another discussion regarding the tension between the divine Wish, as expressed in the Sacred Law, and the existential Will, as manifested by what actually happens in the Cosmos.

THE WISDOM OF BEING
IN THE WORD OF DAVID

Know that since Prophecy and Apostleship are a special divine favor, there is no question of any aquisition [of merit]. I mean [particularly] the legislative Prophecy. His favors to them in this respect are pure gifts and not in any sense rewards for which any compensation will be asked of them, His bestowal on them being a matter of favor and selection. He says, *And We gave to him Isaac and Jacob*,[357] meaning to Abraham, the Friend. Of Job, He says, *And We bestowed*

---
357. *Qur'an*, VI:84.

on him his people and, with them, their like.³⁵⁸ Of Moses He says, *And We gave him from our Mercy his brother Aaron, a prophet*,³⁵⁹ and other similar examples.

They were invested from the beginning, and in all or most of their states, by His name the Bestower. He says of David, *We gave to David, of Ourselves, bounty*,³⁶⁰ not linking it with any notion of a return to be demanded of him, nor is there any suggestion that it was granted as a reward or recompense. When God demands thanks, he demands it of the people, nor does He omit to mention David, so that the people might thank Him for what He has bestowed on David. In David's case it is the granting of a favor and a boon, while in the case of his people a return is required, as He said, *Give thanks, O people of David, for so few of my servants are thankful.*³⁶¹ If the prophets gave thanks to God for his favor and gifts to them, it was not something required of them by God, but something that came voluntarily from themselves, as when the Apostle stood until his legs became swollen, giving thanks to God for forgiving him his early and later sins. When someone spoke to him on the matter, he said, "Shall I not be a grateful servant?"³⁶² God said of Noah, *Indeed he was a grateful servant*,³⁶³ albeit that few of God's servants are so.

The first favor granted by God to David was that He gave him a name, not one of the letters of which is a connecting letter, by which he cut him off from the world and informed us about him by his name alone, the letters being *dāl, alif,* and *waw*. He named Muḥammad, on the other hand, with a name containing letters of connection and disconnection, by which He joined him to Himself and separated him from the world, so combining in his name both states. He did the same for David, but inwardly, not in his name. This is what especially distinguishes Muhammad above David; I mean the information concerning him by his name. In his case it is complete in every respect, as in the name Ahmad, which is of God's wisdom.³⁶⁴

Concerning His favor on David, He also mentions the turning

---

358. Ibid., XXXVIII:43.
359. Ibid., XIX:53.
360. Ibid., XXXIV:10.
361. Ibid., XXXIV:13.
362. Cf. ibid., XLVIII:2. Bukhārī, XIX:6.
363. Ibid., XVII:3.
364. The name Muhammad contains a *dāl*, which does not connect to the letter following it. In this paragraph Ibn al-'Arabī engages in a characteristic exercise in letter symbolism.

back of the mountains and their exaltation. They exalted God because of his exaltation, so that their action might conform with his. Similarly, in the case of the birds, God granted him power and attributed it to him. He also granted him wisdom and the final say in affairs. Finally, the greatest favor and degree by which God singled him out was that He attributed the vicegerency specifically to him, which He did not do for any other human, although there were regents among them. He said, *O David, We have appointed you a vicegerent in the Earth, so judge between men with truth and follow not caprice,*"[365] meaning anything other than My inspiration that comes to your mind in exercising your judgment, *Lest it cause you to err from the path of God,*[366] that is, the way revealed to the apostles. Then He admonishes him, saying, *For those who stray from God's path will be a severe punishment, because they have forgotten the day of reckoning.*[367] He does not say, "If you stray from My way, you will be severely punished."

Should it be pointed out that the vicegerency of Adam was also specified, we reply that it was not as specific as David's, since He said only, *I am going to put a vicegerent on the Earth,* not, *I am going to make Adam a vicegerent in the Earth.*[368] Even if He had said it, it is not the same as saying, *We have made you a vicegerent,*[369] as in the case of David. While the latter statement is unambiguous, the former is not, since no further mention is made of Adam, in what follows, to the effect that it is he who is the vicegerent specified by God. Therefore, consider carefully what God tells us of His servants.

Similarly, in the case of Abraham, the Friend, He says, *I am going to make you a leader [imām] of men,*[370] not a vicegerent. It might be the case if we knew that leadership here means also vicegerency. It cannot be the same, however, because He does not specifically call it vicegerency. A further specification of the vicegerency of David is that it is a vicegerency of judgment, which comes only from God, when He said, *So judge between men with truth,*[371] whereas Adam's vicegerency was probably not of this rank. Adam's regency might have been based on the fact that he had succeeded whoever was there before,

---

365. *Qur'an*, XXXVIII:26.
366. Ibid.
367. Ibid.
368. Ibid., II:30.
369. Ibid., XXXVIII:26.
370. Ibid., II:124.
371. Ibid., XXXVIII:26.

and not because he was God's representative to His creation with the divine power of judgment over them. If indeed he was, so be it, but we are here concerned only with what is clearly specified.

God has, in the Earth, representatives appointed by Him, and they are the apostles. As for the vicegerency at the present time, it derives from the apostles and not from God [directly], since they judge only by what the Apostle has laid down for them and no more than that. There is here, however, a subtle point, which only people like ourselves grasp, that concerns the deriving of criteria for judgment [directly] from what was laid down for the Apostle. The one who derives his vicegerency from the Apostle arrives at his judgments from the Tradition of the Apostle or by his own effort, also inspired by that Tradition. Among us, however, are those who derive it [directly] from God, who are vicegerents appointed by God in the same way and whose criteria come to them in the same way as to the Apostle himself. Such people appear to follow the Apostle only because their judgment in no way contradicts him, as will be the case with Jesus when he will come down and judge, or as in the case of the Prophet in His saying, *Those are they whom God has guided, so follow their guidance.*[372] Such a person is special and worthy in what he realizes concerning the form of derivation, being in the same position as the Apostle who confirmed the Law of the apostles who preceded him. Thus we follow him in his confirmation of them, not the law revealed to those before him. Thus the derivation of judgment, as vicegerent, from God is the same as in the case of the Apostle. Speaking esoterically, we would say of such a one that he is the vicegerent of God and, speaking exoterically, that he is a vicegerent of the Apostle of God.

The Apostle died without appointing a successor, because he knew that someone would later on receive the vicegerency from his Lord and become a vicegerent appointed by God [directly], albeit in conformity with the revealed Law. Therefore, when he knew that, he did not seek to prejudge the matter.

God has vicegerents among His creatures who take from the store of the Apostle and apostles what they have themselves taken, and they know the importance of the preceding apostle, because an apostle is always open to new revelation. The vicegerent himself, however, is not open in this way, as he would be were he an apostle.

---

372. Ibid., VI:90.

When he legislates he propounds only such knowledge and judgments as conform to what the Apostle was given. Thus, outwardly, he is a follower, not an equal, like the other apostles. Consider how the Jews believed in and confirmed Jesus so long as they thought that he had brought no more than Moses, as in the case of the regency today in relation to the Apostle. When, however, he enlarged on or abrogated a judgment established by Moses, Jesus being an apostle, they could not tolerate that, since he was contradicting their preconceptions about him. The Jews were ignorant of the truth of the matter and so demanded his execution, the story being told to us by God in His mighty Book. Being an apostle, he was open to new revelation, either limiting an established judgment or adding to it, limitation being something added, without doubt. The vicegerency today is not of this kind, since only rulings arrived at by personal judgment may be limited or added to, not the Law promulgated on the lips of Muḥammad.

Sometimes a regent might say something that appears to contradict some tradition on a judgment, and it might be imagined that this stems from personal judgment, while it does not. In such a case, the leader in question is not inwardly sure about the apostolic tradition, otherwise he would judge according to it. If, indeed, it is the sort of tradition that is transmitted by one honest man from another, such a one is not immune from fancy or notional transmission. Such things happen today to a viceregent, as they will happen also to Jesus. For when he comes again, he will abolish many established rulings based on personal judgments, clarifying thereby the truth revealed to Muḥammad, and not least in the case of community leaders contradicting each other on a single revelation. We know, of course, that, were a revelation to be sent on the matter, it would agree with one of the conflicting opinions, and that would be the divine judgment on the matter, all else being corroborative, if confirmed by the Reality, so that this Community might be relieved of stress and that God's judgment might be spread throughout it.

As for the saying, "If allegiance is paid to two caliphs, then kill the second," this applies only to the outer vicegerency, which wields the sword.[373] Indeed, even if the two caliphs agree together, one of them must be executed. This is not the case with the spiritual vicegerency, in which no killing is involved, such action being applicable

---
373. Muslim, XXXIII:61.

only to the outer form. This matter of killing in the outer caliphate, which, although it does not enjoy the status of the inner, nevertheless is representative of the Apostle of God, if it be just, must be inspired by the imagined possibility of two gods; *If there were in them gods apart from God, they would bring about corruption,*[374] even if they agreed together. However, we know that if, for the sake of argument, they disagreed, the ruling of one of them would be carried out, so that he would be the god rather than the other.

From this one may deduce that every ruling carried into effect in the world today is the decision of God, since it is only God's decisions that have any effect, in reality, even if it seems to go against the outer established ruling called the Law. That is because everything that happens in the Cosmos is according to the ruling of the divine Will and not [necessarily] in accordance with the rulings of established Law, even though its very establishment derives from the divine Will. Its establishment was brought about in a particular way, the divine Will being concerned with its confirmation (by actualization), but not with guaranteeing its being acted on. The authority of the divine Will is immense, so that Abū Ṭālib al-Makkī[375] called it the Throne of the Essence, since for Itself it determines the effectiveness of the divine decision. Indeed, nothing occurs or fails to occur in existence without the divine Will. When the divine Command appears to be contradicted by what is called "disobedience," it is because it is an indirect [through the medium of prophets or angels] command and not the Existential Command. In the context of the command of the divine Will, no one can ever oppose God in anything He does. That may happen only in the case of the indirect command, so understand. In truth, the Will is concerned only to create the act itself and is not concerned with the agent. Thus, it would be absurd for it not to come into being. In particular instances, however, it may be seen as disobeying God's command, while in others it is regarded as conforming to His command, eliciting praise or blame, as the case may be. If then the matter is as we have said, then all creatures come eventually to felicity, of whatever kind it may be. This is explained by the fact that the Mercy embraces all things and takes precedence over His Wrath, that which precedes going first. When something conditioned by the latter encounters it, the former then takes over

---

374. *Qur'an*, XXI:22.
375. Died A.D. 996, author of the celebrated *Qūt al-qulūb*, Cairo, 1892.

and the Mercy touches it, since no other has precedence. This then is the meaning of the saying that His Mercy precedes His Wrath, conditioning all that comes into contact with it, since it stands at the eventual goal toward which all are traveling. Coming to it is inevitable, so that the attainment of Mercy and the separation from Wrath is also inevitable. The Mercy governs everything that encounters it, according as each thing's state dictates.

> Whoever understands, is witness to what we say,
>   But he who does not is assailed by anxiety.
> There is naught but what we have mentioned, so trust,
>   And be of our own state with respect to it.
> What we have experienced of it we have rehearsed to you,
>   And you have from us what we have given you.

As for the "softening of iron,"[376] it means that hardened hearts are softened by admonishment and warning, as iron is softened by fire. "Difficulty" refers to hearts harder than stone, stone being split and calcified, not softened by fire. He softened the iron for him only so that he could work protective armor from it, as a sign from God. In other words, something may be protected against only by itself, so that one is protected from spears, swords, and knives by armor. Thus in the dispensation of Muḥammad, it is said, "I seek refuge from You in You," so understand.[377] This then is the mystery of the softening of iron, and He is the Avenger, the Merciful, the Giver of grace.

---

376. Cf. *Qur'an*, XXXIV:10.
377. Cf. ibid., IX:118.

CHAPTER XVIII

THE WISDOM OF BREATH IN THE WORD OF JONAH

INTRODUCTORY NOTE

The name of the prophet Jonah is in the title of this chapter because the story of the rescue of Jonah from the belly of the whale and the sparing by God of the citizens of Nineveh helps to illustrate the main theme of the chapter, which is the special nature of the human state and the importance of preserving its life at all costs.

As mentioned in the Introduction, Islam, in keeping with the spirit of all major religious traditions, sees the human state as a special one, being as it is microcosmic, which is to say that it reflects both cosmic and divine realities, part angel, part animal. The Sufis described man as the "Isthmus" [*barzakh*] between God and the Cosmos, that essential link between the Creator and His creation, that all-important medium by which God perceives Himself as manifested in the Cosmos, and by which the Cosmos recognizes its source in God, but which, in isolation, without its cosmic or spiritual reference, is nothing but an absurdity.

Thus the human state, the epitome of which is the Perfect Man, is at once extremely precious and to be valued above all other states of existence, and also pathetic and nonsensical in that, outside the context of the God-Cosmos polarity, it is neither one thing nor the other; indeed, it is nothing at all.

THE BEZELS OF WISDOM

The goal of all human life is the realization of the perfection and completeness implicit and potential in the human state, so that each human birth presents yet another precious opportunity for the fulfillment of one's original potential to be, on the one hand, the faithful representative of cosmic servanthood and, on the other, the perfect transmitter of spiritual dominion. Thus, in this chapter, Ibn al-'Arabī is concerned to show how important it is, both for God and for man, to preserve each human life, as far as is possible, and to destroy it only when human actions effectively cancel the privilege attendant on that state.

As our author says, one of the aims of this human opportunity should be to become, as far as possible, the perfect instrument for God's Self-awareness in the reflected image that is the Cosmos. The best way of doing this, indeed the best of all human acts, is the remembrance [dhikr] of God, not only by mentioning His Name with one's tongue alone, but by imbuing every member and condition with that remembrance, since God is with and remembers everything that remembers Him. Conversely, that human being who completely forgets God has forgotten himself, that is his humanity, as being also divine, so that he forfeits that state and becomes "the lowest of the low" [XCV:5], dissipated and dispersed in the infinite multiplicity of the Cosmos, since it is only by that divine spark within him that he may preserve his unity and integrity as man.

In conclusion, Ibn al-'Arabī discusses the subject of death itself and the states of the Afterlife. He maintains that death, far from being an end—since how can that which is, in truth, nothing other than He come to an end—is rather the dispersal of the various elements and aspects making up this human synthesis and their reassimilation, each to its own kind. Thus, the personal identity and consciousness becomes fully, once again, what it always has been in reality, namely, His Identity, while the various constituent parts of the physical body revert to their original cosmic states, being themselves no more than aspects of His Form. Thus there can be no loss or oblivion in any real sense, seeing that all is nothing other than He Who never dies.

Following on from the subject of death, Ibn al-'Arabī points out that, since the divine Wrath is subordinate to the divine Mercy, the punishment of Hell in the Hereafter cannot be eternal or unmitigated, seeing that all are ultimately and inexorably on the Straight Path, obedient to the divine Will and returning inescapably to their source in Him. Our salvation, therefore, lies ultimately in the inalienable re-

IBN AL-'ARABĪ

ality of the Oneness of Being. According to several of the Sufi masters, even Satan himself had only the best motives for disobeying God's command to prostrate before Adam, in that, perceiving only the ephemeral in man, he could not bring himself to associate what he saw as contingent with God. Thus it is, in truth, only our illusory perception and experience of otherness that is our pain, death, and damnation.

THE WISDOM OF BREATH IN THE WORD OF JONAH

Know that this human creation, in all its spiritual, physical, and psychic perfection, was created by God in His own image, and that none but He has charge of its dissolution, whether by His hand, which is always the case, or by His command. Whoever takes it on himself without God's command wrongs his own soul, transgresses the bounds of God, and seeks the destruction of him whose proper functioning God has ordered. Indeed, solicitude in caring for God's servants is better than [killing them from an excessive] zeal for God.

David desired to build the Holy House and did so several times. However, every time he finished it, it fell down in ruins. When he complained of that to God, God revealed to him, "My House shall not be raised by the hand of one who has spilt blood." David then said, "O Lord, was it not done in Your cause?" God said to him, "Indeed, but are they not My servants?" Then David said, "O Lord, let it then be built by one who is of me." God then revealed to him that his son Solomon would build it.[378]

The moral here concerns the proper maintenance of this human creation, and that its raising up is better than its destruction. Have you not considered how God has ordained the poll tax and the truce for dealing with enemies of the Faith, so that He might spare them? He says, *If they incline to peace, incline to it yourselves and trust in God.*[379] Have you not also considered how, in the case of retaliation, the injured party is encouraged to exact a ransom or to forgive, and that only if he refuses these may the man be killed? Indeed, when there are many injured parties, one of whom is ready to accept payment

---

378. Cf. II Samuel, chap. 6.
379. *Qur'an*, VIII:61.

while the others insist on execution, it is the former, rather than the latter, whose decision is accepted, thus averting the death of the wrongdoer. Also, the Apostle said of the owner of the thong, "If he kills him, he is then no better than he."[380] God says, *The recompense of one evil is an evil like it,*[381] referring to retaliation as an evil action, even though it is legal; *but whoever forgives and does good, his reward is with God,*[382] because he is in His image. So, whoever forgives and does not kill will be rewarded by Him in Whose image he is, since He has most right to him, having created him for that [to be in His image]. This is because God is manifest in the name, the Outer, only through his existence, that whoever preserves him, preserves God.

Man is not blameworthy in himself, but only because of the act that proceeds from him. This act is not the same as his [human] self, and it is of this that we are speaking. Although there is no act [in truth] but God's, some are considered worthy of blame, while others are praised. To pronounce blame for one's own purpose is itself blameworthy in God's sight, since only that which the Law blames is truly blameworthy. The censure of the Law is a wisdom that only God or one who He has taught knows, just as He has ordained retaliation in the interests of preserving humankind and as a deterrent to one who would transgress God's bounds. *In retaliation there is life for you, O you who are intelligent.*[383] Such are the ones who perceive the essence of things and who have discovered the secrets of God's laws. When you have realized that God has care of this human creation and its rearing, you yourself should care for it all the more, which will bring you felicity. That is because, while a man still has life, he has the opportunity to achieve that perfection for which he was created, so that whoever tries to destroy him is seeking to prevent his achieving that for which he was made.

How fine was the saying of the Apostle of God, "Shall I tell you of something much better than engaging the enemy, attacking them and being attacked by them; it is the remembrance of God."[384] That is because only he who remembers God properly appreciates the true worth of this human creation, for it is God Who is the companion of one who remembers Him, and the companion is perceived by the one

---

380. Muslim, XXVIII:32.
381. *Qur'an*, XLII:40.
382. Ibid.
383. Ibid., II:179.
384. Nasā'ī, XXV:24.

who remembers. If the remember does not perceive God, Who is his companion, then he is not a true rememberer, since the remembrance of God flows throughout every part of the [true] servant. This does not mean one who invokes Him with his tongue only, so that only the tongue perceives Him, which is not the same as the perception of the whole man. You should try to understand the mystery implicit in the remembrance of those that are really forgetful. Indeed, that part of the forgetful man which invokes God is undoubtedly present with God, and the one remembered is its companion. The forgetful person [as a whole], however, is not remembering, and He does not accompany one who is heedless.

Man is multiple and not single of essence, while God is single of Essence, but multiple with respect to the divine Names. So also is man of many parts, and the remembering by one part does not imply the remembering by any other part of him. God is with that part which is remembering Him, the rest being described as forgetful. It is necessary that there should be some part of a man that is remembering God and with which God is present, so that the rest of him might survive by His care [for that one part]. The Reality does not, as death, have charge of the destruction of this creation, since it is not a matter of extinction so much as one of severance. God takes him to Himself, *And to Him does the whole matter return.*[385]

When God takes him to Himself, He fashions for him a composite body, not the physical body, of a kind appropriate to the realm to which he has been transferred, which is that of eternal life by virtue of the equilibrium there. There he will never die, nor will his parts be separated again.

As for the dwellers in the Fire, they will indeed eventually attain to felicity, but in the Fire itself, since, after the period of punishment, the Fire must needs become cool and safe, which is their felicity. The felicity of those in the Fire, after the fulfillment of certain rights [of punishment], is similar to that of Abraham when he was thrown into the fire. He was tortured by the sight of it and by what he was accustomed to think of it, being quite sure that it was something that would harm anything that came near it, being ignorant of God's purpose in it for him. However, after all these [mental] tortures, he found it cool and safe, despite what he saw of its color and form. To the people there it appeared as fire, showing that one and the same thing

---

385. *Qur'an*, XI:33.

may appear differently to the various observers of it. Such is the Self-manifestation of God.

Either one may say that God manifests Himself like that or that the Cosmos, being looked at and into, is like God in His Self-manifestation. It is various in the eye of the beholder according to the makeup of that beholder, or it is that the makeup of the beholder is various because of the variety of the manifestation. All this is possible with respect to the [divine] realities. If it were the case that any dead or killed person did not return to God when he died, God would not bring about the death of anyone or command his execution. All is within His grasp, so that there can never be any [real] loss. He commands execution and decrees death, secure in the knowledge that His servant can never escape Him, but returns to Him, as in His saying, *To Him does the whole matter revert*,[386] meaning that all disposal rests with Him, the Disposer, nor is there anything not of His Essence outside Him. Indeed, His Identity is the essence of each thing, which is what inspired the words, *To Him does the whole matter revert.*

---

386. Ibid., XI:123.

CHAPTER XIX

THE WISDOM OF THE UNSEEN IN THE WORD OF JOB

INTRODUCTORY NOTE

The chapter opens with an explanation of the all-embracing nature of the Reality. It is pointed out that God is to be found not only in what is "high," "above," and "lofty," but also in what is traditionally thought of as profane, "low," "below," and "beneath," so that *wherever you turn, there is the face of God* [II:115]. Thus, although the "blowing" breath and radiating light of the Spirit enlivens, it cannot do so without the receptive matrix of the "water" of Nature, which underlies and supports the living structure of the Cosmos [Throne]. Although the Spirit is the spark of the life of Reality, lowly and passive Nature is, correspondingly, the primordial stuff of that life without which no formal life is possible. Indeed, according to the logic of Ibn al-'Arabī's teaching, there is nothing in existence that is not alive in some way or another, since that which is nothing other than He cannot be dead. As he says later in the chapter, we, as Cosmos and creatures, as ephemeral, lowly beings, are in reality His form, while He is, through His all-pervading Spirit, our identity, so that there is nothing at all of which it can be said truly that it is not He.

Before going on to consider the plight of Job and its lesson for us, Ibn al-'Arabī briefly touches on the question of equilibrium and harmony as between the two great currents of cosmic creation and divine reintegration, between His Wrath and His Compassion. He suggests that the question may be resolved only in the ineffable Oneness of Being Itself, but not in our human state, oscillating as it does between the imperative of the divine Wish and the creative impulsion of the creative Will, and in which overemphasis on what is considered "good" inevitably causes imbalance with respect to what is considered "bad," albeit that it exists, by the Will of God.

In discussing Job's plight, our author suggests that true patience is not simply the stubborn refusal to voice a complaint, but rather that it is the intelligent refusal to be tempted by the illusion that any other but God is able to bring relief of suffering. Indeed, supplication to God is, for him, not a sign of impatience, but rather an indication of the essential reciprocity between himself and God, God in him and he in God. Furthermore, suffering is a test and a stimulus from God to awaken His servant to the reality of this relationship, so that failure to respond with supplication is tantamount to heedlessness of His Reality.

THE WISDOM OF THE UNSEEN IN THE WORD OF JOB

Know that the secret of life permeates water, which is itself the origin of the elements and the four supports. Thus did God make *of water every living thing.*[387] There is nothing, indeed, that is not living, just as there is nothing that does not sing God's praises, even if we do not understand its praises, except by divine disclosure. Only the living can offer praise. Therefore, everything is living and everything has its origin in water.

Have you not considered the Throne, how it rests on the water and derives from it? It floats on the water, which supports it from beneath. In the same way, after God had created man as a servant, he became arrogant and aspired to be above Him. In spite of this God supports this servant's "loftiness" from beneath, ignorant as he is of himself, alluded to in his [the Prophet's] saying, "Even if you let down a rope it will fall upon God."[388] This shows that God may be

---

387. *Qur'an*, XXI:30.
388. Tirmidhī, V:58.

IBN AL-'ARABĪ

thought of as "below," as also "above" in His saying, *They fear their Lord above them*,[389] and His saying, *He overcomes His servants*.[390] All below and above belong to Him. Thus, the six directions are manifest only through man, who is in the image of the Merciful.

There is no source of sustenance but God. He said, concerning a group of people, *If they had only abided by the Torah and the Gospel*, going on to be less definite and more general, saying, *and what was revealed to them from their Lord*, which includes all judgments revealed through the apostles and inspired ones. He went on to say, . . . *they would have eaten from above them*, referring to the sustenance from above attributed to Him, *and from below their feet*,[391] which is the sustenance from below that He attributes to Himself on the lips of His Apostle, who transmits His word by His authority.

Were the Throne not on the water, its existence could not be maintained, since the living can be kept in being only by life. Consider how, when someone living dies a normal death, the various parts of his composition break down and his powers are extinguished.

God said to Job, *Urge with your foot, for this is a washing place*,[392] in other words "cool" water, because of the extreme heat of his pain, which God soothed with the coolness of the water. Thus, it is for medicine to lessen that which has increased and to increase that which has grown less, in order to achieve an equilibrium that, however, can be achieved only approximately. We say approximately because evidence of the realities indicates that the act of creation, which occurs with the breaths eternally, constitutes an imbalance in Nature that might be called a deviation or alteration. Similarly, in God there is a desire that is an inclination toward the particular object of desire to the exclusion of any other. Harmony and equilibrium are everywhere sought, but never [truly] achieved. We are thus denied the rule of equilibrium.

In the divine knowledge brought by the prophets, God is described as pleased, angry, and by other attributes. Now pleasure causes anger to cease, while anger brings pleasure to an end. Equilibrium might be said to be the mutual balance of pleasure and anger. However, one who is pleased with someone else is not also angry

---

389. *Qur'an*, XVI:50.
390. Ibid., VI:61.
391. Ibid., V:66.
392. Ibid., XXXVIII:42.

with him, being thought of as one or the other, which indicates a preference. It is the same the other way round. We point this out for the benefit of anyone who might think that the people of the Fire suffer God's Wrath eternally and never enjoy His pleasure, which shows the validity of what we have said. If, on the other hand, as we have also said, the dwellers in the Fire, while remaining in the Fire, are eventually relieved of their tortures, then that is pleasure. Now wrath comes to an end with the alleviation of their pain, since the reality underlying pain is the same as the reality of anger, the angry one being a sufferer who is only trying to avenge himself on the object of his anger by hurting him, so that he might gain relief by passing the suffering he experiences on to the object of his anger.

When one considers the Reality in His transcendence from the Cosmos, then He is far removed from such notions thus limited [by human experience]. If, however, the Reality is the Identity of the Cosmos, then all determinations are manifest from Him and in Him, as in His saying, *The whole matter reverts to Him*,[393] in reality and through spiritual disclosure, and *Worship Him and trust in Him*,[394] from the standpoint of veiled consciousness. Indeed, there is naught in the realm of possibility more wonderful than this Cosmos, which is in the image of the Merciful and which God created in order that His being might become manifest through its appearance. Likewise, man became manifest through the coming into being of the form of Nature.

We are His outer form, while Identity is the directing spirit of that form. That direction can be only in Him and of Him, for He is the First, essentially, and the Last, formally. He is the Outer with respect to the changing of determination and states, the Inner with respect to directing, and *He knows everything.*[395] He is aware of everything and knows by direct perception, not by any deductive thought process, just as spiritual awareness is not achieved by thought. Such is true knowing, all else being guesswork and conjecture, and not knowledge in its true sense.

Job, therefore, was given that water to drink to relieve the anguish of his thirst, which stemmed from the fatigue and distress with which Satan had afflicted him. In other words, he was too far re-

---

393. Ibid., XI:123.
394. Ibid.
395. Ibid., VI:101.

moved from the realities to see them as they are, the perception of which would have put him into a situation of proximity. Everything perceived is close to the eye, even if it be physically remote, for the sight makes contact with it by perception, or else does not perceive it at all. Either that or the object itself makes contact with the sight. There is therefore a certain proximity between the perception and the perceived. Job, however, attributed his affliction to Satan, although it was close to him, saying, "That which is far from me is close to me by reason of its power within me." You know, of course, that distance and proximity are relative notions, having no existence in themselves, despite their quite definite effects on that which is distant and near.

Know that there is a mystery of God in Job, whom He has made a lesson for us and recorded as a story that this Community of Muhammad reads, that it might learn what is in it and become ennobled by contact with its subject, Job.[396] God commends Job for his patience, in spite of his supplication to Him to remove the hurt from him. Now, the supplication of a servant in no way detracts from his patience or his being a good servant, as He says, *Surely he was repentant*,[396] meaning that he turned back to God and not to causes. Although the Reality works through a cause, and although the causes contributing to the cessation of the hurt may be many, the Causer is single. The resorting of the servant to the One Who alleviates the hurt by causes is better than having resort to some particular cause that might not be in accord with God's knowledge concerning the hurt. He might say, "God does not answer me," while he has not called on Him, having merely resorted to a particular cause that is not ordained for that period or moment.

Job, being a prophet, acted according to the wisdom of God, knowing as he did that patience, which most men regard as the restraining of the soul from complaint, is not limited, as we also know, to that, but is rather the restraining of the soul from complaint to what is other than God, not to God Himself. Most people are misled in their view that the one who complains detracts from his acceptance of destiny thereby. That is not the case, since it is not one's acceptance of destiny that is impaired by complaint to God or any other so much as one's acceptance of the thing predestined. What we have been told, however, does not concern the acceptance of what is des-

---

396. Ibid., XXXVIII:41–44.

tined, since the hurt itself is that which is predestined and not destiny itself. Now Job knew that what was implicit in the restraining of the soul from complaint to God, that He might relieve the affliction, was a resistance to divine compulsion. [Such resistance] reveals an ignorance in the person, when God tests him, as to the real nature of what is afflicting the soul, so that he refrains from calling on God to end his pain. In the view of one who is truly aware, one ought to humble oneself and beg God to raise such a thing from one, since, for the inspired one, that alleviation is an alleviation also for God.

God has, indeed, described Himself in terms of hurt when He says, *those who would hurt God and His Apostle.*[397] What greater hurt is there for Him than that He should try you with some affliction or station unknown to you, so that you might beg Him to relieve it, when you are heedless of Him? It is better that you approach Him with the sense of indigence, which is your true condition, since, by your asking Him to relieve you, the Reality Himself is relieved, you being His outer form.

A certain gnostic was hungry and wept because of it, at which someone who had no insight into such matters upbraided him, to which he replied, "He made me hungry only that I might weep." He means that God tried him with an affliction only so that he might ask Him to relieve it, which in no way detracts from his patience, which is the restraining of the soul from complaint to what is other than God. By other than God is meant some particular aspect of God, since He has specified a particular aspect, the aspect of Identity, by which you should call on Him to relieve your distress, and not by other aspects that are called "causes." The latter are nothing other than He as constituting the [principle of creative] particularization in Himself. In asking the Identity of God [God Himself] to lift the affliction from him, the gnostic is well aware that all causes are in Him in particular ways.

This way [of knowing] may be the privilege of only the discreet among God's servants, those worthy to be entrusted with the mysteries of God, for He has trusty servants whom only He knows and who know each other. Thus we have counseled you; so act and ask of Him, may He be exalted.

---

397. Ibid., XXXIII:57.

CHAPTER XX

THE WISDOM OF MAJESTY IN THE WORD OF JOHN

INTRODUCTORY NOTE

The name for John in Arabic, *Yaḥyā*, provides Ibn al-'Arabī with yet another opportunity to find mystical significance in the construction of words. The Arabic name *Yaḥyā* means, as an ordinary Imperfect Indicative verb form, "he lives." What he means is that the father, in this case Zakariah, lives on, essentially in the son, John, or, by extension, that each prophet lives on in the prophet who succeeds him. In the case of Zakariah and John, the physical and the spiritual lines of descent are combined. That is because, as he sees it, the son represents so to speak the embodied essence or seed of his father, in which embodiment both his seed and his name are continued from one generation to the next and thus remembered. As we have seen, in discussing the various modalities of the Spirit [Chap. 15], seed-essence, idea-identity, and word-name are closely related concepts, albeit representing the spiritual reality at different levels of existence. Thus the physical deposition of the seed in the "water" of the mother to produce the son is also a concrete symbol, in the Sufi context, of the spiritual implanting of the divine Name into the worldly mind of the aspirant by way of initiating him into a new life of the spirit, in order to perpetuate the invocation [memory] of His Name [Essence], or of the inspiration of Revelation into the virgin mind of the prophet, to produce a new community of faith and remembrance.

Taking the argument further, we come to the notion that the son, whether spiritual or physical, is essentially identical with the father. It is this notion that underlies the distinction Ibn al-'Arabī makes between John and Jesus, since the relationship of the former to the Spirit is indirect, through his father, while that of the latter is direct, the spiritual seed having been deposited without the intermediary of the human male. For him, this distinction, which he bases on words from the Qur'an [XIX:15 and XIX:33], illustrates the difference between the learning- ['ilm] based faith of the believer and the gnosis-based experience of Identity of the saint-gnostic. In the qur'anic verses quoted, John is blessed by God, in the third person, while Jesus, as a token of Identity, calls down the blessing on himself, after bearing witness to the innocence of his mother, Mary, as being symbolic of the total receptivity of Nature to the act of the Spirit.

THE WISDOM OF MAJESTY IN THE WORD OF JOHN

This is the wisdom of precedence with respect to names, since God names him Yahyā [John], which is to say that the memory of Zakariah lives [yahyā) on through him; *And We did not name anyone before him with that name.*[398] He combined in himself both the attribute [of Prophecy] inherent in all those that have passed on, but whose memory lives on in a son, and the distinction of being named in that way.

He named him John [Yahyā] and his [father's] name lives on like true knowledge, for Adam's memory lived on through Seth, Noah's through Shem, and likewise with other prophets. However, God had never, before John, combined a self-explanatory name with the attribute, except from concern for Zakariah when he said, *Give me from Yourself an heir.*[399] Here he places God before his son, just as Āsiyah mentions the "neighbor" [God] before the "house," saying, [*O my Lord, build for me*] *with You a dwelling in Paradise.*[400]

---

398. *Qur'an*, XIX:7.
399. Ibid., XIX:5.
400. Ibid., LXVI:11. Āsiyah is the name traditionally given to the wife of Pharaoh.

IBN AL-'ARABĪ

So God honored him by fulfilling his need and named him by His attribute so that his name became a reminder of what His prophet Zakariah had asked of Him, since he had stressed the continuance of the remembrance of God in his offspring, a son being the secret essence of his father. ... *who will inherit from me and from the people of Jacob*,[401] being none other than the inheritance of the state of God's remembrance and supplication to Him. Then He tells him of the well-being bestowed on him the day he was born, the day he would die, and the day he would be brought forth living. Here He uses the word "life," which is [the meaning of] his name and informs Zakariah of His bestowal of well-being on his son. God's speech is true and conclusive.

If the [revealing] Spirit had said, *Well-being be upon me the day I was born, the day I will die and the day I am brought forth living*,[402] it would better have expressed the [state of] identity. It is, however, better in that it combines the notion of identity and belief, which is less susceptible to misinterpretation. What was unusual and remarkable in the case of Jesus was his ability to speak [in the cradle], since, in making him articulate, God made his intelligence perfect and effective. It does not follow that everyone thus enabled to speak is sincere in what he says, except one who is attested, like John.

The divine well-being bestowed on John is less susceptible to ambiguity with respect to the divine concern for him than that of Jesus, which he pronounced on himself, even though the situation indicates his proximity to God and sincerity in the matter, since, in speaking in the cradle, he was seeking only to prove the innocence of his mother. Other evidence of this is the dried-up trunk of the palm tree that dropped fresh fruit without being fertilized by the male, just as Mary bore Jesus without the normal sexual union with a male.[403]

Were some prophet to say that his sign and miracle was that a certain wall should speak, and were that wall to say that he was a liar and that he was not the apostle of God, the sign by itself would be valid and would confirm his apostleship, no attention being paid to what the wall actually said.

Since then such a possibility [of misunderstanding] is implicit in the speaking by Jesus in his cradle, when referred to by his mother,

---

401. Ibid., XIX:6.
402. Ibid., XIX:33. These are words uttered by Jesus in the Qur'an.
403. Ibid., XIX:23–34.

the divine well-being bestowed on John is less ambiguous in this respect. Such evidence that he is the servant of God is necessary because of those that assert that he is the son of God, the speaking in the cradle being sufficient in itself. Those who assert that he was a prophet also regard him as the servant of God. There will remain certain possibilities of misunderstanding until, in the future, his veracity with respect to all he uttered in the cradle will become clear; so realize what we have touched on here.

CHAPTER XXI

THE WISDOM OF DOMINION IN THE WORD OF ZAKARIAH

INTRODUCTORY NOTE

The main theme of this chapter is the relationship between the creative Mercy and the objects of its creativity in general, and with the divine Names in particular. The eternal essences of all possible created beings, containing essentially, as they do, all the possible multiplicity and complexity of cosmic state and experience, yearn with the yearning of God to become knowable as existing objects of the Self-consciousness of the divine Subject. As has already been shown, the response to this yearning, this metacosmic labor, is the relieving exhalation of the Breath of the Merciful, which releases the possibilities inherent in the latent essences into the infinite display of cosmic existence.

The first thing that must happen is for the Breath itself to come into being, after which the very principle of objectivity must be established, which Ibn al-'Arabī calls "thingness" [*shai'iyyah*], thus bringing about the polarity Subject-object, both universally as God-Cosmos and particularly as Lord-servant. It is this latter objectivization of the "thing" as servant, as being of the utmost importance for any relationship between latent essence and existential becoming, that probably prompts Ibn al-'Arabī to say, a little later in the chapter, that the "god created in belief" is the first recipient of the Mercy, which concept is very closely related to that of Lord-servant [cf. Chap. 12].

It may seem strange, at first, that Ibn al-'Arabī should speak of the divine Names as things, until it is realized that everything that has anything to do with the creative act, which appears to situate an object outside the divine Essence as something "other," is therefore itself involved in otherness and therefore also in thingness. Now, the divine Names, as has already been mentioned, are precisely various facets of the principle that determines the nature and quality of the relationship, whether individually as Lord-servant or universally as God-Cosmos. They therefore share in the thingness of all existential factors. However, although various and many in existence, they all name the One Named, just as all essences are essentially His Essence, the inevitable return to which is the task of that other obligating "inhaling" Mercy which seeks to resolve thingness in Identity and Uniqueness [cf. Chap. 16].

Finally, that Breath of divine relief without which there would be no Cosmos to experience is the directing Mistress of all becoming, harboring eternally the Mercy of reintegration within Herself.

THE WISDOM OF DOMINION IN THE WORD OF ZAKARIAH

Know that the Mercy of God encompasses everything existentially and in principle, and that the Wrath [of God] exists only by virtue of God's Mercy on it. His Mercy has precedence over His Wrath, which is to say that Mercy is attributed to Him before Wrath. Since every [latent] essence has an existence that it seeks from God, His mercy must embrace every essence, for the Mercy by which He is Merciful accepts the desire of the essence for existence and so creates it. We therefore say that His Mercy encompasses everything existentially and in principle. The divine Names are "things" and stem from one essence.[404]

The first object of God's all-encompassing Mercy is the thingness of that essence which creates the Mercy through the Mercy. There-

---

404. As being objects of the divine Mercy.

fore, the first object of the Mercy's encompassing is itself, then the thingness referred to, and then the thingness of every created being, to infinity, whether of this world or the next, accidental or substantial, complex or simple, without any consideration of purpose or suitability, since the Divine Mercy embraces existentially the suitable and unsuitable alike.

As we have mentioned in *The Meccan Revelations*, only that which is nonexistent exerts influence, and not that which is existent.[405] If the latter seems to exert an influence, it is only by the authority of that which is nonexistent. This knowledge is strange and the question [here considered] is rarely discussed. Only men of imagination may understand it through the spiritual sensitivity they possess, while those devoid of imagination are far from such an understanding.

> The Mercy of God flows in [all] created beings,
>   and courses through the selves and essences.
> The rank of Mercy is the epitome to those who perceive [directly]
>   Sublime to those of discursive minds.

Everything designated by the Mercy is fortunate; there is, however nothing that is not so designated. In designating things, the Mercy creates them, every created thing being the object of Mercy. O friend, do not be distracted from grasping what we are saying by what you observe of afflicted people or what you may believe regarding the torments of the Hereafter which eternally afflict the condemned.

Know that Mercy is inherent in all creating, so that, by the mercy bestowed on pain, pain was created [brought into existence]. Mercy is effective in two ways: first, its effect by essence, which is the bringing into existence of every created essence without regard to purpose or lack of it, suitability or otherwise, having regard only to the essence of every created thing as it is before being brought into existence. Indeed, it beholds it in its latent state, so that it sees "the god created in belief" as one of many latent potentialities on which it bestows mercy by bringing it into existence. We therefore say that, after the Mercy Itself, "the god created in belief" is the first recipient

---

405. *Futūhāt*, I, pp. 275–276.

of Mercy, which has to do with the creation of all created beings. Second, its effect [is] by petition, since the veiled ones, in their belief, ask God to have mercy on them, while the truly inspired ones ask that God's Mercy remain with them. They ask it in God's name, saying, "O God, have mercy on us!"[406] although it is only the remaining of the Mercy with them that is the mercy upon them.

The Mercy has determining power, which really belongs only to the reality conceived of as being inherent in a situation, so that it is, in reality, the Merciful one [the agent], since God has mercy on His intended servants only by the Mercy. When it comes on them, they experience its control in an immediate way. He whom the Mercy remembers, it has mercy upon. The Active Participle is both *raḥīm* and *rāḥim*.

The determining power itself cannot be thought of as a creation, since it is something the [spiritual] concepts [of Name and attribute] require essentially. Indeed, the states (of the Names and attributes) cannot be said to be existent or nonexistent. In other words they are simply relationships, having no true existence. Nor can they be regarded as nonexistent with respect to the determining power, seeing that that in which knowledge resides is called a knower, which is a state. Thus a knower is an essential reality attributed with knowledge. It is not that essence itself, nor the knowledge itself, there being in truth only knowledge and that essence in which the knowledge resides. Being a knower is a state of that essence brought about by its being attributed with this concept [of knowledge]. This attribution of knowledge happens to it, so that it is called a knower. Thus Mercy is, in reality, an attribution of the Merciful that necessitates control, being indeed that which is merciful. He Who causes it to exist in the recipient of Mercy does not bring it into existence to have mercy on the recipient by it, but only to have mercy by it on that which resides within it. God is not a locus for phenomena, nor yet a locus for the bringing of mercy into existence. He is the Merciful, and the Merciful is only such by the residing of Mercy within it. Thus is it confirmed that He is the very Mercy Itself.

There are those with no insight or attainment in this matter who dare not say either that He is the Mercy Itself or that He is the attribute itself, but say that He is not the reality [essence] of the attri-

---

406. Cf. *Qur'an*, XXIII:109.

bute or of anything else, since in their view the attributes of God are not He, nor yet other than He. That is because they can neither deny them nor make them the same as Himself. They therefore turn to this expression, which is quite a good one, although some other would have been closer to the mark and less ambiguous, to the effect that the attributes have no essential reality other than that of Him to Whom they are attributed. They are merely relationships and ascriptions relating the One to Whom they are ascribed with their intelligible essences.

Although the Mercy is universal, it is, in relation to each Divine Name, different, so that God is begged for Mercy by every one of His Names. Thus, it is the Mercy of God, as in the words *My Mercy*,[407] which is all-encompassing, and its ramifications are as many as the divine Names themselves. It is not universal [but particular] in relation to a particular divine Name, as one might say, "O Lord, have mercy on me." Such is the case also with other divine Names, so that even in the case of the Name the Avenger, one seeking revenge might say, "O Avenging One, have mercy on me." That is because the Names are referring to the Essence that is named, while referring, in their [particular] realities, to the various ideas they bear. Thus they may all be appealed to for Mercy in that they all refer to the Essence named by each Name and none other, but not in the sense by which it is different and distinct from other Names. Indeed, [in a sense] it is not distinct from the others since, for the suppliant, it is a reference to the Essence, distinct from the others only by its own essence, the connotation given it by usage representing a reality distinct in itself from any other, even though all of them are used to denote one named Essence. There is no doubt that each Name has an authority of its own to be considered, just as consideration is given to the fact that it refers also to the named Essence.

In this connection Abū'l-Qāsim b. Qissi[408] said that every Name, despite its uniqueness, is named by all the other Names, so that when one gives a Name preference, one is qualifying it by all the Names, however many they are, or how various their realities.

Mercy may be acquired in two ways, by obligation, as in His saying, *I will ordain it for those who are God-fearing and give alms*,[409] togeth-

---

407. Cf. ibid., VII:156.
408. Cf. above, p. 88.
409. *Qur'an*, VII:156.

er with the intellectual and practical qualities He attributes to them, or by divine Grace, which is unlike any [human] action, as in His saying, *My Mercy encompasses everything*,[410] so that *He might forgive you your earlier and later sins*,[411] and, "Do what you will, I have forgiven you."[412] So learn!

---

410. Ibid.
411. Ibid., XLVIII:2.
412. Hanbal, II:492.

CHAPTER XXII

THE WISDOM OF INTIMACY IN THE WORD OF ELIAS

INTRODUCTORY NOTE

Ibn al-'Arabī introduces us, in this chapter, to a particularly interesting microcosmic aspect of the fundamental polarity that features so much in his thought, at the same time hinting at the true nature of gnosis. Related to the suprahuman polarity of God-Cosmos, transcendence-immanence, is the corresponding human polarity of natural desire–intellect, both elements of which are capable of experiencing part of the truth about the Reality, but not the synthetic truth of the Oneness of Being. Later in the chapter, he uses the word *wahm* [fancy, delusion] in place of *shahwah* [desire, lust], while, for the intellect, he uses the single word *aql*. Since they pertain, however, to the human state, neither aspect of human experience is itself divine, but merely reflects and serves to manifest suprahuman realities, in keeping with the nature of that state. Thus, although the microcosmic mode and reflection of the divine Spirit in its Wish for reintegration in the Essence, the intellect cannot properly comprehend either the nature of its vital compliment nor the Oneness of which it is a function, but only transcendental and intangible verities. Similarly, vital desire, or the urge to instinctive experience, although it reflects and manifests the urgent imperative of the divine Will to infinite becoming, cannot comprehend either the principle of its mental compliment, or the Oneness in which both are resolved, but only the actualities of natural life. Since, however, the creative Mercy of the divine Will encompasses the obligating Mercy of the divine Wish, the human intellect, as Ibn al-'Arabī says, is rarely free of the influence of natural fancy that is precisely the human expression of that primordial illusion of otherness and multiplicity without which there would be no vital existence.

As in the case of transcendence and immanence, Ibn al-'Arabī points out that over-emphasis on the claims of either natural desire or the intellect results in the possibility of only partial gnosis, which, in its perfection, is nothing other than immediate knowledge and experience of the all-synthesizing Oneness of Being. To be a true gnostic, therefore, it is not enough, as in the case of Elias, to concentrate exclusively on the intellect, purged of vital urges and susceptibilities, but to experience also, as fully as possible, the inarticulate urge of animal life, devoid of thought and precept, which is after all nothing other the divine life of His Form. Indeed, for any true realization of the full potential of the microcosmic state, the two aspects of human experience must work together mutually, the natural life being inspired and commanded by the intellect, the intellect being tempered and conditioned by life, seeing the presence of the Reality in both as reflecting His Life in Spirit and Spirit in Life. For those in whom one aspect predominates over the other, the predominating aspect acts as a veil concealing the realities of the other, thus preventing any true vision of the Reality.

Toward the end of the chapter he returns to the great mystical paradox implicit in the doctrine of the Oneness of Being. He demonstrates it by saying that it is possible for a cause to be the effect of its own effect, a notion that logic of the usual kind finds difficult, to say the least. This paradox is illustrated by his notion of the latent essences, since the creature who is caused to exist by the Creator is, as the latent essential content of God's knowledge, that which causes Him to become "God."

THE WISDOM OF INTIMACY IN THE WORD OF ELIAS

Elias is the same as Idrīs, who was a prophet before Noah whom God had raised to a high rank. He resides at the heart of the [seven] celestial bodies, which is the sun. He was sent to the settlement of Baalbek. Now Baal is the name of an idol and Bek was the ruler of that place, the idol Baal being special to its ruler. Elias, who was Idris, had a vision in which he saw Mount Lebanon, which is from *lubānah*, meaning a need, splitting open to reveal a fiery horse with trappings of fire. When he saw it he mounted it and felt all his lusts fall away from him. Thus be became an intellect without any lust, retaining no link with the strivings of the [lower] soul. In him God was transcendent, so that he had half the gnosis of God. That is because the intellect, by itself, absorbing knowledge in its own way, knows only according to the transcendental and nothing of the immanental. It is only when God acquaints it with His Self-manifestation that its knowledge of God becomes complete, seeing Him as transcendent when appropriate, and as immanent when appropriate, and perceiving the diffusion of God in natural and elemental forms. Indeed, he sees the Essence of the Reality to be their essence. This is complete gnosis, which the Law, sent down from God, brings, all fancies being determined by this gnosis. For this reason fancies have greater power in this human makeup than the intellects, since the intelligent man, however mature his intellect, is never free of fancy and imagination in what he decides on. Indeed, fancy is the greatest authority in this whole human form. Through it there come the revealed decrees, at once comparing and making Him transcendent. By fancy they liken Him in making Him transcendent, and by the intellect they make Him transcendent in likening Him. Each is [inextricably] bound up with the other, so that transcendence cannot be unaffected by likening, or vice versa.

He says, *There is nothing like unto Him,*[413] where He makes transcendent and likens. He says also, *He is the Hearing, the Seeing,*[414] thus likening Himself. Although the former verse is the greatest expression of transcendence, the word "like" shows that it is not unaffected [in principle] by likening. However, He knows Himself best, and this is the way He has expressed Himself. He says further, *May thy Lord, the Lord of might, be exalted beyond what they describe.*[415] That is, they describe Him only according as their intellects dictate. He therefore puts Himself beyond their insistence on His transcendence, because

---

413. *Qur'an*, XLII:11.
414. Ibid.
415. Ibid., XXXVII:170.

such insistence [in fact] limits Him by reason of the inadequacy of the intellect to grasp such things. Then the revealed decrees bring what the fancies determine. Indeed, God is never without an attribute in which He is manifest, as all Scripture attests and reveals. It is in accordance with that that the peoples act, God having bestowed on them His own Self-manifestation, and they are attached to the apostles as an inheritance. They speak as God's apostles speak.

God knows best where to place His message.[416] The words *God knows best* may be seen in either of two ways. First as predicative of "messengers of God," and second as subjective to "where to place His message," each way revealing a [particular] truth. It is for this reason that we speak of likeness in transcendence and transcendence in likeness. Once this is established we let down the covering and draw the veils over the eyes of the skeptic and the dogmatist, even though both are forms in which God manifests Himself. We are ordered to draw the veil in order that the disparity among forms regarding their readiness [to receive the Self-manifestation] might become clear, and to show that He Who manifests Himself in a form does so only according to the degree of receptivity of that form, so that what is attributed to Him [by that form] is only such as its reality and inherent qualities dictate. Such is the case with someone who has a vision of God in his sleep and accepts it as being God Himself without reservation. In this case, the realities and inherent qualities of the form in which He is manifest in sleep pertain to the sleeper. After sleep what was seen while sleeping might be expressed in terms of something other, which will compel the intellect to recognize God's transcendence [beyond that form]. If the one who interprets it is a man of insight and faith, then it need not necessarily be dismissed in favor of transcendence, since such a man can accord what was seen its due share of transcendence and of that in which He was manifest, since [the name] God is, in reality, but a [verbal] expression, for one who understands what I am talking about.

The spirit and essence of this wisdom is that everything may be divided into that which affects and that which is affected, both of which are denoted by certain expressions. That which affects in every way, in every instance, and in every situation is God, while that which is affected in every way, instance, and situation is the Cosmos. When what we have spoken of comes on you, then attach everything

---

416. Ibid., VI:124.

to its appropriate origin, for that which comes on you is inevitable and always derives from some origin, just as the divine Love springs from the superogatory acts performed by His servant. This is an affect that occurs between that which affects and that which is affected, just as God is the hearing, sight, and powers of the servant by virtue of this Love. This is an affect that is confirmed in the Divine Law and cannot be dismissed, if one is a believer. One of good intelligence will either be aware of a divine Self-manifestation in the natural order so that he grasps what we are saying or, as a Muslim and a believer, will simply believe it because it appears in the *Saḥīḥ*.[417] There can be no doubting the power of fancy to prevail over the intellectual enquirer into what God has brought in this saying, since he is a believer. As for one who is not a believer, he tries to overcome fancy with fancy, imagining, in his rational way, that he has invested God with what that Self-manifestation accorded to him in what he saw. In that case, unknown to him, the fancy will never leave him, being ignorant of himself. Concerning this God says, *Call upon Me and I will answer you*,[418] and, *When My servants ask concerning Me, then I am near to respond to the call of the supplicant when he calls upon Me*,[419] for He does not answer unless there be one to call on Him, even though the essence of the supplicant and of Him Who answers is the same.

There is no real conflict implicit in the variety of forms. They are in fact twofold. All these forms are like the limbs of Zaid. It is quite clear that Zaid is a single personal reality, and that his hand does not look like his foot, head, eye, or eyebrow. In other words he is multiple and single, multiple in form and single in essence, just as man is, without doubt, one in his essence. We do not doubt that 'Amr is not Zaid or Khālid or Ja'far, nor that the various individual parts of this one essence are infinite in existence. Thus God, although One in His Essence, is multiple in forms and individual parts.

If you are a believer, you will know that God will manifest Himself on the Day of Resurrection, initially in a recognizable form, then in a form unacceptable [to ordinary belief], and finally back into a form readily recognized [by belief], He alone being, [throughout], the Self-manifesting one in every form, although it is obvious that one form is not the same as another.

---

417. A collection of Traditions.
418. *Qur'an*, XL:60.
419. Ibid., II:186.

THE BEZELS OF WISDOM

It is as if the single Essence were a mirror, so that when the observer sees in it the form of his belief about God, he recognizes and confirms it, but if he should see in it the doctrinal formulation of someone of another creed, he will reject it, as if he were seeing in the mirror His form and then that of another. The mirror is single, while the forms [it reveals] are various in the eye of the observer.

None of the forms are in the mirror wholly, although the mirror has an effect on the forms in one way, and not in another. For instance, it may make the form look smaller, larger, taller, or broader. Thus it has an effect on their proportions, which is attributable to it, although such changes occur only due to the different proportions of the mirrors themselves. Look then, into just one mirror, without considering mirrors in general, for it is the same as your beholding [Him] as being one Essence, albeit that He is beyond all need of the worlds. As being the divine Names, on the other hand, He is like mirrors [in the plural]. In which divine Name have you beheld yourself, or who is the one who beholds? It is only the reality of the Name that is manifest in the beholder. Thus it is, if you will but understand.

Do not distress yourself nor fear, for God loves courage, even if it be in killing a snake, which snake is nothing other than yourself. Now, to a snake, a snake is a snake in form and reality, nor is anything killed by itself.

Even if the human form is corruptible physically, its [essential] character will maintain it, nor will the imagination desert it. If this is how things are, then it is the guarantee, strength, and defense of the essences [of things], and what strength is stronger than this? You imagine, by fancy, that you have killed [yourself], although the [essential] form survives in the intellect and the fancy, according to its [original] definition. Evidence of this is His saying, *You did not shoot when you shot, but it was God Who shot.*[420] The eye [of the observer] perceived only the form of Muḥammad, which to the physical sight clearly appeared to shoot. This is the form to which God firstly denies the act of shooting, which He then goes on to confirm in the act, finally reaffirming that it was God Who shot in the form of Muḥammad. In this matter, faith is very necessary, so consider His effectiveness in that God was sent down in a Muḥammadan form. It is God Himself Who has related this to His servants, not us, but He Himself. Now, His word is true and to believe it is obligatory, whether one

---

420. Ibid., VIII:17.

grasps the significance of what He has said or not, whether one be a learned man or just a believing Muslim.

An indication of the weakness of intellectual speculation is the notion that a cause cannot be [also] the effect of that to which it is a cause. Such is the judgment of the intellect, while in the science of divine Self-revelation it is known that a cause may be the effect of that for which it is a cause. The judgment of the intellect is sound provided that the speculation is clear and thorough. The most that the intellectual will admit to on this matter, when he sees that it contradicts speculative evidence, is that the essence, after it is established that it is one in the many, as a cause, in some form or other, of an effect, cannot be an effect to its effect, so that that effect should become its cause, while it is still a cause, but that its determination becomes changed by its transformation in forms, so that it may thus become an effect to its own effect, which might then become its cause. This then is as far as he will go, when he perceives that the matter does not agree with his rational speculation. If such is the case in the matter of causality, what scope can intellectual speculation have in other more difficult questions?

There have been none more intelligent than the apostles, God's blessings be on them, and what they brought [to us] derived from the divine Majesty. They indeed confirmed what the intellect confirms, but added more that the intellect is not capable of grasping, things the intellect declares to be absurd, except in the case of one who has had an immediate experience of divine manifestation; afterwards, left to himself, he is confused as to what he has seen. If he is a servant of his Lord, he refers his intelligence to Him, but if he is a servant of reason, he reduces God to its yardstick. This happens only so long as he is in this worldly state, being veiled from his other-worldly state in this world.

The gnostics appear in this world as if they were in worldly forms, by reason of its [apparent] effect on them, but God has transformed them inwardly into their other-worldly state, without a doubt. [Veiled] in their forms, they remain unknown except to one whose inner sight God has uncovered to perceive [spiritual reality], nor may anyone know God in His Self-manifestation, except he be in his other-worldly form. He has already been gathered in [for the Hour] in this world, and is brought forth in the grave, for he can see and witness what you cannot, as evidence of God's caring for certain of His servants.

THE BEZELS OF WISDOM

Whoever wishes to discover this Wisdom of Elias and Idris, which God established twice, then let him know that Idris was a prophet before Noah, and was then raised up and sent down again [as Elias]. Thus, God gave him two missions. He lets him descend from the realm of his intellect to that of his lust until he becomes a pure animal, experiencing what every beast experiences, apart from the *two heavy ones*[421] [man and jinn]. Then he will know that he has realized his animality. Such a one may be recognized by two signs. The first is this revelation, so that he sees who is to be punished and who rewarded in the grave, and sees the dead man as living, the dumb speaking, and the sitting, walking. The second sign is his dumbness, so that even if he wanted to speak of what he sees, he cannot do so. It is this that makes him realize [to the full] his animality. We once had a disciple who had such an experience, but he did not remain dumb and so did not fully realize his animality. When God established me in this station, I realized my animality to the full. I saw things and I wanted to express what I saw, but could not do so, being no different from those who cannot speak. When he has realized all this, he will be transformed into pure intellect, bereft of natural matter. Then he will see things that are at the source of what is manifest in natural forms and will know in an immediate way the origin of this [divine] regime in the forms of nature. If he discovers that Nature is the same as the Breath of the Merciful, then he has received a great favor. If, however, he realizes no more than what we have mentioned, so much gnosis will be enough to condition his intellect. He will then be one of the gnostics and will know experientially [the truth of His saying], *You did not kill them, but God killed them,*[422] since it was only the iron and the striker who killed them and He Who is behind these forms. All in all, the killing and the shooting happened. Thus, the gnostic sees things in principle and in forms, so being complete [in his knowing]. If, in addition to that, he sees the Breath [of the Merciful], he is perfect as well as complete [in his knowing]. He sees only God as being that which he sees, perceiving the seer to be the same as the seen. This is enough, and God is the giver of grace, the Guide.

---

421. Ibid., LV:31.
422. Ibid., VIII:17.

CHAPTER XXIII

THE WISDOM OF VIRTUE IN THE WORD OF LUQMĀN

INTRODUCTORY NOTE

Another way Ibn al-'Arabī has of trying to explain the mutuality and interdependence of the concepts "God" and "Cosmos" is to describe the relationship in alimentary terms. Food is that which is taken into one's body to be disseminated and assimilated for the sustaining of life. At the beginning of this chapter, he says that we, as creatures, are food for Him and that He is food for us. In His divinity, as "God" [*Allāh*], He needs the sustenance of our worship, slavery, and contingency, while we, in our servanthood and creatureliness, need the sustenance of His sufficiency, reality, and power. In His essence, as the Supreme Identity [*huwiyyah*], He needs the nourishment of our latent essentiality, while we, in our latency, need the nourishment of His Consciousness.

Later in the chapter, he makes clear the essential difference between his own view of the nature of things and that of Ash'arite theology. While he agrees with their conclusion that the Cosmos is of one substance, he disagrees with the notion, necessary to exoteric theology, that that substance is, ultimately and essentially, other than or separate from the reality of God.

He concludes the chapter with yet another discussion on the relation of multiple parts to the Single Essence, that each part is none other than the Essence, Which is, in turn, the true identity [reality] of each part.

THE WISDOM OF VIRTUE IN THE WORD OF LUQMĀN

Should the deity wish for Himself sustenance,
 Then the whole of existence is food for Him.
Should the deity wish sustenance for us,
 Then He may be food for us, as He wishes.
His Will is His Wish, so say,
 Of it that He has willed it, so it is what is willed.
He wishes increase and He wishes decrease,
 But what He wills is naught but what is willed.
There is this difference between them, so realize,
 Although from another view they are essentially the same.

God has said, *We brought Luqmān the Wisdom*,[423] and whosoever is brought the Wisdom is granted a great boon. Luqmān, therefore, was the possessor of a great boon, according to the Qur'an and God's own witness. Now Wisdom may be expressed [in words] or may be unexpressed, as when Luqmān said to his son, *O my son, consider this tiny mustard seed, which God would bring forth were it to be [hidden] in a rock, whether in heaven or earth.*[424] This is an expressed wisdom, namely that the bringing forth is God's doing, which is confirmed by God in His Book, the saying not being attributed to the one who uttered it. As for the unexpressed wisdom, it is known by the circumstantial indications, the one for whom the seed is brought forth not being mentioned, since he did not say to his son, "God will bring it forth for you or for someone else." He made the bringing forth general and situated what was brought forth in the heavens or in the earth, to draw the attention of the hearer to His saying, *He is God in the heavens and the earth.*[425] By what was expressed and what was unexpressed, Luqmān realized that God is the essence of everything known, "the known" being a more general term than "the thing," being as indefinite as possible. Then he completes the wisdom and fulfills it, so that

---
423. *Qur'an*, XXXI:12.
424. Ibid., XXXI:16.
425. Ibid., VI:3.

its meaning may be perfected, by saying, *Surely, God is Gracious.*[426] It is also of His grace and kindness that He is the essence of the thing, however named or defined, so that it is referred to by its name only by collusion and usage. Thus one speaks of the heaven, the earth, the rock, the tree, the animal, the angel, sustenance or food, the Essence of everything and in everything being One.

The Ash'arites maintain that the Cosmos is substantially homogeneous, being one substance, which is the same as our saying that the Essence is one.[427] They go on to say that its accidents are different, which is the same as our saying that it is various and multiple in its forms and attributions, so that [its parts] might be distinguished [one from another]. One says of this that it is not that, whether in form, accidental nature, or makeup. One may also say that this is the same as that, with respect to substance, so that the same substance is implicit in defining every form and makeup. We say that it is nothing other than God, while the Ash'arites consider that what is called a substance, even if it is a reality, is not the Reality, which is what is meant by those who understand divine revelation and manifestation. This then is the wisdom of His being Gracious.

Then he [Luqmān] describes Him as being "Experienced," which means knowing by experience, as in His saying, *We will surely test you until We know,*[428] indicating knowledge by immediate experience. God, despite His knowledge of things as they are, speaks [here] of Himself as gaining knowledge, and we cannot deny what God has stipulated of Himself. Here God is distinguishing between knowledge acquired by direct [sensory] experience and absolute knowledge, direct experience being restricted to the faculties. He has said of Himself that He is the very powers of his servant in His saying, "I am his hearing," which is one of the servant's faculties, as also "his sight," and his tongue, foot, and hand, which are his members.[429] It is not merely the faculties that are involved, but also the limbs, which together constitute the servant. Thus the essence of that which is called servant is God, which is not to say that the servant himself is [the same as] the master. That is because the attributions of the essence are differentiated, which is not true of that to which they refer.

---

426. Ibid., XXXI:16.
427. Cf. H. A. Wolfson, *The Philosophy of the Kalam*, Harvard, 1976, chap. 2.
428. *Qur'an*, XLVII:31.
429. Bukhārī, LXXXI:38.

THE BEZELS OF WISDOM

In fact there is nothing but His Essence in all attributions, for He is the One Essence endowed with relationships, ascriptions, and attributes.

It is of the Wisdom of Luqmān in instructing his son that he used the two names *the Gracious, the Experienced*[430] to describe God. This wisdom would have been more perfect had he used the word "is" to denote its being in existence. God relates Luqmān's saying notionally, in the sense that he meant that nothing can add increase to Him. His saying, *God, the Gracious, the Experienced* is God's own saying, since God knew of Luqmān [in eternity] that he would have completed the Wisdom, had he uttered it in a more complete way.

As for His saying, *Even if it be the weight of a mustard seed*,[431] it concerns the one whose food it is, being the same as the "speck" mentioned in His saying, *Whoever does a speck's weight of good will see it, and whoever does a speck's weight of evil, will see it also.*[432] [That which feeds on it] is the smallest feeder, and the mustard seed is the smallest item of food. Were there anything smaller, He would have brought that forth, as in His saying, *God is not shy of coining a similitude, be it a gnat, there being nothing more so.*[433] Because He knows that there is nothing smaller than a gnat, He says, *there being nothing more so*, meaning any smaller. This, as also the verse in the Chapter of the Earthquake [concerning the speck], is the speech of God, so understand. We know that God would not have restricted Himself to the weight of a speck, had there been anything smaller, but would have used it for hyperbole; but God knows best.

As for his use of the diminutive of the word "son," it is a diminutive of mercy, seeing that he counsels him concerning things that will bring him felicity, provided he acts on them. As for the wisdom of his counsel prohibiting him from *associating anything with God, for such association is a terrible wrong*,[434] it is that the divine object of this wrong, which the polytheist describes as divided, is but One Essence. He is, in fact, associating with Him what is nothing other than His Essence, which is the height of ignorance. The reason for this is that one who has no [spiritual] insight into things as they are, or of the

---

430. *Qur'an*, XXXI:16.
431. Ibid.
432. Ibid., XCIX:7–8.
433. Ibid., II:26.
434. Ibid., XXXI:13.

true reality of something when its forms appear various in the one Essence, and does not realize that this variety occurs in one Essence, associates one form with the other in that state [of oneness] and apportions to each form a part of it. Now, concerning an associate, it is well known that that which distinguishes it from that with which it is associated is not the same as that with which it is associated, since the latter is [similarly] distinguished [in some way]. There is then no associate in reality, since each of them has something of its own, from which it is said that an association exists between them. The reason [for such an assertion] is general association. However, if it is truly general, then the independent activity of any particular part annuls that generality. *Say: Call upon God, or call upon the Merciful.*[435] This is the spirit of the matter.

---

435. Ibid., XVII:110.

CHAPTER XXIV

THE WISDOM OF LEADERSHIP IN THE WORD OF AARON

INTRODUCTORY NOTE

The creative Mercy is, once again, a subject for discussion here. Ibn al-'Arabī says that Aaron's Prophethood derived from the divine Mercy, which he goes on to link with the mother of both Moses and Aaron, since motherhood is more representative of the creative Mercy than is fatherhood, which represents rather the more wrathful, obligating Mercy. Earlier in the work he relates the concept of motherhood to Nature and fatherhood to the Spirit. Thus, the infinite Mercy of cosmic becoming in all its luxuriating multiplicity and complexity of forms is thought of in maternal and feminine terms, the very word *raḥmah* [Mercy] being closely related to the word *raḥim* [womb], while the absolute Mercy of spiritual reintegration in all its rigorous simplicity of principle is thought of in paternal and masculine terms. As is only natural, however, within the context of a patriarchal tradition, the male dominates the female, the Spirit rules over Nature, and the Reality as "God" takes precedence over the Reality as Cosmos.

The next main topic of this chapter is that of subjection, of the Cosmos to man, man to God, and of the animal in man to the spirit in man. After pointing out that similars cannot be subject to each other, that a man, as a human being, cannot be subject to another man, as human, he goes on to distinguish between subjection by force of will and subjection by circumstance. Thus, man as servant is subject to the will of his Lord, while man as being part of the Cosmos is circumstantially subject to God. Similarly, as in the case of sustenance and causality, that which is subject may also be said, in a certain sense, to subject its subjecter. Thus God, in His creative and governing role, is, so to speak, responsible and therefore subject to the need and dependence of His creation, just as, in His knowledge of Himself, whether as Essence or as Cosmos, He is subject to what the latent essences give Him to know of Himself.

Now we come to what is, perhaps, one of Ibn al-'Arabī's most daring and profound concepts, that of divine passion [*hawā*]. This word is usually used to denote blind passion, impulse, whim, infatuation, and desire of a most earthly kind. Looking more closely, however, at the various meanings of the Arabic root, one realizes how subtle a concept we are here presented with. Among the meanings of the root *hawā* are to fall headlong, to die, to be wide and deep, wind, air, to blow, space, and abyss. The whole sense, therefore, of the word, as intended here, is that of spontaneously falling passionately in love, hurling oneself, like a rushing gust of wind, into the deep emptiness of the abyss. This experience is, says Ibn al-'Arabī, universal and necessary to the whole notion of worship, since without this desperate urge by the whole to integrate its part and by the part to merge with the whole there would be no love, worship, or affirmation, the consummation of which is in the Oneness of Being.

For Ibn al-'Arabī, this concept is undoubtedly related to his concept of divine Love [*mahabbah*], which is itself another way of describing the Breath of the Merciful, which acts in response to the divine inner yearning for Self-consciousness and thus produces the headlong, outgoing, "blowing" radiation of the Spirit in its urgent desire [*hawā*] to inform and enliven the all-receptive abyss of the matrix of all becoming. In other words, the passionate love-worship that impels man to affirm the real and eternal in his object of worship is nothing but a reflection of the divine desire of the omnipresent Reality to know Itself as Object and, having known Itself, to love Itself to the point of reconsummation, since the worshiper, who is essentially nothing other than He, is only worshiping what is also nothing other than He. Ibn al-'Arabī could not have picked a more suitable word, combining as it does the both the notion of active content and that of receptive container, since every object of love or worship is, in a sense, an assimilating abyss, and every worshiper or lover is a "headlong faller," whether it be the Breath of the divine Mercy releasing the treasure of its essences into the abyss of cosmic existence or the human worshiper pouring out his heart to his deity.

Ibn al-'Arabī brings this chapter to an end by stating something very important, both for his own position with Islam and for the integrity of any mystical tradition. That is that every true gnostic, while inwardly aware of the unrestricted universality of truth, as expressed so often in this work, and of the omnipresence of the Reality in all things, nevertheless conforms outwardly to the doctrinal formulations and ritual practices of that religious dispensation to which his destiny has made him subject by the time and place of his birth and life. In other words his gnosis, if it is true, reveals to him not only the undifferentiated wholeness of the Oneness of Being fundamental to all being and experience of being but also that distinction, differentiation, tension, and otherness are an inescapable aspect of that wholeness which at certain levels requires their due recognition and conformity.

THE WISDOM OF LEADERSHIP IN THE WORD OF AARON

Know that the existence of Aaron derived from the realm of the divine Mercy, according to His saying, *We bestowed on him,* meaning Moses, *of our mercy, his brother Aaron, a prophet.*[436] His Prophethood derived from the realm of the divine Mercy, since, while he was greater than Moses in age, Moses was greater than him in Prophethood. It was because Aaron's Prophethood derived from the divine Mercy that Moses said to his brother, *O son of my mother,*[437] addressing him by reference to his mother and not his father, since mercy pertains to the mother more than the father and is more profuse in its effect. But for this mercy, she would not have the patience to persevere in the rearing of her children.

Then Aaron said, *Do not seize me by my beard nor my hair and do not give my enemies occasion to gloat over me.*[438] All of this is a breath

---
436. *Qur'an*, XIX:53.
437. Ibid., XX:94.
438. Ibid., VII:150.

of Mercy, the reason being that Moses had not looked carefully enough at the tablets he had cast from his hands. Had he done so he would have found in them guidance and mercy, and they would have made clear to him how the affair that angered him had occurred and that Aaron was innocent of it. The Mercy was on his brother, since he did not seize him by the beard in view of his people, because of his advanced age and because Aaron was older than he. Aaron's plea was an act of kindness to his brother, since his Prophethood derived from the divine Mercy, and only such [considerate] behavior was to be expected from him.

Then Aaron said to Moses, *I fear lest you should accuse me of dividing the Children of Israel*,[439] that is to say that you might make me the cause of their division, which was, in fact, the worship of the calf. Some of those who worshiped it did so in emulation of al-Sāmirī, while others held back from that, so that they might consult Moses on the matter on his return. Aaron feared that Moses would attribute their division to him. Moses, however, knew more of the matter than did Aaron, knowing what it was that the followers of the calf were [really] worshiping, being aware that God has ordained that none might be worshiped save Him alone, and that what God ordains surely happens. His rebuke to his brother was because of his [impulsive] rejection of the affair, as also his lack of adequacy [to the occasion]. The gnostic is the one who sees God in everything, indeed, sees Him as the essence of everything. Thus it was Moses who was teaching Aaron, although he was younger than his brother.

Therefore, when Aaron said that to him, he turned to al-Sāmirī and said, *And what have you to say, O Sāmirī?*[440] regarding his action in making the form of a calf from an enemy [the Devil], fashioned from the treasures of the people, thus stealing their hearts for the sake of their wealth. Jesus said to the Children of Israel, "O Children of Israel, every man's heart is where his wealth is. Let, therefore, your wealth be in heaven so that your hearts may be there also."[441] He only calls the wealth *māl* because it is something that by its very nature inclines [*tumīlu*] hearts to its worship, being, by far, the most desired object by reason of the heart's need for it. Forms, however, do not endure, and the form of the calf would undoubtedly have disap-

---

439. Ibid., XX:94.
440. Ibid., XX:95.
441. Matthew, VI:21.

peared had not Moses been so quick to burn it. In his great zeal he burned it and cast the ashes of that form into the sea. Then he said to al-Sāmirī, *Look now upon your god*,[442] calling it a god to reinforce his instruction, knowing well that it was an aspect of divine manifestation. He said, *I will surely burn it!*[443]

Human animality exercises a certain influence on that of the animal by virtue of the fact that God has subjected it to man, and not least because his [true] origin is not animal. The calf, however, was even more subject, since what is inanimate has no will of its own and is at man's disposal, without any resistance on its part. If an animal has the power to offer resistance, it becomes obstinate against what man wants from it. If it has no such power, or if the man's wish happens to coincide with that of the animal, it may then be led submissively to comply with his wish. Similarly, men, like such an animal, may be persuaded to obey some command regarding that by which God has raised him [above the animals] for the sake of some gain he hopes for from his compliance. Such gain is sometimes called wages, as in His saying, *He has raised some of you several degrees above others*,[444] *so that some might subject others.*[445] A man is subject to another only in his animality, not in his humanity, since two similars are mutually exclusive. The superior man might subject another by status through wealth or reputation, that is to say by his humanity, but the other is subject to him, whether through fear or greed, only by his animality, and not by his humanity. One similar is not subject to another, in which respect one has only to consider the mutual conflict among animals by reason of their similarity, similars being mutually exclusive. This is why He said, *And He has raised some of you above others in degree*,[446] the one above not being as the one below in degree. This shows that subjection is a matter of degree.

Subjection is of two kinds, the first being the subjection of the will to him who subjects by overpowering [the will of] the subjected one. This is like the subjection of the slave by his master, even if they be alike in their humanity, or like the subjection by the ruler of his subjects. Thus, even if they are his equals in their humanity, he sub-

---

442. *Qur'an*, XX:97.
443. Ibid. Ibn al-'Arabī has misquoted the words here. They should read, *We will surely burn it.*
444. Ibid., VI:132.
445. Ibid., XLIII:32.
446. Ibid., VI:132.

jects them by degree. The second kind is subjection by circumstance, as with the subjection of a people to the king who orders their affairs, defending them, protecting them, fighting their enemies, and preserving their property and persons. In the case of this subjection by circumstance, the subjects [in a way] subject their ruler. Properly speaking, it is called subjection by rank, which rank governs him. Some kings strive for their own ends, while others realize the truth of the matter and know that by rank they are [inevitably] in subjection to their own subjects, because they recognize their power and right [to their service]. God rewards such a one as He rewards those who know things as they really are. The recompense of such a person is incumbent on God as being involved in the affairs of His servants. Indeed, the whole Cosmos subjects, by circumstance, One Who cannot properly be called subjected, as He has said, *Every day He is busy with some matter.*[447]

Aaron's lack of effective power to restrain the followers of the calf by gaining mastery over it, as Moses did, is a wisdom from God made manifest in the created world, so that He might be worshiped in every form. Indeed, even if that form disappears thereafter, it does so only after it has been, for its worshipers, clothed in divinity, so that every kind of thing is [at some time] worshiped as divine or dominant, and every intelligent person can realize that this must be the case. Nothing in the Cosmos is worshiped, however, except it assume for the worshiper a certain sublimity and enjoy a certain degree in his heart. Thus God is called *The Lofty in degrees,*[448] and not lofty in degree, since He has made many degrees in One Essence. Thus also, He has ordained that none but He should be worshiped in many different degrees, and that each degree should become a context for that divine Self-manifestation in which He is worshiped. The greatest and most sublime of these is passion, as He says, *Do you not consider him who has taken his passion as a god?*[449] It is, indeed, the greatest object of worship, since nothing can be worshiped without it, nor can it be worshiped without His Essence. Concerning this I say:

> By the truth of passion, surely passion begets passion,
>   And but for passion in the heart it would not be worshiped.

---

447. Ibid., LV:29.
448. Ibid., XL:15.
449. Ibid., XLV:23.

Do you not consider how perfect and complete is God's knowledge of things, and how He accomplishes [His will] in the case of one who worships his passion and makes of it a god? He says, *God has caused him to err, knowingly,*[450] error being confusion. Thus He sees that the worshiper worships only his passion because he is driven to obey its urge to worship whatever he worships. Indeed, even his worship of God is motivated by passion, since, had he no passion for the divine Holiness, which is the will to love, he would not worship God or prefer Him to another. The same is the case with everyone who worships some cosmic form and adopts it as a god, since it is only by passion that he can regard it in this way. Every worshiper is under the rule of passion.

Then the worshiper begins to see that, among those who worship, the objects of worship are various and that the worshiper of some particular object of worship accuses those who worship anything else of infidelity. Thus those who have any awareness become confused because of the universality of this passion, indeed, the oneness of passion being the same in every worshiper.

God caused him to err, that is, He confused him *knowingly,*[451] in that every worshiper serves only his passion, by which alone he is moved to worship, whether it conforms to the Sacred Law or not. The perfect gnostic is one who regards every object of worship as a manifestation of God in which He is worshiped. They call it a god, although its proper name might be stone, wood, animal, man, star, or angel. Although that might be its particular name, Divinity presents a level [of reality] that causes the worshiper to imagine that it is his object of worship. In reality, this level is the Self-manifestation of God to the consciousness of the worshiper of the object in this particular mode of manifestation. Because of this, certain people ignorantly said. *We worship them only that they might bring us nearer to God,*[452] but calling them gods when they said, *Would he make the gods into one God, surely this is amazing.*[453] They were not rejecting Him, but showed their amazement, being limited to a notion of multiple forms and the attribution of divinity to them. Then the apostle came and summoned them to one God Who, although recognized, was not

---

450. Ibid.
451. Ibid.
452. Ibid., XXXIX:3.
453. Ibid., XXXVIII:5.

affirmed by them, having shown that they confirmed Him and believed in Him by their words, *We worship them only that they may bring us nearer to God*,[454] knowing that those forms were of stone. Thus the argument was brought against them with His saying, *So, name them!*[455] They, however, named them only in such a way as to suggest that their names possessed a reality.

As for the gnostics, who know things as they really are, they display an attitude of rejection toward the worship of forms, because their degree of knowledge makes them aware that they are, by the authority of the apostle in whom they believe and through whom they are called, believers, subject to the rule of time. Thus, despite their awareness that the polytheists do not worship the forms themselves, but only God in them, by the dominance of the divine Self-manifestation they discern in them, they are nevertheless servants of [their] time. The rejecter, who has no knowledge of how He manifests Himself, is completely unaware of this, since the true gnostic hides all this from the prophet, the apostle, and their heirs. Instead, he orders the polytheists to shun such forms whenever the apostle of the time does so. This they do, adhering to the apostle and seeking the love of God, as He says, *Say: If you love God, then follow me and God will love you.*[456] He is summoning to a god who is eternally resorted to, universally known, but not seen. *Sight cannot reach Him*,[457] but, *He reaches all sight*,[458] by virtue of His subtlety and permeation in the essence of things. The eyes cannot see Him, just as they cannot see the spirits that govern their shapes and outer forms. *He is the Subtle, the Experienced*,[459] experience being immediate tasting, which is His Self-manifestation that is in the forms. Both they and He are necessary, just as one who sees Him through his passion, must worship Him if only you would comprehend; and to God does the path lead.

---

454. Ibid., XXXIX:3.
455. Ibid., XIII:33.
456. Ibid., III:31.
457. Ibid., VI:103.
458. Ibid.
459. Ibid.

CHAPTER XXV

THE WISDOM OF EMINENCE IN THE WORD OF MOSES

INTRODUCTORY NOTE

This is a very complex chapter that deals with many subjects. Certain important themes, however, deserve special note. The first of these is the relationship, dealt with throughout the chapter, between Moses and Pharaoh. The second is the equally interesting relationship between Moses and al-Khidr. Last, he deals again with various aspects of the divine desire to create the Cosmos in a movement of love, the necessity of cosmic ephemerality for the wholeness of the Reality, and the spiritual perplexity experienced by the gnostic who tries to grasp the paradox of divine polarity in Oneness.

In the Qur'an, Pharaoh is the archetype of unbelieving, arrogant, unjust, and self-deifying man, the supreme example of the man who, knowing the truth of divine Unity in his heart, deliberately suppresses that truth in order to arrogate to himself the rights and powers that are properly God's. He thus represents the ultimate abuse of the viceregal function of man by seeking to rule in his own name and to ignore the Law of Heaven. This arrogance is summed up in two words in the Qur'an, *kufr* and *zulm*, the first meaning the deliberate ignoring or concealment of truth for one's own ends, the second being that arbitrary oppression and injustice which is the hallmark of every tyrant. In short, Pharaoh is the embodiment or personification of naked power without principle. Correspondingly, Moses, in the situation described in the Qur'an, represents human commitment and conformity to divine Law, but without the personal power to enforce it. Thus, while Moses has spiritual rank and authority, Pharaoh has actual rank and authority in this world, illustrating, once more, the paradoxical tension between the divine Wish, as symbolized by Moses, and the divine Will, as symbolized by Pharaoh. In other words, Ibn al-'Arabī is suggesting that, despite the apparent godlessness of Pharaoh, the actuality of his power can be nothing other than a particular realization, in the human context, of power as a function of the divine Will to create, the implication being that, inwardly, Pharaoh knows the divine truth, but perforce fulfills his cosmic function in accordance with his own predisposition *in divinis*, even though that function appears entirely reprehensible from the viewpoint of the divine Wish as expounded by Moses. Thus, the dialogue between Moses and Pharaoh, which on the surface appears to be a simple confrontation between right and wrong, good and evil, is in fact an act in the drama eternally being played between the polar principles of the creative Will and the spiritual Wish of God. The inward reality of Pharaoh's faith is reaffirmed at the point of his death.

In the case of the relationship between Moses and al-Khiḍr, which is the name traditionally assigned to the unnamed person whom Moses meets in the Qur'an, we have rather an illustration of the perennial tension between the Sacred Law, represented by Moses and expressing the divine Wish, and the mystic or esoteric knowledge of the gnosis that perceives not only the necessity for and validity of that Law, but also the inescapable validity and necessity of those aspects of cosmic becoming that elude the Law, as also the synthesis of both in the Oneness of Being. Moses, as exponent of the revealed Word as Law, fails to understand, or seems to, either the scope and relevance of the divine Will or the fundamental Oneness in which the conflict Spirit-world is resolved. Al-Khiḍr, on the other hand, while perceiving this failure on Moses' part, nevertheless respects his spiritual rank as a prophet, recognizing also the inevitability of his apparent bias as being necessary to the tension between poles of the divine Reality. In other words, there are certain things revealed by gnosis inwardly, which the prophet and apostle, as in the case of Noah (Chap. 3), cannot take account of outwardly as representative of the spiritual pole, being committed by his function to the rejection of everything, albeit actualized by the divine Will, that does not conform to the divine Wish.

As has been mentioned before, Ibn al-'Arabī sees the outgoing movement of creation as being impelled by Love [*maḥabbah*], that is the divine Love, yearning, or desire to know Himself, to love Himself and ultimately to unite with Himself in the consummation of Reality. As has also been mentioned, this loving movement toward Self-knowledge by creating His cosmic reflection implies the inescapable necessity of what is called the "ephemeral" as an essential element in the attainment of that Self-recognition, as being that necessary cosmic formulation, as object, of what He is in Himself, latently and essentially. This polarity of, on the one hand, the Cosmos essentially implicit in Godhead and, on the other, God spiritually implicit in cosmic forms, with all the seemingly irreconcilable tensions and conflicts inherent in such a polarity, presents the human intellect with a terrible dilemma that can be resolved only by the greatest realization of all, which is to acquire insight into and experience of the Oneness of Being. Awareness of that polar mutuality of God-Cosmos, Wish-Will, Spirit-Nature, throws the aspirant into a state of overwhelming perplexity [*ḥairah*] in which he can only drown to himself, letting go of all partial certainties and sinking into the ocean of divine realities, thus annihilating himself, only to subsist in Him. For such a one there is no "we" and "He," no duality or tension, but only we in Him in us in It in an ineffable experience of Oneness.

THE WISDOM OF EMINENCE IN THE WORD OF MOSES

The wisdom of the slaughter of the male children because of Moses was that the life of each boy killed because of him might revert to him as strength, since each one was killed as being (potentially) Moses. There was no ignorance in the matter, since the life of each boy killed because of him had to revert to Moses, each life being pure and innocent, unsullied by selfish aims and in the state of *Yea, indeed!*[460] Moses was thus a fusion of each life taken in his stead, and

---

460. *Qur'an*, VII:172, That is, in the primordial state of original recognition of the Reality.

everything prepared for each child according to its spiritual receptivity [then] resided in Moses. For Moses, this was a special divine favor not bestowed on anyone before him.

The Wisdom of Moses is manifold and, if God wills, we will include in this chapter as much of it as the divine command dictates to my mind. Indeed, this is the first time I have spoken of such matters.

From his birth Moses was an amalgam of many spirits and active powers, the younger person acting on the older. Do you not see how the child acts on the older person in a special way, so that the older person comes down from his position of superiority, plays and chatters with him, and opens his mind to him. Thus, he is under the child's influence without realizing it. Furthermore, the child preoccupies him with its rearing and protection, the supervision of his interests and the ensuring that nothing might cause it anxiety. All this demonstrates the action of the younger on the older by virtue of the power of his [spiritual] station, since the child's contact with his Lord is fairly recent, being a new creature. The older person, on the other hand, is more distant from that contact. One who is closer to God exerts power over one who is further from Him, just as the confidants of a king wield power over those further removed from his presence. The Apostle of God would expose himself to the rain, uncovering his head to it, saying that the rain had come fresh from its Lord. Consider then, how majestic, sublime, and clear is our Prophet's knowledge of God. Even so, the rain had power over the best of humanity by virtue of its proximity to its Lord, like a divine emissary summoning him in his essence, in a silent way. He exposed himself to it so that he might receive what it had brought from its Lord to him. Indeed, he would not have exposed himself to it but for the divine benefit implicit in its contact with him.[461] This, then, is the message of water from which God created every living thing; so understand.

As for the wisdom related to his [Moses'] being placed in the basket and being cast on the waters,[462] it is that the basket represents his humanity, while the waters represent the learning he acquired through the medium of his body, such as is obtained through the faculty of speculative thought, of sensation and imagination, all of which accrue to the human soul only through the existence of the elemental body. When the soul attaches to this body and is commanded to act

---

461. Cf. Muslim, IX:13.
462. Cf. *Qur'an*, XX:39.

in it and direct it, God allots these faculties to it as a means by which to achieve the direction God wishes for this vessel [basket] in which resides the tranqillity of the Lord. Thus, he was cast on the waters that he might acquire by these faculties all kinds of learning. God told him that even though the directing spirit was the body's ruler, it directed it only through him. God granted to him those powers inherent in humanity and expressed in terms of "the basket" in qur'anic and learned allusions.

The same is true of the Reality's direction of the Cosmos, since He directs it only by itself or by its form. This He does in the same way as the child depends on the engendering of the father, of effects on their causes, of agreements on their conditions, of attested things on their evidence, and of realizable things on their realities. All such things are of the Cosmos, being nothing other than the Reality's working in it, which He does only through it itself. As for our saying, "or by its form," it means the form of the Cosmos, by which is meant the Beautiful Names and sublime attributes by which the Reality is named and described. Whenever we hear one of His Names, we may discover its meaning and spirit in the Cosmos, since He directs the Cosmos only through its form.

Therefore, He has said of the creation of Adam, who is the synthetic link of the attributes of the divine Presence, which is the Essence, to the qualities and actions, "Surely, God created Adam in His Own image,"[463] His image being nothing other than the divine Presence. In this noble epitome, which is the Perfect Man, He created all the divine Names and realities, which issue forth from him into the macrocosm outside him. God made him a spirit for the Cosmos and subjected to him what is high and low, by virtue of the perfection of his form. Just as there is nothing in the Cosmos but gives Him praise, so there is nothing that is not subject to this Man by reason of what is invested in him by the reality of his form. God says, *He has subjected to you, as a charge from Him, all that is in the heavens and the earth,*[464] so that everything in the Cosmos is subject to Man. Whoever [truly] knows this is the Perfect Man, while whoever knows it not is the animal man.

Outwardly, the placing of Moses in the basket and the casting of the basket on the waters is an image of destruction, while inwardly

---

463. Bukhārī, LXXIX:1.
464. *Qur'an,* XLV:13.

IBN AL-'ARABĪ

it meant his escape from death. Thus, his life was spared, as the soul's life is spared from the death of ignorance by learning, as He says *or was dead* from ignorance, *and We revived him* by learning, *and We gave him a light by which to walk among men*, which is the guidance. *[Is such a one] like one in darkness*, that is, error, *never to emerge therefrom*,[465] which means that he will never be rightly guided, and that He has decreed for his soul that he should have no goal to aim at? [True] guidance means being guided to bewilderment, that he might know that the whole affair [of God] is perplexity, which means perturbation and flux, and flux is life. There is no abatement and no cessation, but all is being with no nonbeing. The same is the case with water by which the earth lives and moves, as in His saying, *and it quivers* in its pregnancy, *and swells* in its bringing forth, *and brings forth every joyous pair*.[466] That is to say that it gives birth only to what is like it in Nature. This pairing is the polarity inherent in all that is born or manifest from her. Similarly, the Being of God has a [certain] multiplicity and diversity of Names, because what is manifest of Him in the Cosmos innately requires the realities of the divine Names, so that by it [the Cosmos] and by its Creator the unity of multiplicity is confirmed. In respect to its essence it is single, as the essence of primordial substance is single, but it is multiple in respect to the outer forms it bears within its essence. So it is with God in respect to the forms of His Self-manifestation.

He is the theater of the forms of the Cosmos, taking into account His Unity. How fine is this divine teaching, insight into which is a special favor granted By God to whomsoever He wishes.

When Pharaoh and his people found him in the water by the tree, Pharaoh called him Moses [*Mūsā*], *mū* meaning water and *sā* meaning a tree, in Coptic. Thus, he called him according as he had found him, since the basket stopped by a tree at the water's edge. He intended to kill him, but his wife was inspired by divine words, seeing that God had created her for perfection, as our Prophet said when he attributed to her and to Mary the perfection usually reserved for males. She said to her husband, *Let him be a consolation for you and me*.[467] So it was that she was consoled with the perfection assigned to her, as we have said.

---

465. Ibid., VI:122.
466. Ibid., XXII:5.
467. Ibid., XXVIII:9.

Pharoah's consolation was in the faith God endowed him with when he was [later] drowned. God took him to Himself spotless, pure and untainted by any taint, because He took him in the act of commitment, before he could commit any sin, since submission [to God] erases all that has gone before it. Thus, He made of him a symbol of the loving care He may bestow on whomsoever He wills, lest anyone should despair of the mercy of God, *For, only the unfaithful people despair of the spirit of God.*[468] Had Pharoah been despairing, he would not have hastened to believe [in God].

Moses was, as Pharoah's wife had said of him, *a consolation to you and me and, perchance a benefit to us both,*[469] for God benefited both of them by him, even though they were not aware that he was the prophet at whose hands the kingdom and people of Pharoah would come to destruction. When God had saved him from Pharoah, *His mother's heart became empty,*[470] that is, empty of the anxiety that had afflicted her. Then God kept him from being suckled until he might be brought to his own mother's breast, so that He might make her pleasure in him complete.

Such is also the case with knowledge of the Sacred Law. He says, *For everyone of you We have made a way and a course [minhājā],*[471] that is a path [shir'ah], while *minhājan* [*min-hā jā'a*] means that it came from that way, this being an allusion to the source from which it came, which is sustenance for the law-abiding servant, just as the branch of a tree feeds only from its root. Thus, what is forbidden in one Law is permitted in another, from the formal standpoint. This does not mean that it has always been permitted, since the divine Command is [always] a new creation that is never repeated: so be alert. This is indicated, in the case of Moses, by his being denied a wet-nurse. This is because the real mother is the one who suckles the child, and not the one who bears hm. The mother who bears him carries him as a trust [from the father], and he comes into being in her and feeds on her menstrual blood, all of which happens involuntarily, so that she has no claim on him. Indeed, he feeds only on that which would kill her and make her ill, were it not to discharge from her.

---

468. Ibid., XII:87.
469. Ibid., XXVIII:9.
470. Ibid., XXVIII:10.
471. Ibid., V:48. In proposing a meaning for *minhāj*, Ibn al-'Arabī here seeks to derive its meaning from its sound, as sounding like *min-hā jā'a*, meaning, "it comes from it."

One might say, therefore, that the fetus has a claim on her, seeing that he feeds on that blood and thus protects her from the harm she might suffer were it to remain inside her and not discharge from her or be eaten by the fetus. The wet-nurse is not like that, for by her suckling she promotes his life and survival deliberately. This (voluntary motherhood) was provided by God for Moses from the mother who also bore him. Thus, none other than the mother who bore him was given the right to him, so that she might find consolation also in rearing him and watching him grow on her bosom, *that she might not grieve.*[472]

Thus did God rescue him from the distress of the basket, and he pierced through the darkness of nature by the divine learning that God granted to him, even though he did not [completely] emerge from it. God tempted him many times, testing him in many situations, so that patience with God's trials might be realized in him. The first test was his killing of the Egyptian, which was inspired in him by God and deposited in his inmost heart, although he himself did not know it. He did not really have any interest in killing him, although he did not hesitate when God's command came to him. That is because the prophet is inwardly protected, being unaware of something until God informs him of it. Thus, when al-Khiḍr killed the youth in front of him, Moses disapproved of that, forgetting his own killing of the Egyptian. Then al-Khiḍr said, *I did not do it on my own initiative,*[473] trying to apprise him of his rank, before he was himself informed that he was, although unaware of it, protected against any tendency (contrary to the divine Will). He also showed to him the sinking of the vessel, which symbolized destruction outwardly, while inwardly it meant deliverance from the action of a plunderer. In this he was giving him a comparison with the basket by which he had been encompassed in the water, the outer aspect of which was destruction, deliverance being its inner significance. His mother had done it, only out of fear lest the destroying hand of Pharaoh should sacrifice him in his helplessness before her eyes, despite what God had revealed to her, to the effect that she should not be aware [see]. Although she felt a strong urge to suckle him, she cast him out on the

---

472. Ibid., XXVIII:13. Traditionally, children were entrusted to professional wet-nurses, and not suckled by their mothers.

473. Ibid., XVIII:82. Al-Khiḍr is traditionally the name given to the person whom Moses meets and tries to learn from, as told in the Chapter of the Cave (XVIII). In this account he seems to represent esoteric and mystical knowledge, rather than exoteric and doctrinal learning. The Sufis regarded this figure as a patron.

waters when she feared for his safety; as the proverb goes, "What the eye does not see, the heart does not grieve about." It was not because of something she could see that she feared and grieved for him, having as she did a strong intimation that God might restore him to her, because of her trust in Him. Thus she lived with this feeling, hope and despair jostling within her, so that, when she was inspired by God, she said to herself, "Perhaps this is the messenger at whose hands Pharaoh and the Egyptians will be destroyed." Thus she lived with this feeling and was content with it, it being also [a form of] knowledge.

Then, when he was sought [for the crime he had committed], he left [that place] in flight, outwardly afraid, while inwardly seeking deliverance, since all motivation springs from love, the observer being diverted from this by its other less important causes. That is because the origin [of all motivation] is the movement of the Cosmos out of its state of nonexistence in which it was [latently] until its existence, it being, so to speak, a stirring from immobility [rest]. The movement that is the coming into existence of the Cosmos is a movement of love. This is shown by the Apostle of God in the saying, "I was an unknown treasure, and longed to be known,"[474] so that, but for this longing, the Cosmos would not have become manifest in itself. Thus its movement from nonexistence into existence is the love of the Creator for it [to happen]. Similarly, the Cosmos longs to behold itself in existence as it did in its latency, so that, in every respect, its movement from the latency of nonexistence into existence is a movement of love by the Reality and the Cosmos.

Perfection is loved for itself, so that God's knowledge of Himself, as being beyond all need of the worlds, is for Himself [alone]. There remains only the completion of the degree of Self-knowledge through knowledge of what is ephemeral, which stems from the essences of the Cosmos when they come into existence. The image of perfection is complete only with knowledge of both the ephemeral and the eternal, the rank of knowledge being perfected only by both aspects. Similarly, the various other grades of existence are perfected, since being is divided into eternal and noneternal or ephemeral. Eternal Being is God's being for Himself, while noneternal being is the being of God in the forms of the latent Cosmos. It is called ephemeral because parts of it are manifest to others, which being is manifest to it-

---

474. I have not been able to trace this tradition.

self in the forms of the Cosmos. Thus Being is perfect, the whole movement of the Cosmos being the movement of love for perfection, so understand.

Consider, then, how He relieves the distress of the divine Names in the lack of the manifestation of their effects in the Cosmos. This is because God loves relief, which may be achieved only through formal being, whether high or low. So is it confirmed that movement is for love, there being no movement in existence except for love. Although some of the learned are aware of this, others are made ignorant of it by the impact of more immediate circumstantial factors and their influence over the soul.

Moses' fear of the consequences of his killing the Egyptian was outwardly apparent, although the fear contained within itself the desire [love] for escape from execution. Although he fled when he became afraid, in reality he fled when he began to desire escape from Pharaoh and his designs. He does indeed mention the more immediate and evident cause of his fleeing, which was [to the real cause] as the bodily form is to a man, the desire for escape being implicit, just as the human spirit is implicit in the body. For the benefit of the many, the prophets express themselves on this matter in an outer fashion, limited as they are by the understanding of the hearer. This is because the apostles consider only the generality of men, being well aware of their level of understanding. Our own Prophet said, concerning the question of level in the matter of [worldly] gifts, "I will give a certain man a gift, even though I may prefer another, lest God cast him into the Fire,"[475] since he considered him weak of intelligence and insight and governed by greed and mere instinct. Thus, the knowledge they bring is couched in terms suitable for the lowest understanding, so that one who has no depth of understanding may go no further than the outward forms [of the message], wonder at its outer manifestation, and think that to be the [furthest] limit of knowledge. On the other hand, one of refined understanding, who would probe to the depths for the pearls of wisdom he deserves [to find], says, "This is the outer garment of a king." Thus he examines the quality of the garment and the fineness of its cloth and thereby learns the worth of the one whom it covers, so acquiring knowledge denied to the other, who understands nothing of this. Since, therefore, the prophets, apostles, and their heirs know that such people exist in the

---

475. Bukhārī, II:19.

world, and among their own peoples, they strive to express what they say openly, so as to combine what is outer and public with what is special and inward, so that the special person will understand what the generality understand and more, as is appropriate to that special capacity which distinguishes him from the ordinary man, while those who [who are charged to] convey the knowledge are content with this. This, then, is the wisdom [implicit] in his [Moses'] saying, *I fled from you when I feared you;*[476] he did not say, "I fled from you from a desire for safety and well-being."

Then he came to Madyan and found two maidens and *obtained water for them,* without any payment; *then he went back to the shade* of God and said, *O Lord, I am in dire need of the good you sent down to me,*[477] thus equating his action in obtaining water with the good that God had sent down to him, speaking of himself as being in dire need of God for the good He has. Al-Khiḍr showed to him the wall being rebuilt for nothing, and Moses chided him for that. He then reminded him of his obtaining water without payment and other things he did not mention, until Muḥammad wished that Moses would keep quiet and not interfere until God had related their story to him, so that he might learn what Moses had attained to without being aware of it. Had he been aware of it [in himself], he would not have failed to recognize it in al-Khiḍr, whom God had confirmed to him as purified and equitable. Moses, however, was unaware of God's purification of al-Khiḍr and forgot the condition he had laid down if he were to follow him, which is a mercy for us who are [frequently] forgetful of God's command. Had Moses been aware of it, al-Khiḍr would not have said to him, *what you have no experience of,*[478] which is to say that he knew things of which Moses had no experience, as Moses knew things he did not know. Thus, he was just to Moses.

As for the wisdom implicit in his parting from al-Khiḍr, it is in God's saying, *Do what the Apostle tells you to do and refrain from what he forbids you.*[479] Those of the learned in God who know the true worth of the Apostleship and the apostle need go no further than this saying. Al-Khiḍr, knowing that Moses was an apostle of God, paid careful attention to what he did and said, so that the proprieties

---

476. *Qur'an*, XXVI:21.
477. Ibid., XXVIII:24.
478. Ibid., XVIII:68.
479. Ibid., LIX:7.

might be maintained as regards his position vis à vis an apostle. Moses said to him, *If I ask you anything more, then do not keep company with me.*[480] When, therefore, it happened a third time, al-Khiḍr said, *This is the parting between me and you.*[481] At this Moses said and did nothing, demanding no more of his company, since he recognized the significance of the rank that had prompted him to deny him any further companionship. Moses therefore remained silent and they parted company.

Consider, then, the perfection of these two men in knowledge in their maintaining of the divine proprieties, as also al-Khiḍr's impartiality in recognizing Moses' rank when he said, "I have knowledge from God that you do not have, just as you have knowledge from God that I do not possess." This concession to Moses' knowledge was by way of alleviating the irritation he had caused him by saying, *How can you have patience with that of which you have no experience?*[482] while knowing the loftiness of his apostolic rank, which he himself did not enjoy. This is relevant to the Community of Muḥammad in the story of the pollination of the palm trees. Muḥammad said to his companions, "You have more experience [than I] of what needs to be done in this world,"[483] although there is no doubt that knowledge of a thing is better than ignorance of it. God, therefore, extols Himself as being knowledgeable about all things. Thus, the Apostle recognized that his companions were more knowledgeable about the things of this world, of which he had no experience, since such things are a matter of experience and direct contact, and Muḥammad had no time for such knowledge, being concerned with more important matters. I have brought your attention to a way of behaving that will greatly benefit you if you train yourself to it.

He also said, *My Lord has given me an authority*, meaning the vicegerency, *and made me one of the apostles*,[484] meaning the Apostleship, although not every apostle is a vicegerent. This is because the vicegerent bears the sword and is one who dismisses and appoints governors, whereas the apostle is not such, his only charge being to communicate the message with which he is sent. If he should fight for and protect it by the sword, then he is both a vicegerent and an

---

480. Ibid., XVIII:76.
481. Ibid., XVIII:78.
482. Ibid., XVIII:68.
483. Cf. A. Guillaume, *Life of Muhammad*, O.U.P., 1955, p. 301.
484. *Qur'an*, XXVI:21.

apostle. Thus, just as not every prophet is an apostle, so not every apostle is a vicegerent, which is to say that dominion and rulership are not given to everyone.

As for the wisdom implicit in Pharaoh's question regarding the nature of God,[485] it lies in the fact that it was not asked out of any ignorance on his part, but from experience, to see how consonant his answer would be with his claim to be the Lord's apostle. Pharaoh knew well the rank of apostle through his knowledge [of God], and he duly inferred from Moses' answer the veracity of his claim. He asked the question in a misleading way, to acquaint those present, without their knowing it, of what he himself was aware of in asking the question. When, therefore, Moses answered in the way of one who knows, Pharaoh, to preserve his position, pretended that Moses had not answered the question [properly], so that it might appear to those present, who were weak in understanding, that he knew more than Moses. Therefore, when Moses answered the question in a way that seemed not to answer what was asked, Pharaoh, knowing that he would answer in that way, said to his entourage, *Surely, this messenger of yours is mad*,[486] that is, he is ignorant of what I asked him about, since he does not seem, basically, to know. The question was a valid one, since the question "What?" is concerned with the reality of what is sought, which must be real in itself. As for the imposition of definitions involving genus and species, they are applicable to everything that admits of association. As for Him Who has no genus, His reality in Himself must be quite other than that in any other. Thus, the question is a valid one, according to the people of God, true learning, and sound intelligence, and the answer to it could only have been the one that Moses gave.

Here is a great mystery, since he effectively answered one who had asked about the most essential of all definitions by couching his answer to conform with His own attribution of Himself to the cosmic forms by which He manifests Himself, or in which He is manifest. It was as if he had said in answer to his question, *And what is the Lord of the worlds?*[487] "He in Whom are manifest the forms of the worlds, both on high, which is the heavens, and down below, which is the earth, *if you are certain*,[488] or by which He is manifest." When, there-

---

485. Ibid., XXVI:23: *And what is the Lord of the worlds?*
486. Ibid., XXVI:27.
487. Ibid., XXVI:23.
488. Ibid.

fore, Pharaoh said to his entourage, "Surely, he is mad," as we have mentioned, Moses explained further, so that Pharaoh might recognize his degree of divine knowledge, although he knew that Pharaoh knew it already. Thus he said, *Lord of the East and West*,[489] so combining what is apparent with what is hidden, the outer and the inner and what is between them, as in His saying, *He knows everything.*[490] Also He says, *If you are intelligent*,[491] that is, if you are of those who restrict, the intellect being restrictive. The first part of the answer is for the "certain ones" who are the people of inspiration and [true] being, since He said to them, *If you are certain*,[492] in other words the people of inspiration and [true] being. [It is as if He were saying to them], "I have only informed you of what your inner witness and essential being have made you certain of. If you are not of this kind, but people of intellect, restriction, and limitation, then I answer you with the second part, for God is [also] present in your intellectual proofs." Moses showed himself in both aspects, so that Pharaoh might know his virtue and veracity. Moses knew that Pharaoh knew or was getting to know that, because he had asked what God was, just as he knew that he had not put the question as the ancients did when they asked the question "What?" Therefore, he answered him. Had he thought otherwise, he would have regarded the question as mistaken. Thus, when Moses associated the one asked about with the Cosmos, Pharaoh conversed with him in this fashion, unknown to those present. He said, *If you have a god other than me, I will surely imprison you.*[493] Now, the letter *sīn* in the word *sijn* [prison] is a redundant letter; in other words [he was saying], "I will surely cover [*janna*] [confuse] you,[494] for you answered in such a way as to provoke me into saying what I said to you. You might have said to me, 'O Pharaoh, you are showing your ignorance in threatening me, but how can you separate [us, essentially], seeing that the Essence is One.' " Pharaoh is saying [to him], "It is only the ranks that divide the Essence [apparently], albeit that the Essence cannot [in reality] be divided or separated. My rank now is that of de facto power over you. Although I am you, es-

---

489. Ibid., XXVI:28.
490. Ibid., LVII:3.
491. Ibid., XXVI:28.
492. Ibid., XXVI:24.
493. Ibid., XXVI:29.
494. Here, once again, Ibn al-'Arabī is using Arabic roots for his own purposes, deriving *janna* [hide, cover] from *sijn* [prison].

sentially, I am, nevertheless, different from you in rank." When Moses understood this, he admitted his right, while saying to him that he could not do it [what he had threatened]. Pharaoh's rank demonstrated to Moses that he had power and influence over him because God in the outer form of the rank of Pharaoh had power over that rank in which Moses was manifest in that situation.

Moses then said to him, by way of resisting his threat, *What if I were to present to you something clear and unambiguous*,[495] to which Pharaoh could only reply, *Present it then, if you are truthful*,[496] lest he should appear weak and unjust to his people, who might doubt him, a people whom he despised but who obeyed him. *Surely, they are the evildoers*,[497] that is to say, those who refuse to admit that sound intelligence requires the rejection of what Pharaoh claimed with his words. That is because the intellect reaches a certain limit, beyond which it cannot go, while one possessed of inspiration and certainty can proceed beyond that limit. Thus Moses produces an answer that can be accepted, particularly by one who is certain and intelligent. *So, he cast down his staff*,[498] which was in the form of Pharaoh's rejection of Moses in resisting a response to his summons; *and Lo, it was a manifest serpent*,[499] that is a snake, unmistakably. Thus, the disobedience [of Pharaoh], which is evil, was changed into obedience, which is a good thing, as He says, *God changed their evil deeds into good deeds*,[500] that is, according to [divine] judgment. Thus, the judgment is here manifest in a particular thing in a single substance, since outwardly it is the staff and the snake. As a snake, it devoured the other snakes like it, and as a staff it consumed the other staffs. Thus Moses' argument appeared superior to that of Pharaoh, [as symbolized] in the form of staffs, snakes, and strands. The magicians had strands, which are small threads, while Moses had none, which shows that their powers, in relation to Moses' power, was as that of strands to huge mountains. When the magicians saw that, they became aware of Moses' degree of knowledge, realizing that what they witnessed was not of mortal doing, or, if it were, it could only have come from one whose knowledge is free of all fancy and ambiguity.

---

495. *Qur'an*, XXVI:30.
496. Ibid., XXVI:31.
497. Ibid., XXVII:12.
498. Ibid., XXVI:32.
499. Ibid.
500. Ibid., XXV:70.

IBN AL-'ARABĪ

Have faith, therefore, in the Lord of the worlds, the Lord of Moses and Aaron, the Lord on Whom Moses and Aaron called, since the magicians realized that the people were well aware that it was not Pharaoh on whom Moses had called. It was only because Pharaoh was in a position of power, the man of the moment and vicegerent by the sword, even though he had abused all legal norms, that he said *I am your highest Lord!*[501] That is to say, "Even if all be Lords in a certain sense, I am higher by virtue of the rule I have been granted, outwardly, over you." The magicians, realizing the truth of what he said, far from denying it, confirmed it, saying, *You only judge in the things of this world; so pass judgment, for the state is yours.*[502] Thus, his saying, *I am your highest lord*,[503] was correct, since, even though he was [in essence] God Himself, the form was that of Pharaoh. By the divine Essence [within him], but in the form of falsehood, he cut off hands and feet and crucified people, so that ranks might be acquired that could be acquired only by such action. Causes can never be canceled, because the latent essences make them necessary. They are manifest in existence only in some form or other according as their latent states dictate, there being no way of changing the words [*logoi*] of God, which are nothing other than the essences of created things. In respect of their latency [*in aeternis*], they are called permanent, while, in respect of their existence and manifestation, they are called ephemeral. One might say that some guest has only just come to us today, which does not mean that he had no existence before his appearance [as a visitor]. Thus, God, in His mighty speech, says, which means His sending it forth despite its eternality, *Whenever there comes to them some new reminder from their Lord, they listen to it casually,*[504] and, *Whenever there comes to them some new reminder from the Merciful, they turn aside from it.*[505] The Merciful only comes by Mercy, and whoever turns aside from it may expect the penalty, which is a lack of Mercy. Also His saying, *Their faith will not avail them when they see Our might; the norm of God which has been applied before to His servants,*[506] except

---

501. Ibid., LXXIX:24.
502. Ibid., XX:72.
503. Ibid., LXXIX:24.
504. Ibid., XXI:2.
505. Ibid., XXVI:5.
506. Ibid., XL:85.

to the people of Jonah, which exception does not mean that it will not benefit them in the Hereafter, but means that it will not save them from blame in this world.[507]

Thus, Pharaoh was taken [killed] despite his [sudden] faith, which would also have been the case if he had been certain of dying in that moment. The evidence, however, indicates that he was not certain, since he watched the believers walking along the dry path that had appeared when Moses struck the sea with his staff. Thus, when he believed, Pharaoh was not certain of destruction, unlike the dying man [who only believes] so that death might not touch him. He believed as the Children of Israel believed, although he was [falsely] certain that he would be saved [from destruction]. What he was certain of ocurred, but in a form other than that he had wished for. God saved him from the punishment of the Hereafter in his soul, and also saved his body [corpse], as He says, *Today We will save your body, so that you might be a sign to those that come after you,*[508] lest his people should say that he had merely gone into hiding if his form had disappeared. Although dead, he was visible in his usual form, so that it might be known that it was he. He was thus saved both outwardly and inwardly. One who is condemned to be punished in the Hereafter does not believe, whatever sign he is given, *Until they see the painful punishment,*[509] that is, until they experience the punishment of the Hereafter. It is clear from the Qur'an that Pharaoh was not of that kind. We say further, but God has the last word, that, although people think that he was damned, there is no text to support such a view. As regards his people, that is another story for which there is no place here.

Know that God does not take a man who is dying, unless he be a believer, insofar as the divine warning has reached him. For this reason sudden death and the killing of a man unawares are abhorred. While, in the case of sudden death, the internal breath escapes, but the external breath does not enter, this is not so with one who dies [more slowly]. It is the same with one who is killed unawares, [for example] by being struck from behind. Such a person is taken in what-

---

507. Cf. ibid., X:98.
508. Ibid., X:92.
509. Ibid., X:97.

ever state of belief or unbelief he is in when he dies. The Prophet said, "He will be gathered in the state he was in at death."[510] The dying man, on the other hand, is aware of death and is sure about what is happening, so that he is taken in that state. This is because *kāna* [to be, become] is a word of being that is concerned with the extension of time only by association with states. A distinction must be made, therefore, between an unbeliever who dies in a state of awareness and one who is killed unawares or dies suddenly, as we have mentioned regarding sudden death.

As for the divine Self-revelation and its speaking in the form of fire, it ocurred because of the desire of Moses. God revealed Himself [to him] in [the form of] his desire, so that he might approach and not turn away. Had He revealed Himself to him in any other way, he would have turned away because of the concentration of his interest on a particular purpose. If he had turned away, his act would have rebounded on him and God would have turned away from him also. He, however, was a chosen and favored one, as indicated by the fact that God revealed Himself to him in [the object of] his desire, unknown to him.

> As with the fire of Moses, he saw it as his very need,
> Unknown to him it was indeed the very God.[511]

---

510. I have not been able to trace this saying.
511. See below, p. 274.

CHAPTER XXVI

THE WISDOM OF RESOURCE IN THE WORD OF KHĀLID

INTRODUCTORY NOTE

Two subjects are touched on in this very short chapter. The first is the subject of the Isthmus [*barzakh*], that intermediary world set between life and death, as also between death or nonexistence and life. It is that halfway house between Spirit and Nature, between becoming and reintegration, in which the intangible spirit becomes transformed into physical form and in which or through which forms are transfigured into spirits. It is a subtle world, neither physical nor spiritual, that is the meeting place of Heaven and Earth, between one creative "breath" and another, and between one duration and another.

The other subject is that of intention or wish and its fulfillment, the question being whether an unfulfilled intention or wish merits the same recompense as one that is fulfilled actually. According to the Prophet Muḥammad, men will be judged according to their intentions, which suggests that they do deserve equal recompense. In certain respects, intention and wish have to do with love and desire, while fulfillment has to do with destiny, both of which have to do with essential predisposition. Within the context of the Oneness of Being, every wish is His wish, which cannot but be fulfilled in some way or another.

IBN AL-'ARABĪ

THE WISDOM OF RESOURCE IN THE WORD OF KHĀLID

The wisdom of Khālid b. Sinān resides in the fact that, in his mission, he manifested the Prophethood of the Isthmus. He claimed that he would reveal what was there [at the Isthmus] only after his death. It was therefore ordered that he be disinterred. When he was asked about the matter, he revealed that its regimen was in the form of this world, by which it may be known that what the apostles said in their wordly lives was true. It was Khālid's aim that the whole world should believe in what the apostles told them, so that divine Mercy should be available to all. He was ennobled by the proximity of his mission to that of Muḥammad, knowing that God had sent him as a mercy to the worlds. Although Khālid was not himself an apostle, he sought to acquire as much as possible of the [all-encompassing] mercy of Muḥammad's mission. He was not himself commanded to deliver God's dispensation, but wished, nevertheless, to benefit from it in the Isthmus, so that his knowledge of creation might be greater. His people, however, failed him. A prophet does not speak of his people as failing, but rather as failing him, in that they did not enable him to fulfill his purpose.

Did God, then, allow him to achieve the fulfillment of his wish? While there is no doubt that He did, there is doubt as to whether he attained to the object of his wish, which raises the question as to whether the wish for something to happen is the same as its happening or failing to happen. In the Sacred Law there are many instances that support such an equation. Thus, one who tries hard to attend the congregational prayer, but misses it, is rewarded as if he had attended it. Similarly in the case of one who would dearly like to perform the good deeds possible to rich and wealthy men, his reward is the same as theirs. However, is the similarity in intention or in action, since they combine both intention and act? The Prophet did not pronounce on either one of them. Outwardly, they do not seem to be the same. Thus, Khālid b. Sinān sought to attain both the wish and its fulfillment and thus reap two rewards; but God knows best.

CHAPTER XXVII

THE WISDOM OF SINGULARITY IN THE WORD OF MUHAMMAD

INTRODUCTORY NOTE

The last chapter, named after the Prophet Muḥammad, is, in the main, an extended commentary on the reported saying of the Prophet, "Three things have been made beloved to me in this world of yours: women, perfume, and prayer," which, for Ibn al-'Arabī, serves to illustrate the underlying theme of triplicity in singularity, a subject already touched on in Chapter 11. As has been pointed out, this triplicity in singularity is, in simple terms, the two fundamental poles of the God-Cosmos polarity, the third factor of the relationship between the two, all three elements being united in the Oneness of Being. In the course of his commentary on the saying of the Prophet, which contains three symbolic elements, Ibn al-'Arabī makes some very remarkable and daring statements, the various implications of which he does not fully develop, probably from fear of going too far, conscious as he was of the limits imposed on him by the nature of the Dispensation to which time and place had committed him.

For our author, the three elements used in the saying of the Prophet are perfectly suited to the kind of interpretation and commentary he intended, since each element is associated with a whole constellation of symbolic meanings, each of which helps to illustrate some aspect or mode of triplicity and polarity.

IBN AL-'ARABĪ

The word "women" very well represents the various aspects and nature of the cosmic pole, suggesting as it does multiplicity, nature, form, body, receptivity, fecundity, becoming, beauty, fascination. In short, the feminine symbolizes, microcosmically and therefore in a very succinct way, the very principle of the projected and multifaceted mirror of the cosmic image that reflects to the divine Subject the panoramic beauty of His Own infinite possibility to become, which is nothing other than His Own essential Self, which He cannot but love and desire and into which He pours and "blows" the Breath of His Mercy and Spirit, but which, in absorbing the energies of the divine Will, always threatens the reintegrative imperative of the divine Wish. Similarly, in the human context, the male, as representative of the initiating Spirit, is constantly being attracted by the microcosmic feminine to pour his life and energy into her world of cosmic becoming and natural life experience, threatening always to divert him from the remembrance of the Spirit in Whose Name he acts and of the vicegerency that is his particular function. As Ibn al-'Arabī points out, this total involvement in the complex and multiple demands of cosmic life, symbolized by absorption in sexual union, can be corrected and purged only by the purification of remembering and reintegration into the world of the Spirit, symbolized by the major ablution after such union.

However, just as the Cosmos is nothing other than He, originating in Him, so also woman is nothing other than man and deriving from him, symbolizing for him, therefore, his own servanthood and receptivity vis à vis God. It is for this reason that he says that a man may most perfectly contemplate God in woman, since, in her, he contemplates at once his own servanthood and dominion and in union with her may experience, in microcosmic mode, that fusion of polar experience which is the Reality. According to this view of things, the attracting beauty of woman, far from being a snare to delude man, should rather become for him that perfect reflection, as formal beauty, of his own spiritual truth, being, as she is, that quintessential sign or clue [āyah] from which he might best learn to know his own true self, which is, in turn, to know his Lord.

The second element in the saying is "perfume," which, representing as it does the relating factor in the triplicity, is a very subtle and flexible symbol that lends itself to association with either of the two polar elements. Thus, perfume, aroma, or fragrance is that which at once soothes and incites, drugs and stimulates, may remind one of the delight of woman or the serenity of the sanctuary, and may either sharpen or dull spiritual awareness. In short, it is that not entirely physical nor yet entirely spiritual element that symbolizes at once both the current of the creative Mercy and also the spiritual nostalgia that draws the human spirit back to its source in God. The word used in the Arabic is *ṭīb*, which also carries the idea of goodness, in the sense that in God all is good, whether it be the goodness of what the Will effects, which may seem from the standpoint of the Wish as reprehensible, or whether it be the spiritual goodness of what the Wish demands, which may seem from the standpoint of existential experience hard and painful.

The last element, symbolizing the Spirit and its reflection in man, is "prayer," which seeks to divert man from the world of cosmic concerns and to make him as totally aware as possible of Him from Whom he is and to Whom he is inexorably returning. As with women, it has its own perfume to remind and console the world-weary soul.

As part of his commentary on this saying of the Prophet, Ibn al-'Arabī, true to his usual form, seeks to interpret the linguistic features of the saying in his own special way and to make suggestions of a daring kind. He observes that the word for "three" is, unusually, in the feminine form, and also that the masculine noun "perfume" is placed between two feminine nouns, "women" and "prayer," thus suggesting, although not pursuing, the notion of a certain feminine predominance and all-containing nature. He goes on further to observe that many of the words in Arabic that denote cause, origin, and essence are feminine nouns. This would seem to be an odd suggestion in view of his otherwise firm commitment to a masculine bias, as encouraged by the patriarchal nature of the Islamic tradition. One suspects, however, that this untypical suggestion is yet another way of expressing the idea that the creative Mercy overrides and embraces the obligating Mercy of reintegration and that the positive and essential function of the Cosmic experience overrides its negative and ephemeral nature. Thus the creative Mercy, the word for which in Arabic is feminine and has a close association with the word for "womb," in its complete concern with cosmic becoming and the actualization of infinite possibility, may be thought of as feminine in the same way that the Hindu notion of *māyā*, the world-creating power, is thought of as feminine. In other words, the object of knowledge, whether cosmic or essential, may be thought of as feminine, just as the subject or knower, whether creative or Self-reaffirming, may be thought of as masculine. Thus we are known as a "feminine" aspect of the Reality, whether outer or inner, and we know as a "masculine" aspect of the Reality, whether outwardly or inwardly.

THE WISDOM OF SINGULARITY IN THE WORD OF MUḤAMMAD

His is the wisdom of singularity because he is the most perfect creation of this humankind, for which reason the whole affair [of creation] begins and ends with him. He was a prophet when Adam was still between the water and the clay[512] and he is, by his elemental makeup, the Seal of the Prophets, first of the three singular ones, since all other singulars derive from it.[513]

He was the clearest of evidence for his Lord, having been given the totality of the divine words, which are those things named by Adam, so that he was the closest of clues to his own triplicity, he being himself a clue to himself.[514] Since, then, his reality was marked by primal singularity and his makeup by triplicity, he said concerning love, which is the origin of all existent being, "Three things have been made beloved to me in this world of yours," because of the triplicity inherent in him. Then he mentioned women and perfume, and added that he found solace in prayer.[515]

He begins by mentioning women and leaves prayer until last, because, in the manifestation of her essence, woman is a part of man. Now, man's knowledge of himself comes before his knowledge of his Lord, the latter being the result of the former, according to his saying, "Whoso knows himself, knows his Lord." From this one may understand either that one is not able to know and attain, which is one meaning, or that gnosis is possible. According to the first [interpretation] one cannot know oneself and cannot, therefore, know one's Lord, while, according to the second, one may know oneself and therefore one's Lord. Although Muhammad was the most obvious ev-

---

512. Bukhārī, LXXVIII:119.
513. Cf. above p. 141.
514. Ibid.
515. Nasā'ī, XXXVI:1.

idence of his Lord, every part of the Cosmos is a clue to its origin, which is its Lord, so understand.

Women were made beloved to him and he had great affection for them because the whole always is drawn toward its part. This he explains as coming from the Reality, in His saying regarding the elemental human makeup, *And I breathed into him of My spirit!*[516] God describes Himself as having a deep longing for contact with man when He says to those who long [for Him], "O David, I long for them even more."[517] That is a special meeting. He says further, in a saying on the Antichrist, "None of you will see his Lord until he dies."[518] Indeed, it is hardly surprising that one [God] so described should be longed for. Thus, God longs for those favored ones, seeing them and wishing that they could see Him, although their state does not permit that. It is like His saying, [*We will test them*] *until We know,*[519] although He knows [them] well. Thus, He longs [for them] because of this special quality, which cannot be realized except after death, while their longing for Him is kept fresh by it, as He says, in the Saying of Hesitation, "I do not hesitate in what I do as much as in taking the soul of My faithful servant. He hates death as much as I hate to hurt him; but he must meet Me."[520] He gives him glad tidings instead of telling him that he must die, lest he become distressed at the mention of death, although he may not meet God until after death, as he said, "None of you will see his Lord until he dies." He says, "He must meet Me," the longing of God being because of this attribution.

> The Beloved longs to see me,
>   And I long even more to see Him,
> The hearts beat fast, but destiny bars the way,
>   I groan in complaint and so does He.

Since He has explained that He breathed into man of His spirit, He is yearning [in reality] for Himself. Consider, then, how, because of His spirit, His creation is in His own image.

Since man's makeup is composed of the four elements or humors

---

516. *Qur'an*, XV:29.
517. I have not been able to trace this saying.
518. Muslim, LII:95.
519. XLVII:31.
520. Bukhārī, LXXXI:38.

in the body, His breathing produces a burning, because of the moisture in the body. Thus, by his makeup man's spirit is a fire, because of which God spoke to Moses in the form of fire, in which He put what he wished for. Were his makeup [purely] natural, his spirit would be of light. It is called "blowing" because it comes from the Breath of the Merciful, and it is by this Breath, which is the blowing, that his essence is manifest. It is according to the eternal predisposition of the one blown into that the flaring up is fire and not light, the Breath of the Merciful being deeply implicit in that by which man is man.

Then God drew forth from him a being in his own image, called woman, and because she appears in his own image, the man feels a deep longing for her, as something yearns for itself, while she feels longing for him as one longs for that place to which one belongs. Thus, women were made beloved to him, for God loves that which He has created in His own image and to which He made His angels prostrate, in spite of their great power, rank and lofty nature. From that stemmed the affinity [between God and man], and the [divine] image is the greatest, most glorious and perfect [example of] affinity. That is because it is a syzygy that polarizes the being of the Reality, just as woman, by her coming into being, polarizes humanity, making of it a syzygy. Thus we have a ternary, God, man, and woman, the man yearning for his Lord Who is his origin, as woman yearns for man. His Lord made women dear to him, just as God loves that which is in His own image. Love arises only for that from which one has one's being, so that man loves that from which he has his being, which is the Reality, which is why he says, "were made beloved to me,"[521] and not "I love," directly from himself. His love is for his Lord in Whose image he is, this being so even as regards his love for his wife, since he loves her through God's love for him, after the divine manner. When a man loves a woman, he seeks union with her, that is to say the most complete union possible in love, and there is in the elemental sphere no greater union than that between the sexes. It is [precisely] because such desire pervades all his parts that man is commanded to perform the major ablution. Thus the purification is total, just as his annihilation in her was total at the moment of consummation. God is jealous of his servant that he should find pleasure in any but Him, so He purifies him by the ablution, so that he might once again behold Him in the one in whom he was annihilated, since it is none other than He Whom he sees in her.

THE BEZELS OF WISDOM

When man contemplates the Reality in woman he beholds [Him] in a passive aspect, while when he contemplates Him in himself, as being that from which woman is manifest, he beholds Him in an active aspect. When, however, he contemplates Him in himself, without any regard to what has come from him, he beholds Him as passive to Himself directly. However, his contemplation of the Reality in woman is the most complete and perfect, because in this way he contemplates the Reality in both active and passive mode, while by contemplating the Reality only in himself, he beholds Him in a passive mode particularly.

Because of this the Apostle loved women by reason of [the possibility of] perfect contemplation of the Reality in them. Contemplation of the Reality without formal support is not possible, since God, in His Essence, is far beyond all need of the Cosmos. Since, therefore, some form of support is necessary, the best and most perfect kind is the contemplation of God in women. The greatest union is that between man and woman, corresponding as it does to the turning of God toward the one He has created in His own image, to make him His vicegerent, so that He might behold Himself in him. Accordingly, He shaped him, balanced him, and breathed His spirit into him, which is His Breath, so that his outer aspect is creaturely, while his inner aspect is divine. Because of this He describes it [the spirit] as being the disposer of this human structure by which God *disposes of things from the heaven,* which is elevation, *to the earth,*[522] which is the lowest of the low, being the lowest of the elements.

He calls them women [*nisā'*], a word that has no singular form. The Apostle therefore said, "Three things have been made beloved to me in this world, women ...",[523] and not "woman," having regard to the fact that they came into being after him [man]. Indeed, the word *nus'ah* means "coming after." He says, *The postponed month [nasī'] is an increase in unbelief,*[524] as also selling by *nasī'ah,* that is, "by postponement." Thus he says "women." He loves them only because of their [lower] rank and their being the repository of passivity. In relation to him they are as the Universal Nature is to God in which He revealed the forms of the Cosmos by directing toward it the divine

---

521. Nasā'ī, XXXVI:1.
522. *Qur'an,* XXXII:5.
523. Nasā'ī, XXXVI:1.
524. *Qur'an,* IX:37.

IBN AL-'ARABĪ

Will and Command, which, at the level of elemental forms, is symbolized by conjugal union, [spiritual] concentration in the realm of luminous spirits, and the ordering of premises toward a conclusion [in the realm of thought], all of which correspond to the consummation of the Primordial Singularity in all these aspects.

Whoever loves women in this way loves with a divine love, while he whose love for them is limited to natural lust lacks all [true] knowledge of that desire. For such a one she is mere form, devoid of spirit, and even though that form be indeed imbued with spirit, it is absent for one who approaches his wife or some other woman solely to have his pleasure of her, without realizing Whose the pleasure [really] is. Thus, he does not know himself [truly], just as a stranger does not know him until he reveals his identity to him. As they say,

> They are right in supposing that I am in love,
> Only they know not with whom I am in love.[525]

Such a man is [really] in love with pleasure itself and, in consequence, loves its repository, which is woman, the real truth and meaning of the act being lost on him. If he knew the truth, he would know Whom it is he is enjoying and Who it is Who is the enjoyer; then he would be perfected.

Just as woman [ontologically] is of a lower rank than man, according to His saying, *Men enjoy a rank above them*,[526] so also is the creature inferior in rank to the One Who fashioned him in his image, despite his being made in His image. By virtue of the superiority by which He is distinguished from him, He is above all need of the Cosmos and is the primary agent, the form or image being an agent only in a secondary sense, since the image [man] does not have the primacy, which belongs to God. The eternal essences are similarly distinguished according to their ranks, and the gnostic allots to everything its proper due. Thus it is that Muḥammad's love for women derives from the divine love and because God *Gives to everything He has created*[527] what is its due, essentially. He gives to them according to a merit fixed in the [eternally predisposed] essence of that which is deserving.

---

525. I have not been able to trace this quotation.
526. *Qur'an*, II:228.
527. Ibid., XX:50.

He places women first because they are the repository of passivity, just as the Universal Nature, by its form, comes before those things that derive their being from her. In reality, Nature is the Breath of the Merciful in which are unfolded the forms of the higher and lower Cosmos, because of the pervasion of the expressed Breath in the primordial Substance, particularly in the realm of the celestial bodies, its flow being different in respect of the existence of the luminous spirits and accidents.

Then the Apostle goes on to give precedence to the feminine over the masculine, intending to convey thereby a special concern with and experience of women. Thus he says *thalāth* [three] and not *thalāthah*, which is used for numbering masculine nouns. This is remarkable, in that he also mentions perfume, which is a masculine noun, and the Arabs usually make the masculine gender prevail. Thus one would say, "The Fatimahs and Zaid went out [using the third person masculine plural]," and not the third person feminine plural. In this way they give preference to the masculine noun, even if there is only one such noun together with several feminine nouns. Now, although the Apostle was an Arab, he is here giving special attention to the significance of the love enjoined on him, seeing that he himself did not choose that love. It was God Who taught him what he knew not, and God's bounty on him was abundant. He therefore gave precedence to the feminine over the masculine by saying *thalāth*. How knowledgeable was the Apostle concerning [spiritual] realities and how great was his concern for proper precedence.

Furthermore, he made the final term [prayer] correspond to the first [women] in its femininity, placing the masculine term [perfume] between them. He begins with "women" and ends with "prayer," both of which are feminine nouns, [the masculine noun] perfume coming in between them, as is the case with its existential being, since man is placed between the Essence [a feminine noun] from which he is manifested, and woman who is manifested from him. Thus he is between two feminine entities, the one substantively feminine, the other feminine in reality, women being feminine in reality, while prayer is not. Perfume is placed between them as Adam is situated between the Essence, which is the source of all existence, and Eve, whose existence stems from him. [Other terms] such as *ṣifah* [attribute] and *qudrah* [capability] are feminine. Indeed, whatever school of thought you adhere to, you will find feminine terms prominent. Even the Causalists say that God is the "Cause" [*'illah*] of the Cosmos, and *'illah* is feminine. As for the wisdom of perfume and his putting it after "women," it is because of the aromas of generation in women, the most delightful of perfumes being [experienced] within the embrace of the beloved, as they say in the well-known saying.

When Muḥammad was created a pure servant, he had no ambition for leadership, but continued prostrating and standing [before his Lord], a passive creation, until God effected [His purpose] in him, when He conferred on him an active role in the realm of the Breaths, which are the excellent perfumes [of existence]. Thus, He made perfume beloved to him, placing it after women. He pays respect to the ranks of God in His saying, *Lofty of rank, the Possessor of the Throne*,[528] seeing that He is established on it by His name the Merciful, so that everything encompassed by the Throne is affected by the divine Mercy, as He says, *my Mercy encompasses all things*.[529] It is the Throne that encompasses all things, while the Merciful is its occupant, by Whose reality Mercy permeates the Cosmos, as we have explained many times, both in this work and also in *The Meccan Revelations [Al-Futūḥāt al-makkiyyah]*.[530] God Himself has put perfume [ṭīb, also goodness] in the context of conjugal union with reference to the innocence of ʿĀ'ishah when He says, *Evil [malodorous] women are for evil men and evil men are for evil women, just as good [sweet-smelling] women are for good men and good men for good women, who are innocent of what they allege*.[531] Thus, He speaks of them as sweet smelling, since speaking implies breath, which is of the essence of aroma, coming forth [from the mouth] sweetly or offensively, according to its expression. However, being at source divine, it is all sweet smelling and good, but according as it is approved of [by separative attitudes] or disapproved of, it may be considered good or bad. Of Garlic, Muhammad said, "It is a bush whose odor I detest";[532] he did not say "I detest it." Thus, it is not the thing itself that is to be detested, but only that which issues from it. Such an aversion may be a question of custom, natural antipathy, law, deficiency, or something else. If then the distinction between good and bad is to be made, then Muḥammad was made to love the good and not the bad. Now it is said that the angels are offended by

---

528. Ibid., XL:15.
529. Ibid., VII:156.
530. Cf. II, pp. 390 and 310.
531. *Qur'an*, XXIV:26.
532. Muslim, V:76.

the bad odors arising from the putrefaction associated with this elemental makeup [of man], since he is made of *clay and putrid slime*,[533] that is to say of varying odors, so that the angels find him repugnant by his nature. In a similar way, by its very nature, the dung beetle is offended by the odor of the rose, which, although it has [for us] a fine aroma, is malodorous to the dung beetle. Thus anyone of such a nature, essentially and formally, is repulsed by the truth when he hears it and rejoices in falsehood, as He says, *Those who believe in falsehood and not in God,* describing them as losers, *are the losers who have lost themselves.*[534] Anyone who cannot tell the good from the bad has no perception.

The Apostle of God was made to love only the good in everything, which is [in reality] everything that is. [We might ask] whether there can be anything in the Cosmos that sees only the good in everything and knows no bad. We would say that there is not, since in the very source from which the Cosmos is manifested, which is the Real, we find aversion and love, the bad being that which is loathed, while the good is that which is loved. Now the Cosmos is [created] in God's image [macrocosm] and man has been made in both images [microcosm], so that there cannot be anything that sees only one aspect of things. There are certainly those who can distinguish the good from the bad, that a thing is bad by [sense] experience and good by nonsensual experience, but in whom perception of the good predominates over perception of the bad. As for the idea that one might remove the bad from the Cosmos of created being, such a thing is not possible, since the Mercy of God inheres in both the good and the bad. From its own standpoint the bad is good and the good bad. Indeed, there is nothing good, but seems, in some way, bad to some bad thing, and vice versa.

As for the third element by which the singularity is made complete, it is prayer. He said, "and my solace is in prayer,"[535] because it is [a state of] contemplation, being an intimate discourse between God and His servant. He says, *Remember Me, and I will remember you,*[536] since it is an act of worship equally divided between God and His servant, half for God and half for His servant, as in the authori-

---

533. *Qur'an,* XV:26.
534. Ibid., XXIX:52.
535. Nasā'ī, XXXVI:1.
536. *Qur'an,* II:152.

tative tradition, "I have divided the prayer equally between Me and My servant, a half for Me and a half for My servant who may also have whatever he asks."[537] Thus when the servant says [in reciting *Al-Fātiḥah*], *In the Name of God, the Compassionate, the Merciful*,[538] God is saying, "My servant is remembering Me." When the servant says, *Praise be to God, the Lord of the worlds*, God says, "My servant is praising Me." When the servant says, *The Compassionate, the Merciful*, God says, "My servant is lauding Me." When the servant says, *King on the Day of Judgment*, God says, "My servant is glorifying Me and has yielded all to Me." Thus the whole of the first half [of *Al-Fātiḥah*] belongs to God. Then the servant says, *Thee do we worship and Thee do we ask for help*, and God says, "This is shared between Me and My servant; and for him is whatever he asks," thus introducing an element of participation into this verse. When the servant says, *Guide us on the right path, the path of those whom you have favored, and not the path of those who have incurred Your wrath, nor of those who have gone astray*, God says, "These [verses] are reserved to my servant who may have whatever he asks." Thus these last verses are for the servant alone, just as the first ones belong only to God. From this one may realize the necessity of reciting [the verse], *Praise be to God, the Lord of the worlds*, since whoever omits it has not performed the prayer [properly], which is shared between God and His servant.

Being a discourse, it is also a remembrance, since whoever remembers God sits with God and God with him, as mentioned in the tradition, "I am the companion of him who remembers Me."[539] Now whoever, being perceptive, is in the presence of the one he is remembering, he sees his companion. In such a case there is contemplation and vision, otherwise he does not see Him. From this the one praying will be able to ascertain his degree [of gnosis], that is to say whether he is able to see, in the prayer, in this way or not. If he cannot see Him, then let him worship Him as if he saw Him, imagining Him to be in the *quiblah* during his discourse, and let him listen most carefully to what God might say to him in response [to his prayer]. If he is an *imām* [leader] for his own world [of family or community] and the angels praying with him, he has, in the prayer, the [same] rank as the Apostle, which is to represent God. Indeed, every one who

---

537. Muslim, IV:38.
538. This and the following verses form part of the opening chapter of the *Qur'an*.
539. Cf. Muslim, XLVIII:2.

prays is an *imām*, since the angels pray behind one who prays alone, as is stated by the tradition.[540] When he say, "God hears him who praises Him,"[541] he is letting the people behind him know that God has heard him, to which the angels and others present answer, "O our Lord, yours is the praise," for it is God Himself Who is saying, on the tongue of His servant, "God hears him who praises Him."

Consider, then, the sublimity of the rank of prayer and to what degree of dignity it brings the one who performs it. However, the one who does not attain to contemplative vision in his prayer has not reached its summit and cannot find [true] solace in it, since he cannot see Him with Whom he has discourse. If also he cannot hear the Reality's response, he cannot be listening carefully enough. Indeed, he who is not present with His Lord in prayer, neither hearing nor seeing Him, is not really praying at all, since he does not listen and watch [for God]. While it lasts, there is nothing like the prayer rite to prevent preoccupation with other things.

In the prayer, the most effective element is the remembrance of God, by virtue of the words and actions it comprises. We have, however, described the state of the Perfect Man in prayer, in *The Meccan Revelations* [*Al-Futūḥāt al-makkiyyah*].[542] God has said, *Surely, the prayer prevents much evil and sin*,[543] seeing that the one praying is forbidden to occupy himself with anything else while he is engaged in it. *But the remembrance of God is greater*,[544] that is to say that, within the context of prayer, God's remembering of His servant when He responds to his request is greater. Furthermore, in the prayer, the servant's praising of God is greater than his remembering Him, since all majesty belongs to God. Thus, He says, *And God knows what you fashion*,[545] and, *or who listens and watches*.[546] The listening derives from God's remembering of His servant in prayer.

Thus, of the intelligible movement by which the Cosmos is transformed from nonexistence into existence, the prayer has all three phases, a vertical movement in which the one praying stands erect, a horizontal movement in which the praying one bows and a down-

---

540. Bukhārī, IX:16.
541. These words are part of the prayer rite.
542. Cf. II, p. 468, and III, pp. 296–297.
543. Qur'an, XXIX:45.
544. Ibid.
545. Ibid.
546. Ibid., L: 37.

wards movement, which is the prostration. The movement of man is vertically, that of the animals is horizontally, that of the plants downward, while inanimate things have no real motion, since a stone moves only if some other thing moves it.

In his saying, "and my solace was made to be in prayer,"[547] he does not attribute this to himself, since the Self-revelation of God to one praying comes from God and not the one who is praying. Indeed, had he not mentioned this by himself, God would have ordered him to pray without the [solace of] His Self-revelation to him. Since that came to him as a favor, the contemplative vision is also a favor. He said, "and my solace was made to be in prayer," which means seeing the Beloved, which brings solace to the eye of the lover. This is because the word *qurrah* [solace] comes from the word *istiqrār* [fixing], so that the lover's eye might be fixed [on the Beloved] to the exclusion of all else. It is for this reason that looking around is not permitted in prayer, because in this way Satan seeks to steal something from the prayer of the servant, to deny to him the vision of his Beloved. If God were indeed the Beloved of the one who is [always] looking around him, he would look, in his prayer, only toward the *qiblah*. Every man knows in himself whether his worship is of this kind or not, for *Man sees himself well enough, however many excuses he may give.*[548] Indeed, each man knows the false in himself from the true, since no one is (truly) ignorant of his own state, it being a matter of self-experience.

That which is called prayer has also another aspect in that He has commanded us to pray to Him and has told us that He prays for us, the prayer being both from us and from Him. When it is God Who prays, He does so in His name the Last, as coming after the creation of the servant, being, indeed, the God the servant creates in himself (in his Heart), whether by his reason or through traditional learning. This is the "God of belief," which is various according to the predisposition inherent in that particular person; as al-Junaid said, when asked about the gnosis of God and the gnostic, "The color of the water is the same as that of its container,"[549] which is a most precise answer, showing the matter as it is. This then is the God Who

---

547. Nasā'ī, XXXVI:1.
548. *Qur'an*, LXXV:14.
549. Qushairī, *Al-Risālah*, Cairo, A.H. 1346, pp. 127, 142.

prays for us. Also, when we pray, we bear the name the last, being in the same position as He Who properly has that name. That is because, to Him, we are only as our state dictates, and He sees us only in the form with which we provide Him, since the praying one always lags behind the leader on the race track.

God says, *Everyone of them knows its own way of prayer and exaltation*,[550] which is to say its degree of tardiness in worshiping its Lord, as also its mode of exaltation by which it affirms God's transcendence according to its eternal predisposition. Indeed, there is nothing that does not express its praise of its good and forgiving Lord. This why the worship of the Cosmos in detail, in each of its parts, is not understood (by man). In another way, the pronoun (in the phrase, *His praise*)[551] may also refer to the exalting servant in His saying (by changing the way it is read), *There is nothing, but He exalts its praise*, meaning the praise of that thing. Thus, the pronoun in *His praise* returns to that thing by virtue of the praise uttered on Him in what is believed, since he is only praising the God of his belief whom he has bound to himself. Thus, whatever deeds he performs return to himself. Indeed, he is only [in reality] praising himself since, without doubt, in praising the product, one is praising its producer, its satisfactoriness, or otherwise rebounding upon the one who made it. Similarly, the God of belief is made for the one who has regard for it, being his own production, so that his praise for that which he believes in is self-praise. That is why he rejects the [different] beliefs of someone else, although he would not do so if he were impartial. The owner of this private object of worship, however, is usually ignorant, in that he is wont to object to what someone else believes concerning God. If he were to understand truly what Al-Junaid said regarding the color of the water being that of its container, he would allow to every believer his belief and would recognize God in every form and in every belief. His attitude, however, is merely a matter of opinion and not knowledge. Thus, He has said, "I am in my servant's notion of Me,"[552] that is to say that He is manifest to him only in the form of his belief, whether it be universal or particular in nature. The God

---

550. *Qur'an*, XXIV:41.
551. Ibid., XVII:44, which reads *There is nothing but exalts His praise*.
552. Bukhārī, XCVII:15.

of beliefs is subject to certain limitations, and it is this God Who is contained in His servant's Heart, since the Absolute God cannot be contained by anything, being the very Essence of everything and of Itself. Indeed, one cannot say either that it encompasses Itself or that it does not do so; so understand! God speaks the truth and He is the [sole] Guide along the Way.

BIBLIOGRAPHY

PRIMARY SOURCES

———Bukhārī, Muḥammad B. Ismāʿīl, *Saḥīḥ*, 3 vols., ed. L. Krehl, Leyden, 1862–1868, Vol. IV ed. T. Juynboll, 1907–1908
Dā'ūd, Abū, *Sunan*, 2 vols., Cairo, A.H. 1292.
-Ghazālī, Abū Ḥāmid, *Iḥyā' ʿulūm al-dīn*, 4 vols., Cairo, 1939.
Ibn al-ʿArabī, Muḥyī al-dīn, *Fuṣūṣ al-ḥikam*, autographed ms. Evkaf Musesi, Istanbul, no. 1933. Ed. with commentary by A. A. Afifi, Cairo, 1946. Partially translated by T. Burckhardt, *Sagesse des prophètes*, Paris, 1955.
———*Al-Futūḥāt al-makkiyyah*, Cairo, A.H. 1329, 4 vols.
———*Kleinere Schriften des Ibn Al-ʿArabī*, ed. H. S. Nyberg, Leyden, 1919.
———*Rasā'il Ibnu'l-ʿArabi*, Hyderabad, 1948.
———*Sufis of Andalusia*, trans. R. W. J. Austin of the *Rūḥ al-quds* and *Al-Durrat al-fākhirah*, London, 1971.
———*Tarjumān al-ashwāq*, Beirut, 1961.
Ibn Hanbal, Aḥmad, *Musnad*, 11 vols., Cairo, 1949–1953.
-Jāmī, ʿAbd al-Raḥmān, *Sharḥ ʿalā fuṣūṣ al-ḥikam*, in the margin of Al-Nābulusī's commentary, Cairo, A.H. 1303–1323.
-Makkī, Abū Ṭālib, *Qūt al-qulūb*, 2 vols., Cairo, 1961.
Muslim, b. al-Ḥajjāj, *Saḥīḥ*, 18 vols. in 6, Cairo, A.H. 1349.

BIBLIOGRAPHY

-Nābulusī, 'Abd al-Ghanī, *Sharḥ jawāhir al-nuṣūṣ*, Cairo, A.H. 1303–1323.
-Nasā'ī, Abū 'Abd al-Raḥmān, *Sunan*, Cairo, 1964.
-Qāshānī, 'Abd al-Razz-aq, *Sharḥ 'alā fuṣūṣ al-ḥikam*, Cairo, A.H. 1321.
-Qūnawī, Ṣadr al-Dīn, *Al-Fukūk*, ms. Yusuf Agha, no. 4858.
-*Qur'ān*, Bulāq, A.H. 1342.
-Qushairī, 'Abd al-Karīm, *Al-Risālah*, Cairo, 1940.
-Tirmidhī, al-Ḥakīm, *Kitāb khatm al-awliyā'*, ed. O Yahya, Beirut, 1965.
-Tirmidhī, Muḥammad b. Ismā'īl, *Saḥīḥ*, 2 vols., Cairo, 1937.

SECONDARY SOURCES

Afifi, A. A., *The Mystical Philosophy of Muhid Din Ibnul Arabi*, Cambridge, 1939.
Arberry, A. J., *An Introduction to the History of Sufism*, Oxford, 1942.
Brockelmann, C., *Geschichte der Arabischen Literatur*, 2 vols., Leyden, 1943–1949.
Burckhardt, T., *An Introduction to Sufi Doctrine*, Lahore, 1959.
Corbin, H., *Creative Imagination in the Sufism of Ibn 'Arabī*, London, 1970.
Gardet, L., and Anawati, G., *Mystique musulmane*, Paris, 1961.
Horten, M., *Festagabe Jakobi*, Bonn, 1926.
-Hujwīrī, 'Alī b. 'Uthmān, *Kashf al-maḥjūb*, trans. R. A. Nicholson, London, 1911.
Izutsu, T., *A Comparative Study of the Key Philosophical Concepts in Sufism and Taoism*, I, "The Ontology of Ibn 'Arabī," Tokyo, 1966.
-Jīlī, 'Abd al-Karīm, *De l'Homme Universelle*, trans. T. Burckhardt, Paris, 1953.
Lane, E. W., *Arabic-English Lexicon*, London, 1863–1893.
Lings, M., *A Sufi Saint of the Twentieth Century*, London, 1971.
Massignon, L., *La passion d'al-Hosayn Ibn Mansour al-Hallāj*, 2 vols., Paris, 1922.
Meier, F., "The Mystery of the Ka'bah," in *The Mysteries* [Papers from the Eranos Year Books], London, 1955.
Nasr, S. H., *Three Muslim Sages*, Harvard, 1964.
Nicholson, R. A., *The Mystics of Islam*, London, 1914.
———*Studies in Islamic Mysticism*, Cambridge, 1921.

BIBLIOGRAPHY

Palacios, M. Asin, *Islam Cristianizado*, Madrid, 1931.
Shehadi, F., *Ghazali's Unique Unknowable God*, Leiden, 1964.
Wolfson, H. A., *The Philosophy of the Kalam*, Harvard, 1976.
Yahya, O., *Histoire et classification de l'oeuvre d'Ibn 'Arabī*, Damascus, 1964.
Zaehner, R. C., *Hindu and Muslim Mysticism*, London, 1960.

INDEX TO TEXT

Aaron, 58, 195, 200, 243–248, 264.
'Abd al-Razzaq, 159.
Abraham, 58, 87, 91–95, 99, 100, 101, 113, 166, 199, 201, 210.
Abū al-Su'ūd, 159, 160.
Abū Bakr, 65, 99.
Abū Jahl, 171.
Abū Madyan, 159, 160.
'Ād, 132.
Adam, 87, 219, 272, 277; and angels, 52; creation of, 180, 253; and divinity, 50–59; as mirror, 51; as prophet, 66; as Regent, 56, 57, 98, 201.
Ahmad, 200.
'Āishah, 121, 278.
'Alī, 158.
'Amr, 191, 232.
The Ancient of Days, 55.
Angels, 51, 52, 53, 67, 85, 121, 178, 180, 181, 196, 204, 238, 247, 274, 278, 279, 280, 281.
Antichrist, 273.
Apostles, 46, 73, 116, 117, 134, 136, 151, 152, 160, 161, 165, 168, 169, 170, 175, 194, 201, 202, 203, 214, 231, 234, 235, 247, 258, 259, 260, 261, 268; Seal of, 66, 67.
Apostleship, 160, 168–169, 199, 220, 259, 260.
Asaf Ibn Barkhiyah, 192, 193.
Ash'arites, 154, 192, 238.
Āsiyah, 219.

Baal, 230.
Bek, 230.
Being, 199–205; Absolute, 135, 150; coming into, 141, 142; contingent, 55, 70, 115, 116, 118, 123, 124; cosmic, 56; and Cosmos, 123; created, 65, 66, 73, 83, 84, 92, 93, 106, 107, 116, 130, 135, 224, 225, 279; essential, 54, 70, 262; Eternal, 257; existent, 53–54, 84, 239, 272; of God, 254, 257; individual, 53, 57, 106; Itself, 132; of man, 178; necessary, 54; and nonbeing, 254; Oneness of, 133; of Reality, 124, 125; relative, 57, 85, 86, 92, 150; true, 262; Unity of, 107.
Belief, 137, 149, 151, 152, 194, 224, 225, 232, 233, 255, 265, 266, 279, 283, 284.
Bezels of Wisdom, 45.
Bilqīs, 189, 192, 193, 194, 195.
Bistāmī, Abū Yazīd al-, 101, 102, 148, 179.
Book of Theophanies, 153.
Breath, 148, 153, 154, 155, 193, 208–211; Divine, 180, 181, 275; and Jesus, 174, 176; of the Merciful, 135, 148, 179, 235, 243–244, 274, 277; Realm of, 278.

Caliphs, 85, 203, 204.
Chosroes, 189.
Command, creative, 87, 141, 154; divine, 50, 51, 52, 62, 63, 66, 114, 116, 117, 133, 159, 160, 169, 170, 171, 178, 182, 183, 194, 195, 196, 197, 204, 208, 211, 252, 255, 256, 259, 276, 282; Existential, 204; and Reality, 183.
Compassion, 148, 179, 188–197.
The Compassionate, 188, 189, 192, 280.
Consciousness, of God, 184; of man, 184, 247; of self, 81.
Contemplation, 77, 81, 98, 148, 159, 275, 279, 280, 281, 282.
Cosmos, and Being, 123; and causality, 126, 142, 253, 277; creation of, 55, 141, 148, 215, 279; dependency of, 126; and divine Name, 78, 125, 148, 254, 258; existence of, 50, 57, 257, 281; forms of, 51, 56, 73, 74, 135, 136, 180, 254, 257, 258, 261, 275, 277; and God, 150, 180, 211, 231, 246, 262, 275, 276; and Mercy, 278; as mirror, 51; movement of, 258, 281; origin of, 273; and

INDEX

path, 195; and Reality, 50, 55, 56, 57, 73, 93, 123, 124, 148, 215, 253, 279; transformation of, 153, 154, 281.

Creation, 101, 114; act of, 214; of Cosmos, 55, 141, 148, 215, 279; and God, 114, 134, 153, 158, 161, 165, 166, 168, 170, 181, 202, 208, 252, 254, 273, 274, 275, 276; of man, 54, 55, 79, 95, 126, 127, 136, 137, 190, 195, 210, 245, 273, 274; and Mercy, 223, 224; nature of, 158; new-, 153, 154, 155, 255; preserved, 51; and Reality, 51, 102, 103, 109, 132, 134, 136, 141, 142, 166, 191; renewal of, 193, 194.

Creator, 87, 98, 141, 180, 196, 254, 257.

David, 58, 193, 194, 199–205, 208, 273.

Decree, 193, 230, 231; of God, 160, 165, 166.

Dead, raising of, 176, 177, 178, 179.

Demons, 189, 190.

Destiny, 165–171, 216, 217.

Determination, of being, 53; divine, 50, 86, 152, 165, 166, 215; essential, 57, 86, 165, 185; eternal, 62; and form, 93, 234; and knowledge, 53, 54; and Lord, 78; and Mercy, 225; of Names, 65; and Reality, 87, 92, 93, 94, 117, 215; and Spirit, 73.

Devil, 100, 244.

Dispensation, 113, 114.

Divinity, acts of, 177; and Adam, 50–59; aspects of, 107, 247, 275; and dependency, 148; gifts of, 62, 63, 65, 70; Identity, 178; Image of, 52; manifestations of, 58, 78, 80, 234, 245; Modes of, 135; shadow of, 123.

Dominion, 189, 190, 192, 195, 196, 223–227, 261.

Dreams, 121, 122.

Duality, 75.

Elevation, 275; of degree, 83, 84, 85, 88, 89; of God, 85, 88; of position, 83, 84, 85, 88, 89.

Elias, 58, 229–235.

Eminence, 58, 251–266.

Enoch, 58, 83–89.

Esotericism, 202.

Essence, of Being, 123, 135; contingent, 123, 124; created, 224, 264; determined, 93; divine, 91, 126, 264; eternal, 51, 85, 93, 94, 115, 116, 118, 123, 131, 133, 264, 276; gifts of, 62, 65; and God, 85, 189, 223, 244, 248; of God, 78, 95, 108, 125, 126, 161, 162, 179, 180, 182, 210, 211, 232, 237, 239, 246, 253, 264, 275; inner, 74; Itself, 109, 284; latent, 64, 92, 94, 115, 118, 123, 158, 161, 182, 223, 264; of man, 178, 179, 210, 233, 238, 252, 274; and Mercy, 223, 224, 225, 226; and Names, 50, 88, 108, 126, 226; and One, 150, 153, 158, 223, 232, 238, 239, 240, 246; of the Reality, 50, 52, 95, 125, 126, 148, 230; spiritual, 57; Throne of, 204; and triplicity, 141; Unique, 85, 86, 87; Unity of, 126, 154, 158, 190, 191, 210, 232, 233; unmanifest, 92, 93, 95.

Eve, 277.

Exaltation, 58, 73–81, 201, 283.

Existence, coming to, 167, 224, 257, 281; and Cosmos, 50, 57, 257, 281; dependent, 54, 55, 57; determined, 55; earthly, 121; essential, 125; individual, 53, 54; latent, 167, 257; and light, 123; manifest, 85, 94; and Mercy, 51, 224, 225; and nonexistence, 159, 161, 193, 225, 257, 281; potential, 123, 224; real, 124; and Reality, 50, 93, 115; relative, 125, 133, 135; source of, 277.

Exotericism, 202.

INDEX

Ezra, 58, 165–171.

Al-Fātihah, 290.
Fire, 170–171, 210, 215, 258.
The Folk, 45, 51, 69, 102, 107, 130, 138, 169.

Gabriel, 121, 122, 174, 175, 176, 177, 178, 196.
Ghazālī, Abū, Hāmid al-, 93.
Gospel, 131, 214.
Gnosis, 69, 77, 80, 93, 101, 102, 103, 121, 130, 132, 133, 134, 137, 149, 150, 151, 165, 169, 178, 185, 188, 217, 235, 244, 248, 272, 276, 280; forms of, 234; of God, 230, 282; heart of, 137, 147, 148, 149; perfection of, 160, 166, 247; and power, 158, 159, 162.
God, agents of, 159, 276; attributes of, 54, 55, 68, 76, 79, 88, 126, 133, 135, 150, 166, 178, 180, 190, 191, 214, 220, 225, 226, 231, 238, 239, 261; blessing of, 186, 234; as Breath, 148, 155, 273; call to, 70, 75, 76, 77, 78, 132, 197, 216, 217, 232, 240; and creation, 114, 134, 142, 153, 158, 161, 165, 166, 168, 170, 181, 202, 208, 252, 254, 273, 274, 275, 276; dispensation of, 160, 268; effects of, 113; face of, 84, 137, 138; fear of, 55, 57, 103, 226, 259; as First, 55, 69, 85, 125, 135, 136, 189, 215; forgiveness of, 184, 186, 200, 227, 283; friends of, 168, 169; glorification of, 52, 124, 280; gifts of, 63, 64, 67, 68, 69, 134, 165, 168, 189, 193, 196, 199, 200, 201, 235, 237, 252, 254; Identity of, 126, 130, 132, 136, 149, 150, 151, 152, 153, 182, 191, 211, 215, 217; image of, 153, 208, 209, 215, 253, 273, 274, 275, 276, 279; immanence of, 74, 75, 76, 230; intimate of, 91, 95, 99, 101; jealousy of, 133, 274; kingdom of, 77; as Last, 55, 69, 85, 125, 135, 136, 189, 215, 282; limitations to, 74, 75, 134, 135, 138, 150, 165, 231; longing for, 273, 274; manifestations of, 78, 79, 80, 86, 95, 142, 147, 149, 152, 155, 178, 179, 182, 189, 209, 211, 215, 231, 232, 238, 247, 248, 254, 261, 283; messengers of, 231, 268; Nature of, 261, 262; nearness to, 132, 220, 248, 252; is One, 78, 106; Path of, 129, 130, 201, 248, 280; pleasing of, 55, 108, 114, 115, 214, 215; praise of, 45, 63, 74, 75, 92, 94, 95, 109, 127, 213, 280, 281, 283; Presence of, 62, 132, 137, 181, 253; Regent of, 52, 202, 260, 261, 264, 275, 280; remembrance of, 209, 210, 220, 279, 280, 281; return to, 211, 216; servants of, 45, 62, 63, 67, 68, 108, 113, 130, 132, 136, 138, 142, 149, 152, 167, 168, 169, 170, 178, 179, 182, 183, 184, 185, 186, 189, 191, 196, 197, 200, 201, 208, 211, 213, 217, 220, 225, 233, 234, 238, 246, 264, 274, 279, 281, 283, 284; shadow of, 123, 124, 127; son of, 221; submission to, 186, 194, 195, 255, 280; thanks to, 200; transcendence of, 63, 73, 74, 75, 76, 134, 230, 231, 283; Unity of, 106, 107, 108, 125, 126, 254; veiled, 56, 107, 118, 149, 153, 185, 231; as Watcher, 184–185; witness to, 152, 184, 185; worship of, 78, 138, 149, 151, 183, 215, 244, 246, 247, 248, 279, 280, 282, 283; wrath of, 55, 204, 205, 214, 215, 223, 280.
Grace, 205, 227, 235, 238.

Heart, 101, 114, 147–155, 166, 244, 282, 284; of gnostics, 137, 147, 148, 149.
Heaven, 110, 134, 195, 237, 244, 261, 275; seven, 180, 229–230.
Hell, 103, 109, 131, 138.

INDEX

Holiness, 58, 83–89, 247.
Hūd, 58, 129–138.
Humility, 177, 217.
Huwairith, Umm al-, 116.

Ibn al-Shibl, Abū al Su'ūd, 159, 160.
Ibn Masarrah, 95.
Ibn Qā'id, Abū 'Abdallāh, 159.
Ibn Qissi, Abū al-Qāsim, 88, 226.
Idrīs, 229, 230, 235.
Imagination, 79, 99, 100, 101, 102, 120, 121, 122, 124, 125, 197, 224, 230, 232, 233; Plane of, 120, 121, 151.
Incarnation, 177.
Inspiration, 69, 166, 201, 204, 214, 217, 225, 256, 262, 263.
Intellect, 70, 76, 81, 101, 150, 230, 231, 232, 233, 235, 262, 263; and knowledge, 51, 77, 125, 166, 181, 234; and universals, 53.
Intelligibles, 53, 54, 57, 116, 123.
Intimacy, 58, 229–235.
Isaac, 58, 87, 98–103, 199.
Islam, 113, 115.
Ishmael, 58, 106–110.
Israel, 195, 244, 265.
Isthmus, 268.

Jacob, 58, 113–118, 122, 199.
Ja'far, 232.
Jerusalem, 166.
Jesus, 58, 174–186, 202, 203, 220, 244.
Jews, 203.
Job, 58, 63, 199, 213–217.
John, 58, 219–221.
Jonah, 58, 208–211, 265.
Joseph, 58, 99, 120–127.
Judgment, Day of, 280.
Junaid, al-, 148, 282, 283.

Khālid, 58, 232, 268.
Kharrāz, Abū Sa'īd al-, 86.
Khatīm, Qais b. al-, 157.
Khiḍr, al-, 256, 259, 260.
Knowledge, absolute, 238; acquired, 194, 238, 258; contingent, 53; of Cosmos, 123, 181, 191; dependency of, 161; degree of, 84, 248, 257, 263; esoteric, 131; and essence, 65, 93; eternal, 53; of God, 54, 62, 64, 65, 66, 74, 75, 76, 79, 85, 92, 93, 94, 95, 98, 115, 132, 136, 137, 138, 150, 151, 161, 162, 165, 166, 167, 179, 182, 190, 191, 194, 209, 211, 214, 215, 216, 217, 230, 231, 238, 247, 252, 257, 260, 261, 262, 268, 273, 281; from God, 260; increase of, 169, 196, 197; and knower, 53, 94, 132, 225; of law, 255; limitations of, 52, 53, 258; of Lord, 107, 153, 181, 272; of Muhammad, 118, 122, 186, 197, 252, 268, 277; of mystery, 166; and perception, 51; perfection of, 134, 166, 235, 260; of predispositions, 62, 63, 70; of Reality, 52, 53, 56, 64, 99, 115, 117, 123, 133, 137, 151, 182, 183; of self, 52, 54, 64, 74, 126, 132, 153, 181, 272, 282; spiritual, 69, 93, 131; symbol of, 196, 197; unitary, 79; of universals, 53.

Last Day, 185.
Law, 46, 66, 125, 168, 169, 202, 203, 204, 209, 230, 232, 255, 268.
Leadership, 58, 243–248.
Light, 58, 120–127, 181, 254, 274; of faith, 161.
Lord, fear of, 108, 214; glorification of, 52; and God, 80, 106; and man, 125, 137; pleasing of, 106, 107, 138, 143; serving of, 78, 80, 103, 107, 108, 148, 183, 214, 234; transcendence of, 52.
Lot, 58, 157–162.
Love, 58, 91–95, 186, 232, 233, 248, 255, 257, 258, 272, 274, 276, 277, 279.
Lucifer, 56.
Luqmān, 58, 237–240.

Macrocosm, 135, 279.
Majesty, 58, 219–221, 281.
Makki, Abū Ṭālib al-, 161, 204.

INDEX

Man, annihilation of, 80, 81; being of, 178; and Cosmos, 253; creation of, 57, 208, 209, 213; definition of, 73, 74; and God, 54, 55, 79, 95, 126, 127, 136, 137, 190, 195, 210, 245, 273, 274; Great-, 51, 135; and individuality, 116; knowledge of, 53; as manifestation, 52, 54, 55; Nature of, 273, 279; Perfect, 51, 52, 55, 56, 84, 88, 149, 253, 281; perfection of, 209, 272; and Reality, 77, 93, 95, 124, 135; spirit of, 274; as Vice-Regent, 51, 52, 77, 98.
The Manifest, 55, 69, 73, 85, 86, 92, 125, 135, 136.
The Many, 87, 88.
Mary, 174, 175, 176, 177, 178, 220, 254.
Mastery, 58, 157–162.
The Meccan Revelations, 65, 224, 277, 281.
The Merciful, 67, 78, 84, 98, 101, 188, 189, 192, 205, 214, 215, 225, 240, 264, 277, 280; Breath of, 135, 148, 179, 235, 243–244, 274, 277.
Mercy, 46; divine, 114, 130, 152, 157, 189, 205, 223, 224, 225, 226, 243, 244, 255, 264, 268, 278, 279; as embracing, 204, 227, 268, 278; and existence, 51; and giving, 189, 190; kinds of, 189, 190, 226; of Lord, 143; and Names, 67, 192; object of, 224; obligating-, 189, 190, 226; and Reality, 147.
Messiah, 177.
Michael, 95.
Microcosm, 279.
Miracles, 160–161, 220.
Monasticism, 114.
Moses, 58, 181, 194, 195, 200, 203, 243, 244, 246, 251–268, 274.
The Mosul Revelations, 81.
Muḥammad, 66, 132, 158, 189, 214, 217; Community of, 194, 196, 197, 203, 216, 260; dispensation of, 205; form of, 233; heirs of, 77, 78, 79, 80, 84, 122; and law, 46, 203; as Lord of Men, 67; and Moses, 259; name of, 200; power of, 161, 190; and Qur'ān, 76, 114; sayings of, 74, 76, 86, 92, 99, 117, 122, 151, 157, 160, 182, 190, 196, 209, 213, 254, 257, 258, 260, 266, 275, 278; and singularity, 58, 272–284; spirit of, 100; states of, 186; Traditions of, 56, 92, 125, 133, 134, 147, 148, 190, 202, 280; and visions, 45, 58, 121.
Mukhallad, Taqīb. al-, 100, 101.
Multiplicity, 55, 78, 79, 85, 87, 116, 125, 126, 153, 238, 254.
Muslim, 232, 234.
Mu'tazilite, 152.
Mystery, 50, 64, 80, 102, 106, 116, 162, 165, 166, 192, 197, 205, 216, 217, 261.

Names, and Cosmos, 78, 125, 148, 254, 258; divine, 52, 55, 63, 65, 67, 68, 78, 85, 88, 95, 107, 108, 113, 126, 127, 148, 150, 151, 153, 166, 169, 180, 181, 183, 188, 190, 191, 192, 210, 233, 225, 226, 231, 233, 239, 253, 258, 278, 282; essences of, 50, 68, 88, 108; gifts of, 62, 65, 67; infinite, 68; manifestation of, 52, 54, 68, 80, 254; and Reality, 92, 124, 125, 191, 192, 233, 253; uniqueness of, 226.
Nature, 81; and creation, 158, 214; darkness of, 256; of Destiny, 169; Essential, 87, 165; form of, 180, 215; and Mercy, 235, 277; servant of, 116, 117; taint of, 175; Universal, 51, 87, 275, 277.
Night Journey, 196.
Noah, 58, 73–81, 200, 219, 229, 235.

Obedience, to Command, 141, 143, 159, 196, 204; to God, 45, 113, 117, 170.

INDEX

Obligation, 189, 190, 196.
One, 131, 216; Eternal-, 53, 148; and God, 78, 106, 109, 130, 192; and multiplicity, 55, 79, 126, 153, 234; and Name, 126; and opposition, 86; Reality, 108; Unity of, 158.

Paradise, 107, 108, 109, 138, 170, 171, 219.
Passion, 246, 247, 248.
Path, 129, 130, 131, 132, 134, 158, 195, 196, 197, 201, 284.
Patience, 216, 217, 243, 256, 260.
Pharaoh, 194–195, 254–258, 261–265.
Planes, of Divinity, 109, 141; of existence, 102; of Imagination, 120, 121, 151; of Reality, 52.
Polarity, and man, 274; and Names, 166; and Nature, 180; of qualities, 55, 56; and Reality, 274.
Polytheism, 75, 239, 248.
Power, of concentration, 160, 161; divine, 191, 202, 230, 238, 263; and fancies, 230, 232; of Gabriel, 175; and gnosis, 158, 159, 162; of Mercy, 225; and miracles, 160, 161; of souls, 195; of subjugation, 195.
Prayer, 113, 183, 190, 268, 277, 279–283.
Predisposition, 62, 63, 65, 70, 149, 165, 167, 168, 276, 282.
Prophecy, 168–169, 174–186, 199, 219, 243, 244, 268.
Prophets, 46, 98, 151, 158, 165, 166, 167, 168, 170, 184, 200, 204, 214, 216, 219, 220, 221, 229, 235, 243, 248, 255, 256, 258, 261, 268, 272; Seal of, 66, 67, 272.
Providence, 114, 120, 138, 152.

Reality, 46, 98–103; attributes of, 68, 88, 92, 253; and causality, 126, 216; and Cosmos, 50, 55, 56, 57, 73, 123, 124, 148, 215, 253, 257, 279; and creation, 51, 102, 103, 109, 132, 134, 136, 141, 142, 166, 191, 210, 273, 274; definition of, 74, 136; and Destiny, 167; divine, 73, 79, 261; Essence of, 50, 52, 95, 125, 126; essential, 53, 56, 57, 69, 83, 94, 95, 131, 134, 135, 159, 166, 225, 226; eternal, 166; face of, 81; form of, 86, 137; and Heart, 147; Himself, 93, 133, 217; Identity of, 73, 124, 151, 191; knowledge of, 52, 53, 56, 64, 99, 115, 117, 123, 133, 137, 151, 182, 183; limitations of, 134, 135, 138, 150; manifestations of, 73, 78, 88, 92, 93, 95, 101, 117, 124, 125, 135, 149, 151, 279; messenger of, 170; mirror of, 65; and path, 130; permeates all, 57, 92; and power, 50; and servants, 53, 134; shadow of, 123, 124; and transcendence, 73, 87, 215; transformation of, 136, 150, 151; and triplicity, 142.
Religion, of created beings, 113; and God, 113, 114, 115; practise of, 113, 114, 183.
Resource, 58, 268.
Resurrection, 137, 170, 171, 232.
Revelations, 45, 46, 54, 57, 64, 65, 76, 94, 109, 114, 120, 121, 131, 132, 134, 141, 160, 166, 167, 169, 170, 201, 202, 208, 214, 231, 235, 238, 256, 266, 275.

Sacrifice, 98, 99, 100, 256.
Saints, 68, 69, 160, 165, 169, 170; Seal of, 66, 67.
Saintship, 168–170.
Sāliḥ, 58, 140–144.
Salvation, 170, 265.
Sāmirī, al-, 175, 244, 245.
Sanctification, 52.
Satan, 45, 100, 122, 215, 216, 282.
Scriptures, 73, 94, 114, 131, 133, 231.
Self, -consciousness, 81; essential, 69, 77, 87, 103, 124, 127, 165; and God, 107; knowledge, 52, 54, 64, 74, 126, 132, 153, 181, 272, 282.

INDEX

Self-Knowledge, 94, 151, 257.
Self-limitation, 134.
Self-manifestation, 87, 110, 148, 149, 150, 151, 152, 155, 211, 230, 231, 232, 234, 246, 247, 248, 254.
Self-revelation, 50, 65, 70, 79, 87, 93, 99, 107, 115, 166, 234, 266, 282.
Self-subsistent, 125.
The Self-sufficient, 54, 56, 57, 126, 127, 148, 180.
Seth, 58, 62–70, 219.
Shem, 219.
Shu'aib, 58, 147–155.
Sin, 68, 76, 117, 200, 227, 255, 281.
Singularity, 58, 272–284.
Solace, 282.
Solomon, 58, 188–197, 208.
Sophists, 154.
Soul, 117; lower, 46, 230; restraining of, 216–217.
Sphere, of Divinity, 51; seven higher, 84; seven lower, 84; of Sun, 81, 84.
Spirit, of Cosmos, 135; and form, 73; and God, 178, 196, 273, 275; and Jesus, 174, 175, 176, 220; men of, 66.
Stations, 235; of the Apostle, 160, 186; divine, 95; of Eternity, 45; of knowledge, 182; of prophecy, 101; of Sanctification, 45; spiritual, 252; of synthesis, 196; of weakness, 160.
Substance, and accidents, 154; and Cosmos, 238; Primordial, 153, 180, 254, 277.
Sufis, cf. also the Folk; 153.
Substitutes, 159, 160.
Symbols, 196, 255, 256, 263, 276.
Synthesis, 56.

Theosophists, 153.
Throne, 204, 213, 214, 278.
Tirmidhī, al-, 77.

Torah, 131, 214.
Transcendence, 52, 231; divine, 182; of God, 63, 73, 74, 75, 76, 134, 230, 231, 283; and Jesus, 176; and limitation, 73; and Reality, 73, 87, 215.
Triplicity, 141, 142, 272.
Tustarī, Sahl al-, 98, 106.

Unity, 106, 107, 108, 125, 126, 129–138.
Universals, 53.
The Unmanifest, 55, 69, 73, 85, 86, 92, 125, 135, 136.
'Umar (b. al-Khaṭṭab), 66, 100, 196.
The Unseen, 167, 182, 213–217.

Virtue, 58, 237–240, 262.
Visions, 45, 98, 99, 100, 101, 122, 144, 153, 230, 231, 280, 281, 282; Veridical, 121.

Way, cf. Path.
Will, free, 192; of God, 70, 94, 114, 122, 141, 159, 166, 204, 235, 247, 252, 256, 276; of Lord, 124; of Reality, 117; and subjection, 245.
Wisdom, divine, 70, 200, 216; expressed, 237; and law, 209; manifestations of, 58; unexpressed, 237.
Wish, divine, 166, 185, 190, 191, 197, 237, 253, 254.
Women, 272, 273, 274, 275, 276, 277, 278.
Word, 51, 135, 141, 175, 176, 233.
Worship, of God, 78, 138, 149, 151, 183, 215, 244, 246, 247, 248, 279, 280, 282, 283; and passion, 246, 247, 248.

Zaid, 191, 232, 277.
Zakariah, 58, 219, 220, 223–227.

INDEX TO PREFACE, INTRODUCTIONS AND NOTES

Aaron, 241.
Abdel-Kader, A., 148.
Abraham, 90, 164.
Abū al-'Abbās of Ceuta, 7.
Abū Jahl, 171.
Abū Madyan, 4, 159.
Adam, xii, xiv, 18, 50, 83, 208; as archetype, 47, 49; as God's representative, xii, 35; as word, 16, 17, 35.
Afifi, A. A., 12, 13, 23, 24, 34, 106.
Amin, A., 157.
Angels, 47, 49, 174, 206.
Apostles, 38, 60, 61, 112, 164, 199, 250.
Arberry, A.J., 21.
Archetypes, 32, 35, 37, 47, 49, 91, 97, 111, 120, 147, 157.
Ash'arites, 23, 147, 154, 236.
Ashraf, al-, 11.
Āsīyah, 219.
Atomism, 154.
Austin, R.W., 2.
Averroes, 2, 6.
Ayyubid, 9.

Badawi, A., 1.
Bargès, J.J.J., 159.
Beatrice, 7.
Being, xiii, 198–199; created, 32, 157, 163, 164, 222; divine, 47; essential, 32; experience of, 243; identity of, 112; Oneness of, 19, 24, 25, 26, 27, 30, 31, 32, 33, 35, 37, 39, 48, 71, 73, 113, 120, 128, 129, 145, 174, 199, 208, 213, 228, 229, 242, 243, 252, 267, 269; and polarity, 113; and Reality, 40.
Bezels of Wisdom, xii, 11; importance of, 18; and mysticism, xi, xvii, 9, 13, 18–21, 25; organization of, 16–17, 20; text of, 17; translation of, 12, 16, 17, 18; studies of, 13, 17, 21.
Bible, xii.
Bilqīs, 188.
Bistāmī, al-, 23, 107.
Breath, 206, 222, 223; of the Merciful, 28, 60, 120, 140, 147, 163, 172, 222, 242, 243, 270.
Brethren of Purity, 23.
Brockelmann, C., 23.
Buddhism, 23.
Bukhārī, 56, 67, 86, 92, 121, 125, 130, 134, 150, 151, 158, 168, 182, 184, 189, 190, 196, 200, 238, 253, 258, 272, 273, 281, 283.
Burckhardt, T., 12, 16.

Christ, xii, xiii.
Christianity, xii, xiii, xviii, 10, 16, 20, 22, 23, 111, 112.

295

INDEX

Command, Creative, 31, 33, 140, 163; of God, 50, 90, 111, 112, 208; Obligating, 31, 33, 111.
Compassion, 187, 213.
Corbin, S.H., 13, 19, 22, 23, 24, 28, 35, 36, 106.
Cosmos, becoming of, 96, 140, 145, 147, 241, 250, 270, 271; creation of, 27, 35, 47, 49, 72, 90, 119, 120, 147, 172, 173, 187, 198, 213, 249; and God, 27, 30, 31, 32, 34, 47, 48, 61, 83, 90–91, 97, 98, 104, 105, 111, 112, 120, 140, 157, 164, 188, 206, 207, 222, 223, 228, 236, 242, 252, 269, 270; nourishment of, 91; and polarity, xiii, 31, 35, 47, 48, 49, 82, 112, 140, 188, 206, 222, 228, 252, 269, 270; and Reality, 241; shadow of, 119–120.
Creation, of Cosmos, 27, 35, 47, 49, 72, 90, 147, 172, 173, 187, 249; and Destiny, 164; and determinism, 32; and God, 32, 33, 35, 36, 83, 90, 91, 120, 129, 147, 163, 187, 206, 242; instant to instant, 154, 188; and light, 120; and love, 252; and mercy, 29, 31; and polarity, 28, 29, 104, 128, 140, 146, 173; recurring, 146.
Creator, xiii, 30, 31, 35, 83, 97, 120, 147, 229.
Culme-Seymour, A., 12.

Dante, 7, 15.
Da'ūd, 197.
David, 61, 198–199.
Decree, 32, 33, 163, 164.
Destiny, 32, 157, 163, 164, 243, 267.
Dispensation, 269.
Divinity, absolute, xiii; consciousness, 35, 119, 172; gifts of, 60–62; identity of, 32, 40; light of, 35, 119, 120; omniscence of, 32; and polarity, 26, 30, 31, 33, 96, 129, 249; power of, 35, 36, 49, 157, 187, 249; presence of, 49, 90; and punishment, 33, 106; and reward, 33; transcendence of, 27; unity of, 249; wisdom of, xi, xiv, 17, 18; worship of, 30; wrath of, 106, 128, 207, 213.
Dominion, 222.
Duality, 105, 139.

Eckhart, 16, 20.
Elias, 228–229.
Eminence, 249–251.
Enoch, 82.
Essence, and Cosmos, 147; divine, xiii, 47, 105, 218–219, 223, 236, 237, 242, 252, 270; eternal, 222; gift of, 61, 243; Itself, 140; latent, 32, 61, 91, 104, 105, 120, 140, 146, 147, 163, 187, 229, 236; knowledge of, 91; of man, 105; Reality as, 120; and reintegration, 228; spiritual, 97; unmanifested, 120.
Esoterism, xiii, 3, 8, 14, 112, 164, 250.
Evans-Wentz, W.Y., 36.
Eve, 35, 83.
Exaltation, 71.
Existence, becoming of, 33, 164; cosmic, 164, 188, 243; created, 83; as gift, 60, 61, 187; particular, 146.
Exotericism, 9, 18, 71, 112, 129, 236.
Expiration, 60.
Ezra, 163.

Fatima bint al-Muthannā (of Cordova), 3.
Fuṣūṣ al-ḥikam, cf. *Bezels of Wisdom*.

Gabriel, 174.
Ghazālī, 22, 24.
God, and Cosmos, 27, 30, 31, 32, 34, 47, 48, 61, 83, 90–91, 97, 98, 104, 105, 111, 112, 120, 140, 164, 188, 206, 222, 223, 228, 236, 242, 252, 269, 270; essence of, xiii, 47, 105, 218–219, 223, 236, 237, 242, 252; identity of, 207, 219, 223,

INDEX

236, 237; identity with, 90–91, 105, 147, 212, 213, 219, 252; image of, 35, 49, 72, 187, 207, 252, 270; knowledge of, 27, 28, 33, 91, 105, 112, 120, 146, 157, 229, 242, 252; and man, 32, 47, 49, 97, 98, 129, 164, 198, 229, 241, 252, 271; manifestations of, xiii, 33, 72, 146, 206; messengers of, xii; names of, 30, 37, 47; nature of, 18, 146; as One, 83, 97, 223; permeation of, 90–91, 112; and polarity, xiii, 31, 34, 37, 47, 48, 49, 82, 83, 96, 112, 188, 206, 222, 228, 252, 269; religion of, 111; separation from, 40, 72, 82, 97, 106, 120; unity of, 71, 187, 249; wisdom of, 16; worship of, 20, 49, 82, 91, 106, 236, 242, 243.
Gnosticism, 3, 23, 61, 72, 73, 97, 98, 105, 145, 146, 156, 157, 219, 228, 229, 243, 249, 250.
Guillaume, A., 66, 260.

Hajji Khalīfah, 100.
Hallaj, al-, 23, 24, 102.
Hanbal, 100, 134, 196, 227.
Harūn, A., 157.
Hasār, Muhammad al-, 7.
Heart, 97, 98, 145, 146.
Heaven, 35, 97, 140, 249, 267.
Hell, 72, 106, 140, 207.
Heresy, 20, 24, 71.
Hinduism, 14, 23, 26, 271.
Holiness, 82.
Horten, M., 23.
Hūd, 128.
Hujwīrī, al-, 85, 98, 100.
Husaini, S.A.Q., 13.

Ibn al-'Arabī, acceptance of, xiv, 4, 8–12, 15, 16, 20, 22, 24; disciples of, 11, 17, 22; family of, 1, 2, 11; life of, 1–12; and mysticism, xi, xvii, 4, 5, 10, 13, 14, 15, 18, 20, 21, 22, 24, 25, 128, 229; sources of, 22–23; studies of, 13, 17, 21, 22, 28; and Sufism, xiv, xvii, 2–4, 7–9, 12, 14, 20–23, 29, 37; teachers of, 2–4, travels of, 4–11.
Ibn al-'Arabī, works of, cf. also *Bezels of Wisdom*; editions of, 12; translations of, 12; *Dīwān*, 11; *Al-Futūḥāt al-makkiyyah*, xiv, xv, xvii, 2–13, 18, 20, 21, 25, 28, 29, 38, 40, 65, 134, 224; *Hilyat al-abdāl*, 13; *The Interpreter of Desires*, 7, 10; *Meccan Revelations*, cf. *Al-Futūḥāt al-makkiyyah*; *Mir'āt al-ma'ānī*, 23; *Mosul Revelations*, 8; *Rasā'il Ibnul 'Arabī*, 12; *Sufis of Andalusia*, 2, 3, 4, 6, 8, 11, 12, 36, 40, 134, 159; *Tarjumān al-ashwāq*, 7, 8, 12.
Ibn al-'Arīf, 23.
Ibn Barrajān, 23.
Ibn al-Fārid, 15, 24.
Ibn Masdanīsh, 1.
Ibn Qisyi, 4.
Illusion, 28, 39, 40, 48, 98, 208, 213, 229.
Imagination, Creative, 18, 23, 27, 96, 98, 119, 140; and man, 98; and Real, 28.
Imru 'l-Qais, 116.
Intellect, and desire, 228, 229; human, 252; Universal, 30, 173.
Intimacy, 228–229.
'Irāqī Fakhr al-Dīn al-, 15.
Isaac, 96, 119.
Ishmael, 104.
Islam, esotericism of, xiii; exotericism of, 9, 18, 71; law of, 1, 6, 10, 20; and man, 198, 206; and mysticism, 9, 16, 20, 22, 25, 30, 41, 243; and prophets, xii, 38; religion of, 111; and saints, 37; spirituality of, 14, 271; theology of, xiii, 9, 20, 71.
Isma'ilis, 23.
Isthmus, 34, 72, 206, 267.
Izutsu, T., 13, 22, 24.

INDEX

Jacob, 111.
Jāmī, al-, 17.
Jeffrey, A., 12.
Jesus, 18, 172, 174, 176, 188, 219, 220.
Jīlanī, al-, 159.
Jīlī, 'Abd al-Karīm al-, 10.
Job, 212–213.
John, 218, 219.
Jonah, 206.
Joseph, 119.
Jung, C.G., 8.
Justice, 152.

Kabbalism, 23, 24.
Kay Kaus, 9, 10, 11.
Khālid, 267.
Kharrāz, Abū Sa'īd al-, 85.
Khiḍr, al-, 249, 250, 256.
Knowledge, xiii, 139, 270, 271; of God, 27, 28, 33, 91, 105, 112, 120, 146, 157, 229, 242, 252; of Reality, 61; of self, 61, 91, 105, 164.
Koran, cf. under Qur'an.

Lane, E.W., 26.
Law, 1, 6, 10, 20, 199, 250; of Heaven, 249.
Light, 35, 38, 119, 212.
Lord, 145, 146; and creation, 83; servants of, 20, 31, 49, 104, 105, 222, 223, 242.
Lot, 156.
Love, 28, 29, 39, 90, 242, 249, 252, 267.
Luqmān, 236–237.

Macrocosm, xii, 26, 35, 96, 119, 173.
Majesty, 218.
Malik al-'Ādil, al-, 9, 11.
Man, condition of, 34, 37, 62, 119, 198, 206; and Cosmos, 241, 242; divinity of, 207; and God, 32, 47, 49, 97, 98, 129, 164, 198, 229, 241, 252, 271; as God's agent, 34, 198, 270; life of, 207; as microcosm, xii, 34, 35, 36, 72, 97, 119, 198, 229; nature of, xii, 18, 35, 157; Perfect, 34, 35, 37, 38, 61, 97, 145, 206; power of, 35, 36, 37, 157, 164; and Reality, 40, 98; as servant (slave), 34–35, 37, 49, 146, 198, 213, 236.
Mashā'is, 23.
Mary, 174, 219.
Massignon, L., 23, 102.
Mastery, 156.
Matthew, 6:21, 244.
Meier, F., 8.
Mercy, Breath of, 28, 60, 120, 140, 147, 163, 172, 222, 242, 243, 270; creative-, 29, 31, 60, 187, 222, 229, 241, 271; divine, 18, 106, 129, 147, 187, 188, 207, 223, 241; and love, 29; obligating, 229, 241, 271; and reality, 129, 145.
Metaphysics, xiv, 3, 23, 32, 48.
Mevlevi, 15.
Microcosm, 26, 96, 206, 228, 270; man as, xii, 34, 35, 36, 72, 97, 119, 198, 229.
Miracles, xiv, 36, 37, 98, 156.
Monism, 16, 26.
Moses, 18, 249–251, 256.
Muhammad, xii, 17, 171, 200; light of, 38; as Perfect Man, 97; and sainthood, 37, 38; as Seal, 61; sayings of, 7, 72, 267, 269, 271; and singularity, 269–272; Traditions of, 1, 22, 27, 28, 97, 105, 188, 199.
Muḥāsibī, al-, 24.
Multiplicity, 105, 139, 146, 222, 229, 270.
Muslim, 100, 121, 203, 209, 252, 273, 278, 280.
Mu'tazilites, 152.
Mystery, xiii, 25, 32, 39, 48, 164.
Mysticism, xiii, 2, 19, 40; Christian, xviii, 16, 22; and experience, 25, 219; Jewish, 23; and Ibn al-'Arabī, xi, xvii, 4, 5, 10, 13, 14, 15, 18, 20, 21, 22, 24, 25, 128, 229; and Islam, 9, 16, 20, 22, 25, 30, 41, 243; of number, 83; and Sufis, 3, 9, 14, 18; Tibetan, 36.

INDEX

Nābulusī, al-, 17.
Name, gift of, 61; of God, 30, 37, 47, 49, 83, 105, 120, 146, 218, 222, 223; oneness of 105; of names, 30; Supreme, 30, 48, 49, 146; universal, 83, 105.
Nasā'ī, 209, 272, 275, 279, 282.
Nasr, S.H., 13.
Nature, 252, 267, 271; cosmic, 48, 83, 112; and God, 49, 83; of God, 18, 146; of man, xii, 18, 35, 157; as Mother, 173, 241; original, 172; of reality, 128, 212; and Spirit, 173-174, 212, 219; Universal, 30.
Neoplatonism, 22, 23, 24.
Nicholson, R.A., 10, 15, 16, 37, 65, 85.
Noah, 18, 19, 71, 72.
Nyberg, H.S., 12.

Old Testament, xii, xiii.
The One, 139, 147.
Oneness, of Being, 19, 24, 25, 26, 27, 30, 31, 32, 33, 35, 37, 39, 48, 71, 73, 113, 120, 128, 129, 145, 174, 199, 208, 213, 228, 229, 242, 243, 252, 267, 269; Essential, 140; experience of, 252; of God, 83, 97, 223; of Perception, 26, 27, 39, 48; and polarity, 249, 250; and Reality, 128, 188; and transcendence, 228.

Palacios, Asin, 12, 15, 23, 95.
Pantheism, 26-27.
Paradise, 140.
Pharaoh, 219, 249, 250.
Platonism, xiii.
Plotinus, 23.
Polarity, and creation, 28, 29, 104, 128, 140, 146; of Creator and creation, xiii, 31, 34, 47, 48, 49, 82, 104, 111, 112, 173, 188, 206, 222, 228, 252, 269; and divinity, 26, 29, 31, 33, 96, 129, 249; and nonpolarity, 48; and Real, 27-31, 33, 34, 39, 40, 111, 112.

Predisposition, 60, 61, 83, 104, 113, 146, 164, 187, 250, 267.
The Prophet, cf. under Muhammad.
Prophets, xi, xii, xiii, xiv, 16, 18, 20, 38, 61, 164, 172-174, 188, 198, 199, 218 219, 250.

Qāshānī, al-, 17.
Qunawī, Ṣadr al-Dīn al-, 9, 15, 17.
Qur'an, xi, xii, 1, 18, 21, 22, 49, 71, 72, 104, 111, 128, 173, 198, 249, 250.
Qur'an, I: 1, 75, 92; II: 16, 77; II: 20, 79; II: 25, 153; II: 26, 239; II:30, 52, 85, 201; II: 43, 183; II:49, 100; II:57, 161; II:88, 159; II:115, 40, 137, 138, 213; II:116, 80; II:117, 178; II:124, 201; II:132, 113; II:152, 279; II:166, 152; II:179, 209; II:186, 63, 232; II:188, 114; II:210, 50; II:228, 276; II:253, 165; II:255, 29, 135; II:257, 168; II:259, 166, 167; II:260, 166; II:272, 161; III:10, 168; III:19, 113; III:21, 143; III:26, 77; III:31, 248; III:47, 38; III:49, 176; III:91, 150, 151; IV:1, 57, 87; IV:133, 94; IV:150, 73; IV:171, 175; V:18, 180; V:48, 255; V:66, 131, 214; V:109, 185; V:110, 176, 177; V:116, 182; V:117, 182-185; V:118, 184-186; V:119, 115; VI:3, 237; VI:38, 103; VI:59, 167; VI:61, 214; VI:84, 199; VI:90, 202; VI:91, 81; VI:101, 136, 215; VI:103, 248; VI: 122, 179, 254; VI:124, 231; VI:132, 245; VI:149, 93, 115, 143, 160; VII:33, 133; VII:54, 134; VII:122, 195; VII:150, 243; VII:156, 188, 190, 226, 227, 228; VII:172, 251; VIII:17, 233, 235; VIII:61, 208; IX:21, 143; IX:29, 177; IX:37, 275; IX:118, 40, 205; X:90, 195; X:92, 265; X:97, 265; X:98, 265; XI:33, 210; XI:56, 130, 134; XI:57, 135, 143; XI:80, 157, 158;

299

INDEX

XI:112, 117; XI:123, 84, 92, 211, 215; XII:4, 122; XII:5, 122; XII:43, 99; XII:87, 255; XII:100, 122; XII:108, 78; XIII:33, 78, 248; XIV:27, 33; XIV:47, 109; XV:26, 279; XV:29, 178, 273; XVI:40, 141; XVI:50, 214; XVI:70, 158; XVI:71, 165; XVI:125, 161; XVII:2, 77; XVII:15–44, 188; XVII:23, 78; XVII:44, 195, 283; XVII:55, 165; XVII:110, 240; XVIII:68, 259; XVIII:76, 260; XVIII:78, 260; XVIII:104, 153; XIX:5, 219; XIX:6, 220; XIX:7, 219; XIX:15, 219; XIX:17–21, 175; XIX:19, 175; XIX:23–34, 220; XIX:33, 219, 220; XIX:53, 200, 243; XIX:54, 109; XIX:57, 84, 85; XIX:85, 78; XIX:86, 131; XX:5, 84; XX:39, 252; XX:50, 68, 107, 149, 166, 168, 276; XX:55, 80; XX:72, 264; XX:86–89, 175; XX:94, 243, 244; XX:95, 244; XX:97, 245; XX:114, 150, 169, 196; XXI:2, 264; XXI:22, 204; XXI:30, 213; XXI:37, 62; XXI:78–79, 194; XXI:79, 194; XXI:91, 50; XXII:5, 254; XXII:34, 79; XXIII:109, 225; XXIII:118, 183; XXIV:26, 278; XXIV:41, 283; XXV:19, 115; XXV:45, 124; XXV:46, 124; XXV:70, 263; XXVI:5, 264; XXVI:21, 259, 260; XXVI:23, 261; XXVI:24, 262; XXVI:27, 261; XXVI:28, 262; XXVI:29, 262; XXVI:30, 263; XXVI:31, 263; XXVI:32, 263; XXVII:12, 263; XXVII:29, 189, 192; XXVII:30, 188; XXVII:40, 192; XXVII:42, 194; XXVII:44, 194; XXVII:60, 84; XXVII:107, 87; XXVIII:9, 254, 255; XXVII:10, 255; XXVIII:13, 256; XXVIII:24, 259; XXVIII:56, 161, 171; XXVIII:82, 256; XXVIII:88, 84; XXIX:45, 281;

XXIX:47, 134; XXIX:52, 279; XXIX:64, 191; XXX:7, 159; XXX:54, 158; XXXI:12, 237; XXXI:13, 239; XXXI:16, 237–239; XXXII:5, 275; XXXIII:21, 197; XXXIII:57, 217; XXXIV:10, 200, 205; XXXIV:13, 200; XXXV:15, 127; XXXV:32, 79; XXXVI:10–11, 33; XXXVII:102, 87, 99; XXXVII:105, 99; XXXVII:164, 94; XXXVII:170, 230; XXXVIII:5, 247; XXXVIII:26, 55, 56, 199, 201; XXXVIII:30, 193; XXXVIII:35, 189; XXXVIII:36, 195; XXXVIII:39, 196; XXXVIII:41–44, 216; XXXVIII:42, 214; XXXVIII:43, 200; XXXVIII:75, 85, 181; XXXIX:3, 78, 247, 248; XXXIX:9, 136; XXXIX:47, 152, 153; XL:15, 246, 278; XL:53, 74; XL:60, 63, 232; XL:85, 264; XLI:53, 54; XLII:9, 176; XLII:11, 75, 76, 135, 191, 230; XLII:27, 166; XLII:28, 67, 168; XLII:40, 209; XLIV:10, 180; XLV:13, 195, 253; XLV:23, 246, 247; XLVI:9, 118, 160; XLVI:16, 109, 115; XLVI:24, 132, 133; XLVI:25, 133; XLVII:31, 64, 182, 238, 273; XLVII:35, 84; XLVIII:2, 200, 227; XLVIII:25, 185; XLVIII:32, 245; L:15, 154, 193; L:16, 132; L:22, 132; L:29, 161; L:37, 150–152, 165, 281; LV:29, 80, 246; LV:31, 235; LVI:85, 131; LVII:4, 195; LVII:7, 77, 159; LVII:27, 114; LVII:32, 262; LIX:7, 259; LXVI:11, 219; LXVIII:1, 30; LXVIII:42, 93, 170, 171; LXXI:2, 76; LXXI:5, 75, 76, 77; LXXI:7, 80; LXXI:10, 75; LXXI:11, 77; LXXI:12, 77; LXXI:21, 77; LXXI:22, 77; LXXI:23, 78; LXXI:24, 19, 79; LXXI:25, 79, 80; LXXI:26, 80;

INDEX

LXXI:27, 80, 81; LXXI:28, 81; LXXIII:9, 159; LXXV:14, 282; LXXV:17, 76; LXXVIII:1, 84; LXXIX:24, 264; LXXX, 181; LXXX:38, 143; LXXX:39, 143; LXXXI:6, 79; LXXXI:38, 348; LXXXIII:7, 174; LXXXV:22, 30; LXXXIX:28, 107; LXXXIX:29, 107, LXXXIX:30, 107; XCV:5, 132, 207; XCVIII:8, 108; XCIX:7–8, 239; CXII, 126.
Qushairī, 282.

Rāzī, al-, 129.
Reality, consciousness of, 39, 49; and Cosmos, 241; divine, xiv, 10, 33, 50, 236, 250, 252; as Essence, 120; and God, xiv, 33, 82, 120, 146, 213, 241, 242; Itself, 82, 83, 97, 105, 128, 140, 145, 146; and man, 40, 272; and polarity, 27, 28, 29, 30, 31, 33, 34, 39, 40, 111, 112, 228, 229, 270; presence of, 37, 39, 229, 243; unity of, 26, 29, 37, 40 73, 97, 128; wholeness of, 249.
Religion, 111–112, 173.
Resource, 267.
Revelation, xii, xiv, 13, 164, 174, 188, 199, 219.
Rūmī, Jalāl al Dīn, 10, 15, 22, 24, 129.

Saints, 36, 37, 38, 60, 61, 72, 164, 199, 219.
Sālih, 139.
Salvation, 31, 128, 139, 146, 207.
II Samuel 6, 208.
Sarrāj, Abū Nasr al-, 65.
Satan, 49, 50, 208.
Scripture, 199.
Seal, of apostles, 60; of Muhammadan Sainthood, 6, 8, 38, 60; of prophets, 38.
Self-actualization, 34.
Self-consciousness (awareness), 27, 29, 39, 48, 49, 60, 164, 187, 207, 222, 236, 242.
Self-experience, 72, 105, 112.
Self-knowledge, 32, 39, 91.
Self-manifestation, 33.
Self-polarization, 96.
Self-realization, 27, 28, 29, 49, 112, 140.
Self-recognition, 252.
Self-sufficiency, 47, 187, 236.
Self-subsistent, 29.
Seth, 60–62.
Shādhilī, Abū al-Hasan al-, 15.
Shams, 3.
Shehadi, F., 93.
Shīrazī, Qutb al-Dīn al-, 15.
Shu'aib, 145, 146.
Singularity, 269–272.
Solomon, 187, 188.
Soul, xi, 82, 173, 271.
Spirit, xiv, 30, 38, 50, 111, 172–174, 188, 212, 218, 228, 229, 242, 251, 252, 267, 270, 271; as Father, 173, 241; of Muhammad, 38.
Spirituality, of Islam, 14, 271; of Sufism, xii, 9, 20, 22; and transcendence, 82.
Sublimity, 104.
Sufis, xi, xiv, 6, 198, 206, 208; and exegesis, 18, 19; and God, xiii; and Ibn al-'Arabī, xiv, xviii, 2, 3, 4, 7, 8, 9, 12, 14, 20, 21, 22, 23, 29, 37; and Law, 10; metaphysics of, 32; and mysticism, 3, 9, 14, 18; spirituality of, xii, 9, 20, 22; teachings of, 3, 10, 27; Way of, 1, 2, 6, 40.
Suhrawardī, 'Umar al-, 10, 15.
Symbols, 119, 120, 139, 147, 218, 269, 270, 271.

Tirmidhī, 66, 80, 213.
Tirmidhī, al-, 23.
Triplicity, 105, 139, 140, 269, 270.
Truth, 34, 129, 146, 157, 228, 243, 249, 250.
Tustarī, Sahl al-, 98.

Unity, 128, 139, 140, 145, 249.
Uryani, Shaikh al-, 3.

INDEX

Valiuddin, A., 26.
Virtue, 236.
Visions, xiii, 8, 17, 38, 119.

Will, creating-, 40, 213, 251; divine, 19, 31, 32, 33, 41, 104, 111, 112, 113, 140, 163, 164, 188, 207, 213, 228, 229, 250, 252, 270, 271; existential, 199; free, 32, 33.
Wisdom, divine, xi, xiv, 17, 18, 198, 199; of God, 16; and Muhammad, 38.
Wish, divine, 31, 32, 40, 111, 112, 113, 163, 164, 188, 199, 213, 228, 229, 250, 251, 267, 270, 271.
Wolfson, H.A., 154, 238.
Word, 35, 173, 174, 188, 250.
World, cf. under Cosmos.
Worship, 20, 30, 49, 82, 91, 106, 236, 242, 243.

Yahya, Osman, 17, 23, 66.

Zaehner, R.C., 23, 101.
Zakariah, 218, 222.